Brexit, Facebook, and Transnational Right-Wing Populism

DISCOURSE, POWER AND SOCIETY

Series Editors: Martin J. Power, Amanda Haynes, Eoin Devereux, and Aileen Dillane

Discourse is understood as both an expression and a mechanism of power, by which means particular social realities are conceived, made manifest, legitimated, naturalized, challenged, resisted and reimagined. This series publishes edited collections, monographs and textbooks which problematize the relationship of discourse to inequality, exclusion, subjugation, dominance and privilege. In doing so, the linkages between discourse, modes of social organization, lived experience and strategies of resistance are addressed.

Titles in the Series

Public and Political Discourses of Migration: International Perspectives, edited by Amanda Haynes, Martin J. Power, Eoin Devereux, Aileen Dillane and James Carr

The Discourse of Neoliberalism: An Anatomy of a Powerful Idea, by Simon Springer

Poor News: Media Discourses of Poverty in Times of Austerity, by Steven Hawkins and Jairo Lugo-Ocando

Framing Austerity: Print Media Portrayals of the Public Sector during the Irish Financial Crisis, by Aileen Marron

Discretion in Welfare Bureaucracies: Understanding Decision-Making in the Context of Rule Ambiguity, by Majka Ryan

Brexit, Facebook, and Transnational Right-Wing Populism, by Natalie-Anne Hall

Brexit, Facebook, and Transnational Right-Wing Populism

Natalie-Anne Hall

LEXINGTON BOOKS
Lanham • Boulder • New York • London

Published by Lexington Books
An imprint of The Rowman & Littlefield Publishing Group, Inc.
4501 Forbes Boulevard, Suite 200, Lanham, Maryland 20706
www.rowman.com

86-90 Paul Street, London EC2A 4NE

Copyright © 2024 by The Rowman & Littlefield Publishing Group, Inc.

All rights reserved. No part of this book may be reproduced in any form or by any electronic or mechanical means, including information storage and retrieval systems, without written permission from the publisher, except by a reviewer who may quote passages in a review.

British Library Cataloguing in Publication Information Available

Library of Congress Cataloging-in-Publication Data

Names: Hall, Natalie-Anne, author.
Title: Brexit, Facebook, and transnational right-wing populism / Natalie-Anne Hall.
Description: Lanham : Lexington Books, [2023] | Series: Discourse, power and society | Includes bibliographical references.
Identifiers: LCCN 2023037040 (print) | LCCN 2023037041 (ebook) | ISBN 9781666914719 (cloth) | ISBN 9781666914726 (ebook)
Subjects: LCSH: Facebook (Electronic resource)--Influence. | Online social networks--Political aspects--Great Britain. | European Union--Great Britain. | Populism--Great Britain. | Right-wing extremists--Great Britain. | Communication in politics--Great Britain.
Classification: LCC HM743.F33 H344 2023 (print) | LCC HM743.F33 (ebook) | DDC 302.30285--dc23/eng/20230828
LC record available at https://lccn.loc.gov/2023037040
LC ebook record available at https://lccn.loc.gov/2023037041

Contents

List of Figures	vii
Acknowledgments	ix
Introduction: Facebook, the EU Referendum, and Its Populist Aftermath	1
SECTION I: EXPERIENCES	19
Chapter 1: Becoming Engaged in Brexit and Right-Wing Populist Politics on Facebook	21
Chapter 2: Meaningful Online Engagement Practices in the Pro-Brexit Facebook Milieu	51
SECTION II: IDEOLOGY	77
Chapter 3: The Pro-Brexit Facebook Metanarrative	79
Chapter 4: Racisms and White Victimhood in Pro-Brexit Engagement on Facebook	99
Chapter 5: Anti-Leftism and Right Victimhood in Pro-Brexit Engagement on Facebook	119
SECTION III: KNOWLEDGE	143
Chapter 6: Brexit, Facebook, and Epistemic Battlegrounds	145
Conclusion: Taking Back Control?	173
Appendix: Participant Characteristics	183

References 185
Index 217
About the Author 223

List of Figures

Figure 2.1 Posts by Content Type

Figure 2.2 Posts by Content Source—Full Participant Group

Figure 2.3 Posts by Content Source—Participant Group Excluding Eileen

Acknowledgments

This book would not have been possible without the generosity of a number of people. Thank you to the Economic and Social Research Council for funding this research, and the Department of Sociology at the University of Manchester for supporting it. Thank you to my PhD supervisors, James Rhodes and Hilary Pilkington, who guided me through the process of the research so thoughtfully and have continued to support me unwaveringly since. Thank you to the research participants who gave up their time and so openly shared their views and experiences. Thank you to Maisie Tomlinson, Jaime Garcia Iglesias, Renée Ward and the "pyjama writing group" for helping me find more hours in the finite day. Thank you to the generous and patient colleagues and dear friends who kindly gave up their time to provide feedback on the manuscript, including Hayley James, Yutaka Yoshida, and Neema Begum. Thank you to my virtual office mate Brendan Lawson, who provided helpful feedback, intellectual guidance, and moral support. A particularly special thanks goes to my academic bestie, Neta Yodovich, who offered feedback on multiple chapters, invaluable advice on the publishing process, and lent a loving ear to my various related and unrelated grumblings. Finally, I am immeasurably grateful to Owen Abbott, my academic role model, intellectual inspiration, career advisor, personal marketing consultant, proofreader, training partner, cheer squad, and pillow, who also happens to be the unrivalled love of my life.

Introduction

Facebook, the EU Referendum, and Its Populist Aftermath

In March 2018, *The Observer* and *The Guardian* uncovered accusations that the personal data of millions of Facebook users had been illegally harvested and used to target individuals with political advertising (Cadwalladr and Graham-Harrison 2018). It was alleged that a firm called Cambridge Analytica had been employed by recently successful right-wing populist campaigns to generate psychological profiles of voters for the targeting of specific campaign messaging online. This was regarded as more violating than the increasingly normalized sale and exploitation of social media-generated personal data to commercial advertisers, not least because the data were gathered disingenuously. Results from purported personality quizzes were coupled with unconsented scraping of personal information and "Friends" lists from the platform, contradicting Facebook's Terms of Use and, some have alleged, with corporate Facebook's knowledge (Risso 2018; Zuboff 2019). This was also a particularly unsettling development because it linked such privacy concerns with the notion of a new threat to the integrity of electoral politics and democracy.

In the UK, the Cambridge Analytica story quickly became a scandal that received much press and even parliamentary attention (Lusher 2018). This controversy centered on accusations that the firm had been involved in influencing the result of the 2016 "Brexit" referendum in which the UK voted to leave the European Union (Cadwalladr and Graham-Harrison 2018). Whether or not this actually occurred is unclear; the conclusions of the UK's Information Commissioner in 2020 (BBC News, 2020b) stand in contrast to testimony by whistleblowers (Lewis and Hilder 2018; Martin 2018a). Facebook (now known at a corporate level as Meta) was, however, handed a record fine by the Commissioner for failing to protect user data from being harvested and used for political purposes,[1] and Leave campaigners too were fined for unrelated breaches of personal data (BBC News 2020b). Even before the Cambridge Analytica scandal broke in 2018, the success of Leave at the ballot box was being partly attributed to its zealous campaign on social media (Hänska and Bauchowitz 2017; Lilleker and Bonacci 2017), with Vote Leave having reportedly spent 98 percent of their funds there, including funding nearly a billion targeted adverts (Moore and Ramsay, 2017).

Regardless of the level of involvement of the disgraced Cambridge Analytica, the construction of this scandal can be said to reflect broader narratives among certain Remain supporting media, academic, and parliamentary actors that sought to rationalize the result of the EU referendum. These attempts were underpinned by an assumption that democracy had gone wrong or been hijacked. From the announcement of the result until the Cambridge Analytica story broke, disingenuous populist politicians, bus-strewn campaign lies, and tabloid-propagated racism were all the object of analyses that sought to provide explanations for the outcome (e.g., Peat 2017; Pencheva 2016; The Independent 2018). Remain activists petitioned and took to the streets to demand a "People's Vote" on any negotiated deal on the grounds that the public did not know what they were voting for in the referendum (BBC News 2016b; 2019a). In Scotland, calls for independence were renewed amid claims that the nation was being "dragged" out of the EU against its will by voters in England and Wales (BBC News 2016a). As Walkerdine (2020, 144) notes, "[t]he majority concern since the result has focused on the gullibility of ordinary people as well as their xenophobia" (see also Moss et al. 2020). The White working class was particularly implicated (despite the middle classes making up a larger proportion of the Leave vote, Antonucci et al. 2017), rehearsing standard classist stereotypes of bigotry and cultural impoverishment (McKenzie 2017).

Now it seemed it had been discovered that social media was to blame. According to this narrative, trust in online content over institutions of authority had driven "emotionally charged, value-based decision making" in the referendum, and the outcome of the vote was deemed a symptom of a "post-truth" condition (Marshall and Drieschova 2018). In this way, the fallout from the Cambridge Analytica scandal is illustrative of the notion, at least among some commentators at the time, that the referendum result was somehow invalid—the British public in its right (unmanipulated) mind would never have voted to leave the EU.

The current study is set in this post-EU referendum period, 2017–2019. The divisions inflamed by the referendum meant that identities of Leaver and Remainer had become salient categories with which to structure social life in Britain, and they remain so at the time of writing (Tyler et al. 2022; see also Hobolt et al. 2020; Curtice 2019). Britain's exit from the EU—or "Brexit"—was a consistently dominant news issue. Then Prime Minister Theresa May, a self-confessed Remainer, was struggling to negotiate an exit deal with the EU. Although Britain has now left the union, in 2018 and 2019 when the fieldwork for this project took place, that goal seemed almost insurmountable. May was tasked with satisfying the 52 percent who had voted to Leave, the UK Parliament whose members' support skewed toward Remain, *and* the remaining twenty-seven member states, all while ameliorating the negative impact of Brexit on the UK's economy and international reputation (Allen 2018). The futile outcome of these efforts was captured in her populist successor Boris Johnson's hugely successful 2019 General Election campaign slogan: "Get Brexit Done" (Cutts et al. 2020). These were ideal conditions for right-wing populist politicians, media, and other actors to exploit discontent by claiming that the democratic mandate of the referendum was under threat.

Within this context, the current study combines interview and immersive observational research to trace the experiences of UK-based users who became engaged with Brexit and related right-wing politics on Facebook. As we shall see throughout the chapters that follow, many of these individuals had become politicized around these issues through their use of Facebook. This book examines the relationship between these passionate political stances and this technology. It asks what role Facebook played in the online political engagement of these individuals, and how this fits into broader landscapes of transnational right-wing populism online. With this book, I aim to build a sociological understanding of the motivations, meanings, and consequences behind these online, right-wing populist political engagement practices.

BREXIT AND TRANSNATIONAL RIGHT-WING POPULISM ONLINE

The Leave campaign and support for Brexit have been characterized as populist (e.g., Calhoun 2017; Cox 2017; Norris and Inglehart 2019). This was articulated in the campaign's appeals to "little" and "ordinary people," the "dispossessed" whose victory was proclaimed on the day of the result (Clarke and Newman 2017, 109). The key populist tenets of people-centrism and anti-elitism were also integral to the conceptualization of the referendum result as a protest vote against disenfranchisement, enshrined in the populist discourses of the "left behind" that emerged after the referendum (e.g., Ford 2016; Freedland 2016; Goodwin and Heath 2016).

However, the implications of the findings in this book go far beyond understanding support for Brexit and its consequences for British society. The EU referendum result has been held up as both symptom and harbinger of a new era of reactionary racism and right-wing populism that is said to be afflicting democracies the world over. Beneath its local specificities, online engagement with Brexit is a microcosm of the contemporary, global phenomenon of engagement with right-wing populism through social media. In the 2010s, the world saw the right-wing authoritarian regimes of Bolsonaro in Brazil and Duterte in the Philippines; the Hindu nationalism of Modi in India; the historical revisionist nationalism of the Abe faction in Japan; the illiberalism of Orbán in Hungary; the dog-whistle politics of asylum seeker treatment by Australia's government; and the growth and disproportionate media coverage of far-right political parties in France, Italy, Spain, Sweden, and the Netherlands (Curato 2017; Mondon and Winter 2020; Mudde 2019; Narusawa 2013). In the same year that Britain voted to Leave the EU, Donald Trump was elected to the U.S. presidency. The two events have much in common, from their characterization as some of the most divisive and reverberating electoral events in these countries' histories, to the nostalgic populist promises of their respective campaign slogans "Take Back Control" and "Make America Great Again."

Each of these events is not only a product of domestic context but is also underpinned by important global social phenomena. They take place in an era where the growing use of social media to engage with politics intersects with the post-9/11 demonization of Muslims, migrants, and minority-rights activists. Although the Cambridge Analytica incident highlighted above was framed by the news media as a shock exposé, allegations of the influence of social media in the successes of Brexit and Trump came as no surprise to those studying the role of these technologies in generating support for racism and right-wing populism. Since the early 2010s, researchers had been observing that "Web 2.0" had grown into a hostile arena for discussion of contentious politics, particularly with regard to race and immigration (e.g., Due 2011; Loke 2012; Steinfeldt et al. 2010). In 2014, one study found more than 10,000 instances of English language racist and ethnic slur terms per day on Twitter alone (Bartlett et al. 2014). While some pointed to this as evidence of the prominence of racism in society, unmasked by the freedom of online anonymity, others emphasized the role of the affordances of online platforms themselves in shaping attitudes (A. Brown 2018). Theories like "echo chambers" and "filter bubbles" have since been developed in attempts to conceptualize how the increasing visibility of once extreme ideas, combined with algorithmically-driven consumption of content on social media, could potentially be polarizing and radicalizing political attitudes (Colleoni et al. 2014; Quattrociocchi et al. 2016; Ribeiro et al. 2017).

By the year of the EU referendum and Trump's election, a *Time* magazine cover went so far as to proclaim that we are "losing the Internet to the culture of hate" (Stein 2016). This claim was prompted in particular by the emergence of the Alt-Right, which began in the United States but would influence online right-wing culture in various parts of the world (J. Berger 2018). The Alt-Right is one, albeit important, strand of a White "identitarian" mobilization that is truly transnational (De Bruin 2022; Froio and Ganesh 2019; Phillips and Yi 2018). Across the Atlantic, in Australasia, and even in South and East Asia, the mutual incorporation of shared themes, logics, terminologies, and strategies link these online subcultures and movements (Davis 2019; Fujioka and DeCook 2021; Leidig 2021). Although cross-national networking has been a feature of the far-right for many decades (Jackson and Shekhovtsov 2014), the capacities for this have been dramatically accelerated and expanded by the advent of the internet and social media. Social media facilitates bottom-up content production and serendipitous encounters with ideologies, but far-right and right-wing populist actors have also taken advantage of the capacities of online technologies for dissemination, recruitment, and exchange of ideas, and to foster cross-national collective identities and worldviews (Busbridge et al. 2020). Not only a transnational ideology but also a transnational hegemonic project is said to have emerged (Stewart 2020).

These spheres may originate, coagulate, and organize online, but they have real offline consequences. Cynical and disparate as it may be, the Alt-Right movement is credited with mobilizing a portion of Donald Trump's support base in the lead-up to the presidential election. Donald Trump even selected as chief strategist Steve Bannon, the executive chairman of the Alt-Right-aligned Breitbart News (Mirrlees 2018). In addition to far-right terrorism, these transnational online spheres have prompted vast crowds to gather for deadly events such as the "Unite the Right" rally and the January 6 Capitol Hill insurrection. On an everyday level, the "mainstreaming" (Mondon and Winter 2020) of far-right ideologies that social media facilitates has fueled an increasingly hostile environment for minoritized individuals, characterized by racist lynchings, unaccountable police brutality, transgender murders, and intersectional microaggressions (Banaji et al. 2019; Koram 2020; Transgender Europe 2022).

This mainstreaming occurs not only via the incorporation of these ideologies into the political positions, policies, and rhetoric of mainstream political actors, but through the discursive framing of the far-right as the populist voice of the people (Brown et al. 2021). In this way, while right-wing populists are not always far-right, and the far-right does not always focus on populist appeals, the two spheres are inextricably interlinked, interdependent, and overlapping. As we shall see in this book, engagement with Brexit on Facebook in the post-referendum period was closely connected to both. Studying online political engagement around Brexit is revealing of the contemporary condition of globally mediated right-wing politics. Examining how "Brexiteers" engaged with U.S. Trumpism or Australian immigration policy, for example, is ultimately an investigation into the transnational appeal of right-wing populist claims. Through a case study of online engagement with Brexit and the issues seen as related to it, this book aims to shed light on the global phenomenon of online right-wing populism, and the racist, nativist, and illiberal ideologies on which it is predicated.

UKIP AND THE ROAD TO BREXIT

As much as support for Brexit on Facebook is linked to this transnational phenomenon, like all political causes it has also grown out of a particular domestic context. Long before the Leave campaign's alleged employment of Cambridge Analytica, this support had been developing among segments of the British public. Euroscepticism began as a simmering concern over the UK's first application for European Communities membership in the 1960s, but came to the fore with events like the ratification of the Maastricht Treaty in 1992 (Gifford 2006). The following year, the United Kingdom Independence Party (UKIP) would emerge, and would go on to become the most prominent advocates of Brexit. The subsequent rise of UKIP illustrates something fundamental to support for Brexit—that this cannot be understood simply as skepticism toward EU governance, but is intimately intertwined with nativism. This can be seen in the way UKIP's electoral popularity would only grow once it embraced concerns around immigration (Ford and Goodwin 2014). In particular, the accession to the EU of Poland and Hungary in 2004 and Romania and Bulgaria in 2007, accompanied by the press' demonizing depictions of immigrants from these countries (Fox et al. 2012) and from other nations hoping to join (Ker-Lindsay 2018), added to the momentum of UKIP's campaign. In 2014, UKIP won a landslide victory in Britain's European elections in what were described as the union's most Eurosceptic elections to date (Treib 2014). The party also gained a significant share of the vote in the 2015 General Election (Goodwin 2015). Indeed, more voters were expected to support UKIP that year had it not been for the success of Conservative Party leader David Cameron's fateful election promise to hold a referendum on Britain's membership in the EU (Green and Prosser 2016).

By the time the referendum was scheduled and the Leave campaign began, the EU was given as one of the top three important issues facing the nation by 20 percent of voters, up from just 3 percent five years earlier (Ipsos MORI 2022), and Leave already had a one point lead on Remain in the polls (Dahlgreen 2016). Thinly veiled nativist and Islamophobic statements and policies (Gupta and Virdee 2018), and a slew of scandals among UKIP members and leaders (BBC News 2018; Stockham 2015), exposed the Leave campaign's fraught relationship with the issue of immigration and race and the central role of cultural racism in support for Brexit. Indeed, negative attitudes toward immigration have been revealed as a key predictor of support for Leave (Goodwin and Milazzo 2017). This racism was neither new nor fleeting, having been a central feature of British politics for many decades (Barker 1981; Garner 2010; Solomos 2003). Analyses of the Leave campaign have also pointed to the key role played by nostalgic nationalism in mobilizing support for Brexit (Campanella and Dassù 2019; Clarke and Newman 2017). Within this, the specter of colonialism looms large, with appeals to a "Global Britain" working to invoke "warm collective memories of a now lost world where Britain was the global hegemon of the capitalist world economy" (Virdee and McGeever 2018, 1805). This allure was made possible through erasure of the racisms, inequalities, and subjugations at the heart of the history of the imperial project (ibid.). In other words, the driving forces behind Euroscepticism in Britain are multiple, complex, political, and social, in no way limited to the impact of Leave's 2016 social media campaign.

THE UNMATCHED IMPORTANCE OF FACEBOOK

Nonetheless, social media platforms have become important arenas for engagement with political issues, and for Brexit this has been true both before and after the referendum (Brändle et al. 2022). Through these technologies, support for Brexit has been experienced, discovered, expressed, and enacted. This is not confined to official campaign material, as political content is also created, modified, and circulated by individual social media users and interest groups. On Facebook, dozens of Pages and Groups emerged specifically around support for Leave, some boasting followings in the hundreds of thousands (Brändle et al. 2022; Lee 2019). Long-time Brexit campaigner Nigel Farage's Page garnered over one million Likes, and Britain First—which has shared many of its stances and supporters with UKIP (Davidson and Berezin 2018)—was Liked by more than two million users before it was permanently banned from the platform (Hern and Rawlinson 2018). Pro-Brexit content has also been produced and Shared by a large number of other right-wing personalities and groups to vast quantities of Followers, from Conservative MPs Boris Johnson and Jacob Rees-Mogg to notorious anti-Islamist campaigner and former English Defence League (EDL) leader "Tommy Robinson."[2]

These large followings are a symptom of the popularity of Facebook itself. Facebook is the most used social media platform in the world (Kemp 2021). Its user numbers have continued to rise, undeterred by scandals like that around Cambridge Analytica (Dixon 2023). In Britain, it is by far the most popular social networking site, used by 79 percent of the population at the time of this fieldwork (O'Dea 2018) and 53 million people in 2022 (Dixon 2022). Over the years, Facebook has burrowed into social life in many societies, and users are motivated to stay on the platform by the relationships they maintain there and the power of their routine practices (Lupton and Southerton 2021). The research on which this book is based focused on Facebook users precisely for this reason. Disproportionate attention has been given to the relationship between Brexit and social media on rival platform Twitter (see Hall 2022c). This is in line with broader trends in the study of populism and hate online (see Jacobs et al. 2020). Such trends have come about perhaps because Twitter has (until recently) provided capability through application programming interfaces, or APIs, to scrape content for research, and because the character limit and simplicity of format facilitate analysis of the content Posted there. However, not only is Twitter a less significant platform in the UK in terms of number of users, but these users are more heavily concentrated among the young and highly educated (Mellon and Prosser 2017; Sloan 2017), meaning older and less-educated cohorts are in fact more likely to use Facebook than Twitter. According to Lord Ashcroft's highly-regarded polling, it is precisely these cohorts who were most likely to have voted Leave in the EU referendum (Ashcroft 2016).

THE FOCUS OF THIS BOOK

This book is about the phenomenon of political engagement with pro-Brexit and surrounding right-wing populist politics on Facebook. The term "political engagement" is used throughout to mean, broadly, a state of being "engaged with" political topics, causes and issues, which in Berger's (2009) definition encompasses both activities in (being "engaged *in*") and attention to (being "engaged *by*") political issues and processes. In the study of political social media use, this concept thus captures both the activities individuals undertake online (and offline) and the meanings they make of them, or their ideological consequences. As will become clear, the users in this study were engaged with Brexit and surrounding issues on Facebook, in that they were engaged (or affected) *by* the content they encountered and its inherent ideologies, and actively engaged *in* Sharing this content with the conscious intention of spreading awareness in the hope of effecting change.

I refer to the sphere in which this engagement was taking place as the "pro-Brexit Facebook milieu." This was an at times loose, at times tight, coagulation of dozens of Pages and Groups where content in support of Brexit—and frequently other right-wing causes—was Shared, discovered, appreciated, discussed, revised, and redistributed. Moving within this milieu, a user could encounter the same meme or Follower on multiple Pages or Groups. At the same time, any two individual users may never come across each other, and no two Pages or Groups were exactly alike. I call the users who engaged with these Pages and Groups as part of their support for Brexit "pro-Brexit Facebook users." This choice of terminology is deliberately neutral, so as to encompass the widest possible range of levels and styles of engagement. Few pro-Brexit Facebook users considered themselves "members" of a community or movement. Facebook afforded them the ability to engage with the content in the milieu without any formal commitment. And while the term "user" falls short of recognizing that these individuals also led offline lives, into which they carried the same political stances, I choose it to reflect the focus of this book on the impact of their online activities.

The current study also has a particular focus on those who did not grow up with the internet, or roughly those whose birth year falls before 1980 (see Palfrey and Gasser 2008). Social media use has been on the rise among older age groups, with Facebook the most popular outlet for this (Ofcom 2017). Thus, while much research has focused on the use of social media by younger generations, including for political participation and expression (e.g., Edgerly et al. 2018; Ekström and Shehata 2018; Loader et al. 2014; Macafee and De Simone 2012; Penney 2018; Schuster 2013; Sveningsson 2014; Vraga et al. 2015; Vromen et al. 2016; Yamamoto et al. 2015; Zhou and Pinkleton 2012), there is an important case for investigating the political social media use of those who have been experiencing the adoption of, and adaptation to, use of the internet later in life (Vošner et al., 2016). Any research into older groups' social media use has tended to focus on the 65+ cohort, and the needs or deficiencies of this group which either act as barriers to adoption of technology or can be ameliorated by it (Beneito-Montagut et al. 2022). Such research rarely examines these individuals' social media use in its own right, let alone as a form of engagement with politics.

The focus in this book on those who did not grow up with the internet is not intended to homogenize the relationship with technology of a whole generation of users, to legitimize a moral panic over the effects that this technology may have on any one age group, or to make assumptions about media literacy. Rather, it is to acknowledge the significance of having to adopt digital connectivity in adulthood, which should be understood as part of a broader experience of adapting to a rapidly changing world. For those born before 1980, this includes living through the neoliberal project that was Margaret Thatcher's prime ministership, the end of the Cold War, a sizeable increase in ethnic, cultural, and religious diversity in Britain, and huge progress in many areas of minority rights recognition. While such change is certainly no prerequisite for, nor predeterminate of, conservative political stances, as we shall see throughout this book, these contexts were important to the pro-Brexit Facebook users examined in this study. Indeed, the strong relationship between age and voting intention in the 2016 referendum broadly mirrors other survey findings about attitudes toward immigration, multiculturalism, and transgender rights (British Social Attitudes 39 2022).

RESEARCHING FACEBOOK SOCIOLOGICALLY: A USER-CENTRIC METHOD

This book makes a further important contribution to our understanding of online, right-wing populist political engagement by re-evaluating how it is studied. While there has been much public and academic discussion about the potential for social media milieus to disinform, polarize, or radicalize, little is yet known about how individuals actually engage with contentious content on social media and the effect this has on their social and political lives (Hall 2022c). I contend that this is because existing studies have tended to focus on collecting and analyzing social media content and behavioral traces that can be quantified, such as Likes or Shares. These methods are less suited to understanding experiences, intentions, and subjective meaning-making, or to investigating social phenomena in context. They have been accused of inherent positivist assumptions, of taking a superficial, decontextualized or reductive approach to social media data, and of ignoring "the embeddedness of the media into society's power structures and social struggles" (Fuchs 2017, 40).

Studies into the relationship between social media and Brexit have included the use of computational techniques to attempt to measure the influence of "bots" during the referendum campaign (Bastos and Mercea 2019; Gorodnichenko et al. 2018; Howard and Kollanyi 2016), the extent of the circulation of "rumours, conspiracy theories and propaganda" about Brexit (Dobreva et al. 2019, 144), information consumption patterns around Brexit (Bossetta, Segesten, and Trenz 2018; Bossetta, Segesten, Zimmerman, et al. 2018; Del Vicario et al. 2017), and patterns of emotional expressions on social media in the aftermath of the referendum (Bouko and Garcia 2020; Rosa and Ruiz 2020). Discourse analysis has also been conducted on the content of particular Posts or Pages related to Brexit (Bonacchi et al. 2018; Fuchs 2018b; Lilleker and Bonacci 2017; Spring and Webster 2019).

All of these studies represent the emergence of a field of "social media analysis" in political communication, fueled by excitement over new computational capabilities. However, the objects of these analyses are the materials available for users to engage with and the artifacts of some of these users' interactions with it. These artifacts are not windows into social reality, nor do they provide access to users' "true" sentiments (Langlois and Elmer 2013; see also Hogan 2010). Behavioral traces left on social media are shaped by specific norms and expectations there, by imagined audiences (Marwick and boyd 2011), and by the logics and affordances of each platform (van Dijck and Poell 2013). Focusing on such artifacts alone provides little insight into the lived realities within which these arise or their actual ideological consequences. It cannot tell us which content is meaningful to individuals and in what ways, or their motivations for consuming and circulating such content and engaging with the ideologies contained therein (Latzko-Toth et al. 2016). Thus, a reliance on such studies limits our understanding of social media use to the data it produces, severing its connection with individuals' "offline" lives. It obfuscates the social and cultural conditions under which these online behavioral traces are produced, and the consequences of this for politics and for society. As Hine (2015) argues, we must treat the digital as embedded, embodied, and every day if we are to research its use in a sociologically meaningful way. This necessitates seeking the interpretations of users themselves (Geertz 1977).

Meanwhile, in sociological accounts of support for Brexit, theoretical works dominate while empirical investigations—close-up work in particular—remain limited. As noted above, quantitative findings have pointed to the link between the Brexit vote and opposition to immigration, and analysis of campaign material has emphasized the importance of racism, nationalism, or populism (Ashcroft 2016; Campanella and Dassù 2019; Clarke and Newman 2017). However, the limited interview studies that have been conducted with Brexit supporters have mostly focused on class-based explanations and downplayed the importance of racism (e.g., Balthazar 2017; Koch 2017; McKenzie 2017; Walkerdine 2020). These studies, in turn, have been criticized for perpetuating "methodological whiteness" that assumes a link between class and race, and a "left-behind" discourse that legitimizes racism (Bhambra 2017). Crucially, little sociological attention has been paid to the role of social media in (enduring) pro-Brexit sentiment, with most sociological accounts studying this as an offline phenomenon and failing to acknowledge the crucial role of online spaces that I have outlined above.

Acknowledging this important research gap, this book is based on a multi-method, close-up, interpretive study. I developed a novel, user-focused method combining two rounds of in-depth interviews with immersive qualitative observations. The aim of this method was to privilege users' accounts of how they engaged with pro-Brexit and related right-wing content on Facebook and the significance of this engagement to their social and political lives. Fifteen pro-Brexit Facebook users were identified, based on them having publicly Shared at least one piece of pro-Brexit content on Facebook in the past month. These individuals consented to having their Posts observed for a one-month period, as well as participating in an interview both before and after these observations.[3] The interviews ranged from about half an hour to almost 2.5 hours in length, with the average length being around seventy-five minutes. There was no attrition, and all individuals participated in all three aspects of the study. Most of the initial interviews took place via Facebook video chat, and most of the follow-up interviews in person in local cafes or pubs, or at participants' homes. I carried out all of the interviews and immersive observations myself between July 2018 and May 2019, at the height of critical media coverage of then-Prime Minister Theresa May's negotiations with the EU.

Rather than using computational techniques to analyze the content that the participants Posted to Facebook during the observation period (as is often the case with studies of political phenomena on social media) I observed each of the Posts in its original context, taking detailed field notes that I used to help inform a situated understanding of these individuals' social media lives. Immersing myself in participants' Facebook Timelines, I followed links Posted to other sites, and read, watched or otherwise examined the content there to deepen my understanding of the milieu in which they were engaged. Particularly intriguing Posts by each individual were also used as prompts in their follow-up interview to elicit interpretations and encourage discussion on and around enigmatic themes. My full field diary for the study consists of details of 3,693 Posts, including images, videos, news articles, blog items, or simple text. Following the consent-based approach of this study, no details were collected or stored about Posts or Comments made by any individuals other than the study participants, including Posts by Friends on their Timelines. These immersive observations gave me unique and invaluable insights into the pro-Brexit Facebook milieu, the discussions and interactions there. In this project, as primacy was given to the meanings attributed by the participants themselves as social actors, the Posts observed were used to "thicken" the interpretations of participants and augment my understanding of their online world. Throughout this book, unless otherwise stated, all quotes from participants represent comments made in interviews as opposed to remarks they Posted on Facebook. Images from Facebook Posts are not reproduced here, as like much social media content, their original authors are near impossible to ascertain and to obtain proper consent from. Furthermore, given the particularly evocative power of images and the often discriminatory or hateful nature of the content in the milieu, I do not care to add to their dissemination.

The participants of this study occupied a range of social classes and geographical locations within England and Wales.[4] Their ages ranged between forty and seventy-three; eight were male and seven female. Basic demographic details can be found in the Appendix. All names are pseudonyms assigned by myself. No deliberate attempt was made to recruit from minority ethnic groups, and all of those who agreed to participate were White British. Although certainly not all Leave voters identify as White British (Begum 2023), the majority do (Ashcroft 2016). Meanwhile, Whiteness has been described as playing an important role in the sorts of racist and nationalist tropes that were significant to the Leave campaign (Valluvan and Kalra 2019). A sample limited to White Britons, while unable to explore the full complexities of inter-ethnic relations in Britain that contributed to support for Brexit, affords an opportunity to focus on the role of race, including transnational White consciousness, in online engagement with Brexit and right-wing populism.

The socially harmful nature of some of the attitudes expressed by the participants of this study both online and offline meant that researcher-participant relationships presented certain ethical issues. Building a degree of trust with participants was necessary to encourage them to openly share their interpretations with me in interviews, particularly given my status as a member of academia, a group often demonized in the milieu as "liberal elites." However, developing close or empathetic relationships would clearly have been ethically problematic and risked legitimizing these attitudes through "White complicity" (Applebaum 2010; Esseveld and Eyerman 1992). Meanwhile, Pilkington (2019) argues one may research and attempt to understand a group without "siding" with them or "faking" friendship. I therefore chose a strategy of "deflection" (Waldner and Dobratz 2019) and "vigilance" (Foste 2020) in interviews, whereby I demonstrated active listening but neither feigned agreement with nor actively challenged participants' problematic views. Although some researchers advocate a more transparent approach (e.g., Blee 2002), given the sensitization around Leave-Remain identities, this would likely have driven participants away or caused interviews to deteriorate into conflict.

STRUCTURE OF THE BOOK

This book is divided into three sections, each representing a salient layer of engagement with Brexit on Facebook that emerged from the testimony of the users themselves. Each of these interrelated facets sheds light on the fundamental question of what this engagement meant to these individuals. The first section, "Experiences," asks which online practices were seen as most meaningful by the users, and how this came to be so. It thus contributes to our understanding of what the affordances of the internet and social media bring to bear on right-wing populist mobilizations. Chapter 1 examines the routes by which these users came to be politically engaged on Facebook, based on their own accounts of this transformative process. It identifies a crucial conjuncture for the politicization of individuals who had otherwise been largely politically disengaged, namely between the technological opportunities provided by Facebook, the discursive and sociopolitical opportunities found in the offline realm, and the rise to prominence of Brexit as a mainstream political issue. This conjuncture crystallized pre-held grievances and propelled individuals into intense online political engagement. The findings challenge the idea that mobilization of online support for right-wing populism can be explained by attending to social media architectures alone, highlighting the need for processes to be situated within their social, political, and historical contexts.

Chapter 2 turns to participants' online practices in order to elucidate the role played by Facebook in the ways in which these individuals engaged with pro-Brexit and right-wing populist politics. Focusing on what the users described as the two most significant types of practices—finding and Posting content—the analysis reveals the aspects of the Facebook platform that made engagement with Brexit meaningful. These included its logics of automation, visuality, and Sharing, which were themselves shaped by the constraints of the attention economy and the system of surveillance capitalism. Within a sociopolitical context that pro-Brexit Facebook users saw as devaluing and disempowering, Facebook both afforded and encouraged them to become politically engaged in ways that made them feel socially valued and in control. However, it also put limitations on the continuity of these practices, through its potential to place burden on users' relationships, emotional well-being, and the constant threat of temporary and permanent platform bans.

The second section of the book, "Ideology," focuses on the ideological substance of pro-Brexit engagement on Facebook. It asks which ideas gave this engagement its appeal, and does so through the lens of narratives. Chapter 3 demonstrates how an overarching "metanarrative" gave the milieu its ideological nucleus: a story of a covert global agenda from above to force left-wing change, to the detriment of ordinary people. The designation of villains, victims, and heroes of the plot points to the role of democracy, freedom, and traditional values as evaluative criteria within the metanarrative, and reveals the importance of populist configurations. The integration of ideas borrowed from far-right conspiracy theories also illuminates the power of social media and Brexit to extend the reach of the transnational far-right.

Chapters 4 and 5 then unpack the two main types of ideology that underpinned engagement in the pro-Brexit Facebook milieu. Chapter 4 explores the role of racism, a force often implicated in support for Brexit but rarely the focus of studies into manifestations of Brexit on social media. Racist ideologies, including differentialist racism, cultural racism, nativism and Islamophobia, are revealed to play a prominent role. Chapter 5 turns to anti-leftism, whose relationship to support for Brexit has yet to be explored. Analyzing how anti-leftism is operationalized in the narratives of pro-Brexit Facebook users reveals how it is at once an extension of the "loony left" folk devil of the Thatcher era and a product of the absorption of ideas from the transnational far-right. Together, these two chapters illuminate the existence of two key forms of indignation driving engagement in the pro-Brexit Facebook milieu: White victimhood and Right victimhood.

The third section, "Knowledge," focuses on the importance of knowledge—broadly construed to encompass notions of facts, information, and truth—to engagement in the pro-Brexit Facebook milieu. In Chapter 6, I examine the users' relationship with knowledge in light of the characterization of Brexiteers, in both popular and academic discourse, as misinformed, irrational, and driven by emotions. Doing so reveals how these individuals sought to assert their epistemic capital (Maton 2003) in order to reclaim a stake in political knowledge production and subvert what they saw as a pro-left regime of truth. The chapter demonstrates how this both reflects, and constitutes an important part of, a broader transnational movement within online right-wing populism toward weaponizing "facts" as part of a contemporary struggle for cultural hegemony.

The final chapter, "Taking Back Control?" concludes this volume by synthesizing the findings of each of the empirical chapters to generate an understanding of engagement with Brexit and right-wing populist politics on Facebook as a sociological phenomenon. It highlights the way in which Brexit became an effective vehicle for the grammar of right-wing populism to appeal to individuals who came to see themselves as disempowered, within the context of enduring racisms and experiences of liberal social change, and how this was operationalized through the phantom grievances of both White victimhood and Right victimhood. The chapter draws on evidence from the preceding analysis to demonstrate how Facebook not only provided an opportunity to exercise a sense of political agency, but also to connect with far-right ideas that would perhaps not have otherwise found themselves salient in a Eurosceptic milieu. I highlight how these insights were only able to be garnered through a methodological and epistemological approach that privileged the meaning-making of the individuals actually engaging in this milieu.

A NOTE ON TERMINOLOGY AND LIMITATIONS

It is necessary to provide clarification on the use of additional key terms which have already begun to appear in this introductory chapter. Firstly, it should be noted that in this book, functions of social media platforms are denoted by capitalizing the first letter, for example, Post, Share, Like, Friend, Timeline, Newsfeed. This is to avoid confusion with the lay use of these terms; for example, the difference between sharing one's thoughts with a friend through a letter in the post, and Sharing one's thoughts with one's Friends via a Post to one's Facebook Timeline.

My decision to use the terms "right-wing populist," "racist," and "far-right" throughout this book to characterize the phenomenon of political engagement that linked the pro-Brexit Facebook milieu to likeminded mobilizations across the world, was not taken lightly. As Mudde (2019, 5) notes, choice of terminology is not a trivial matter in this arena as such definitions are also used to set the limits of social, democratic and legal acceptability. Choosing the term that individuals or groups use to describe themselves is one strategy toward avoiding misrepresentation and coheres with an interpretivist epistemology. However, this would rely on an articulated (and consistent) self-awareness by these individuals, something which is not characteristic of the disparate milieus and fluid participation online.

No one term can begin to adequately describe the complexities of the exclusionary, reactionary, and racist right-wing ideologies and movements which are plaguing societies around the world. While right-wing populist parties and opportunistic conservative politicians are not the same as, for example, far-right groups or the Alt-Right movement, we cannot pretend that these do not interact and overlap, in their actors, ideologies, targets and aims. At the same time, choosing any one feature shared by all of these mobilizations, such as racism or illiberalism, does not do justice to the variegated and composite ways in which they draw their support. "Populism" as a research field has been (I would argue, aptly) criticized for constituting somewhat of an academic bandwagon, for failing to agree on the definition of the object of its analysis, and for constructing a purely political phenomenon that obscures the pervasive role of racism in support for these parties and movements (Brubaker 2017b; Rooduijn 2019). At the same time, focus on the "far-right" is said to contribute to the construction of racism as the property of an extreme fringe, which results in a failure to confront the endemic nature of racism in society and its everyday consequences for racialized individuals.

Although it is therefore at best impractical and at worst impossible to choose an umbrella term with which to refer to the phenomenon under investigation here, an analytic focus is nonetheless necessary to advance the discussion. Right-wing populism is a useful concept for understanding the *appeals* at play in the pro-Brexit and related right-wing milieus online, which were central to mobilizing the forms of indignation that this study finds drove the online political engagement of users. A strong appeal to the "will of the people," juxtaposed against a democratically illegitimate "elite"—which scholars tend to agree is the fundamental tenet of "populism" (Mudde 2007)—was inescapably pivotal in the rhetoric of the Leave campaign and in the content Shared in the pro-Brexit Facebook milieu. My use of the term populism is not meant to legitimize the demands of right-wing populists as somehow the voice of a virtuous majority. On the contrary, I use the term consciously, to bring focus to the use of such discursive constructs by racist and right-wing actors to generate appeal and bring an aura of legitimacy to their exclusionary, hateful, and illiberal ideas.

I have chosen to use this term with the modifier "right-wing" not only to differentiate the phenomenon from what is sometimes termed "left-wing populism," whose targets and aims tend to be fundamentally different, but also to highlight the central role of a range of (culturally, rather than economically) right-wing ideologies to this. I also use the category of "right-wing" throughout the book to describe the broader gamut of content with which the participants engaged. Here too I use this to mean culturally, rather than economically right. Where this short-hand is used, it is not done so to dismiss the importance of racist, discriminatory and at times far-right ideology in the content in question. Rather, my intention is to be as all-encompassing as possible while incorporating an implicit recognition of the real and mutually reinforcing relationship between these more extreme forms of right-wing politics and more "mainstream" right-wing ideology.

Where possible, I refer to attitudes or behaviors by more specific terms. This includes the use of "racism," which is meant here to refer to all forms of racism, including "cultural" and "biological" racism and forms of racialization. While Islamophobia is considered a form of racism, where relevant I refer to it specifically, so as to acknowledge the particularly salient nature of attitudes toward Islam and Muslims within the milieu under study and within global contemporary racism more broadly. Similarly, I use the term "nativism" not to refer to a phenomenon distinct from racism, but to acknowledge the importance of attitudes toward immigration, ethnic-cultural-religious diversity, entitlement, and belonging in contemporary racisms (Huber et al. 2008). Those movements and political actors who openly profess to seek the creation of White ethno-states, often without ostensibly claiming to represent the will of the people as populists do, I refer to in this book as "far-right," rather than "radical right" or "extreme right," as the radical right is more closely associated narrowly with political parties, and the extreme right narrowly with violent acts, neither of which are prerequisites for the social media mobilizations with which the pro-Brexit Facebook users interacted online.

Because the participants of this study came to comprise a group who were mostly very actively politically engaged in Publicly Sharing content on Facebook, the analysis and conclusions drawn in this book apply more to this group than to social media users casually interacting with right-wing content. However, the participants of this study were generally neither extremists in terms of their worldviews nor radical in terms of their lived experiences. Many of the ideas that they expressed in their Facebook Posts had more than niche appeal. At the same time, these individuals were part of a startlingly large, transnational milieu of racist, nativist, and right-wing populist online political actors. Thus, observations about these participants' practices, narratives, and attitudes toward information and information-seeking offer important insights into the real potential for Facebook to politically engage users around contentious topics and the implications of this.

Finally, it is important to note that the interpretive approach of this book, which seeks to give voice to and understand participants and their meaning-making on their own terms, is not intended to condone or legitimize the positions or attitudes they express. To do so would be to diminish the racialization and discrimination experienced by many of the minoritized groups who are targeted by these attitudes. This book does seek, however, to understand and engage with the experiences of participants in so much as they are real to them. Whether or not participants' sense of disempowerment reflected a political reality is not under investigation here. What is important is that this feeling or experience of disempowerment, as will be revealed in the coming pages, was real in its consequences. Furthermore, as Clarke and Newman (2017, 109) note, oversimplification of the issue of Brexit support into a binary whereby "either Brexit people are racists or they are decent people who have suffered [. . .] is analytically unsustainable and politically unhelpful." It collapses the complexity of social relations and denies the plurality and fluidity of the identities, values, and attitudes people hold, which can be at times internally incompatible or even contradictory. The aim of this book is to shed light on this complexity, as it elucidates the elaborate nexus between the contemporary phenomenon of Euroscepticism, long-standing discontent with immigration and social change, and the evolving role of social media in politics.

NOTES

1. The firm has admitted no liability (BBC News 2019b).

2. "Tommy Robinson" is the name by which Stephen Yaxley-Lennon calls himself (Cleland 2020).

3. One participant, Olivia, incurred a permanent ban from Facebook toward the beginning of her observation period. She continued Posting on other social media platforms, and I obtained permission from her to observe this on the platform with the most similar interface to Facebook, called MeWe. The content she chose to Post on MeWe may have differed from what she would have Posted on Facebook due to, among other things, differences in permitted content and the imagined audience for Posts. However, as this study focused on users' interpretations of their online practices, this is not deemed to have had a significant impact on the findings.

4. The study was limited to these two nations to avoid introducing into the small participant sample the complexity of the unique socio-historical contexts and nationalisms of Scotland and Northern Ireland, where Brexit did not receive majority support in the referendum (R. Harris and Charlton 2016; Henderson et al. 2017).

SECTION I

Experiences

Chapter 1

Becoming Engaged in Brexit and Right-Wing Populist Politics on Facebook

> Social media probably changed my son's views as well as mine. [. . .] If you was thinking it ain't that bad in the EU and then you watch some of the stuff on social media and you think "bloody hell, I didn't know it was that bad." [. . .] That gives you the impetus to [. . .] push on and get out of it. (Kirk, male, 60s, London)

As set out in the previous chapter, this book focuses on the sense-making of individuals in order to understand how and why they engage with right-wing populism on social media. To this end, the first section examines users' experiences of such engagement, based on their own narratives. Answering the question of which online practices were seen as most salient by pro-Brexit Facebook users, and how this came to be so, can help reveal what it is that the affordances of the internet and social media bring to bear on right-wing populist mobilizations. This is particularly important in an age in which society is reckoning with the social and political consequences of the ubiquity of social media.

This chapter focuses on the processes or "trajectories" of becoming engaged in this form of online politics. It asks how everyday individuals come to be so engaged, and to what extent the online environment itself contributes to the way these politicizations play out. While privileging participants' accounts does not preclude the potential for them to reinterpret past experiences (Pilkington, 2016), I seek here to understand what such experiences *mean* to these individuals so as to elucidate the impact of social media insomuch as it is real to them. The findings raise important questions for how we should understand the role of the online environment in such processes and the potential for right-wing populist mobilizations within our current techno-social and political moment.

SOCIAL MEDIA AND TRAJECTORIES TOWARD RIGHT-WING POLITICAL ENGAGEMENT

The popularization of social media has had a profound impact on politics and the way many people engage with it. In line with this and in recognition of concurrent gains made by the right in a number of countries, significant academic and public concerns have been raised about the alleged ability of social media platforms like Facebook to "polarize" or "radicalize" individuals, and the dangers of this for democracy (Sunstein, 2018). A body of research has thus turned to investigating the potential role of social media in mobilizing support for right-wing populism and other divisive forms of politics (for reviews of this literature, see Marwick, Clancy, and Furl 2022; Tucker et al. 2018; Zhuravskaya, Petrova, and Enikolopov 2020).

Popular theories like "echo chambers" and "filter bubbles" were some of the first used to conceptualize the political effects of social media. They focus on these platforms' ability to filter out opposing views when tailoring content to user interests. Such filtering is said to reinforce views and contribute to political polarization, among the alleged outcomes of which is an ever more right-leaning segment of society (Ross Arguedas et al. 2022). However, empirical evidence on the existence and effects of these phenomena remains inconclusive and in some cases conflicting (Wollebæk et al. 2019). While echo chambers have been found to exist in insular spheres such as anti-vaccination communities (Van Raemdonck, 2019), other studies conclude that echo chamber effects depend on dispositional and topic-related factors (Barberá et al. 2015; Dubois and Blank, 2018), or that it is primarily those users who are more extreme in their ideologies who interact less with opposing views (Bright, 2017). There is also evidence that social media users do in fact actively seek out opposing viewpoints, albeit that this may be simply for the purpose of seeking confrontation (Karlsen et al. 2017). In fact, this confrontation may itself contribute to polarization by promoting defensive reactions and strengthening in-group resolve (Bail et al. 2018; Hwang, Kim, and Huh 2014; Kim and Kim 2019). These complexities and inconsistencies point to the limitations of technologically deterministic accounts that are unable to consider the embeddedness of online interactions within offline lives, with all of the socio-cultural specificity that this entails.

Since the events of 2016 and the ensuing concern about a "populist moment" (Mouffe 2019), focus has shifted somewhat from polarization processes to social media's alleged "affinity" with populism. These include the mass dissemination capabilities of these platforms, their subversion of mainstream media filtering, their ability to directly link charismatic figureheads to their followers, and the way they allow re-contextualization and reinterpretation of news (Engesser et al. 2017; Gerbaudo 2018). In his theoretical exploration of this relationship, Krämer (2017) touches upon the individual-level processes through which users may self-socialize into right-wing populism via social media. He posits that "concepts and interpretations of social phenomena" encountered online serve to crystallize latent attitudes and grievances (ibid., 1302). Social media platforms then provide unique opportunities to express, consolidate, and inter-subjectively confirm one's right-wing populist "identity." This process is partly prompted by online interactions with those with opposing views, which serve to "confirm one's status as a critical outsider" (ibid., 1302), a hypothesis supported by some of the findings about the role of confrontation in reinforcing political dispositions.

However, without empirical evidence on the actual experiences of users and what these experiences mean to them, we cannot know whether or how such a process of online right-wing populist (self-)socialization actually occurs, or the role of mechanisms like "echo chambers" or "filter bubbles" in this. A body of qualitative, interpretive work is developing in the field of "online radicalization," with a greater focus on individual experiences (e.g., Pilkington and Vestel 2021; McDonald 2018; Koehler 2014). However, becoming engaged with right-wing populist politics online is not the same as being "radicalized." Marwick et al. (2022) have argued that there are serious limits to the utility of "radicalization" as a frame for understanding the online spread of right-wing ideas, given among other things the concept's imprecision and its inextricable links with the post-9/11 security-driven scholarship targeting Islamist extremism. Though the definition of radicalization is contested, it is broadly understood as a process of adopting violent extremist ideologies (regardless of whether the individual goes on to commit violent acts) (Zhang and Davis 2022). Violent ideology was not a central feature of the pro-Brexit Facebook milieu and the users in the current study generally did not espouse violence. Although these individuals were intensely and passionately engaged, as we shall see in section II many of the ideologies at the core of this engagement were underpinned by ideas that were not necessarily new or by any means niche. Rather, as the vast numbers of Likes and Followers amassed by accounts like UKIP and "Tommy Robinson" on social media attest, they had a certain broad appeal. In this sense, the pro-Brexit Facebook milieu is an example of how transnational right-wing populist spaces may lie at the enigmatic intersection between increasingly "mainstream" right-wing populist content and fanatical dedication to these issues. Scholarship on online radicalization, with its focus on cognitive and affective journeys toward reverence or moral justification of heinous acts, is thus less useful for informing the study of the trajectories under investigation here.

USER EXPERIENCES OF BECOMING ENGAGED ONLINE

Evidence from the narrative accounts of pro-Brexit Facebook users can help to fill this gap in our understanding of the trajectories by which people become engaged with right-wing populist politics online. The individuals I spoke to had undergone significant processes of politicization. Interviews and observations revealed that they were intensely engaged in online right-wing populist politics. They spoke passionately about Brexit and about Facebook, and reported spending several hours daily discovering and distributing content online about Brexit and the political issues they saw as related to it. However, this online engagement was relatively new to them. As little as six months prior to the project fieldwork, these individuals had been more sporadic, primarily social, users of Facebook, in many cases not particularly interested in politics at all.

Attention to the lived experiences articulated in these individuals' trajectories allows us to connect online practices to offline lives in ways that cannot be achieved by the strategies of online-only data collection so relied upon by studies of political social media use. Thus, in the analysis that follows, I present evidence in the form of pen portraits that contextualize the analysis within each individual's broader experience of their trajectory. Examining these individuals' accounts of how and why their transformations occurred reveals the complexities and specificities of such trajectories. Together, they cannot be reduced to a singular typology or explanatory process. It is, however, possible to identify common salient forces that come to bear on these trajectories, beyond those determined by the architectures of social media.

In the following sections, I group the salient forces that featured in these individuals' accounts into discursive opportunities, sociopolitical opportunities, and technological opportunities, before addressing the unique power of the issue of Brexit to crystallize these. I conceptualize these as opportunities for they are not determining factors. The individuals in question ultimately possessed the agency to decide whether or not to become involved in pro-Brexit and right-wing populist engagement on Facebook. These external aspects did, however, provide the conditions for the trajectories to take place, and facilitated the transformations these individuals experienced. The analysis reveals the significance of the conjuncture at which these processes occurred—between historically-embedded racism, growing sociopolitical frustrations, the rise of political social media, and the emergence of Brexit as a salient right-wing populist issue within British politics. In many of the testimonies, Brexit was a key catalyzing force and social media an important enabler, but this form of politics would not have appealed were it not for the significant contexts of racism, Islamophobia, and misgovernance surrounding Britain in the leadup to the referendum. In short, for those engaged in pro-Brexit politics on Facebook, technological opportunities converged with discursive and sociopolitical opportunities to form a unique conjuncture at which the issue of Brexit was able to crystallize grievances and propel individuals into online political engagement.

Discursive Opportunities

When recounting how they came to be engaged, the pro-Brexit Facebook users articulated a range of experiences that they interpreted as motivations or triggers. Such interpretations were made possible by prominent discursive frames, which were a product of the ongoing salience of exclusionary ideologies within British society. In other words, this context created discursive opportunities (Ferree et al. 2002) for experiences to be understood as evidence of particular phenomena, and for these experiences to become meaningful to individuals in ways that motivated their online right-wing populist engagement.

Anti-multiculturalist Discourse

A key component of the backdrop to the pro-Brexit Facebook users' trajectories was the development of anti-multiculturalism and the nativist and culturally racist discourses that this has engendered. These discourses have been circulating for decades in the media and been promoted in the rhetoric of politicians (Kundnani 2002; Vertovec and Wessendorf 2010), infamously including David Cameron's pronouncement in 2011 that multiculturalism was "dead" (Sealy 2014). Coupled with neoliberal discourses of meritocracy, they have produced ways of describing and understanding diversity, entitlement, and belonging that have embedded themselves into everyday narratives within communities (Beider 2015; Hewitt 2005; Rhodes 2010). Such discourses feature heavily in the ideological underpinnings of the pro-Brexit Facebook milieu that will be examined in section II of this book.

Carl's trajectory illustrates well the role of the discursive opportunities provided by anti-multiculturalism. Carl was a self-employed van driver in his fifties, born, bred, and living in Northwest England. While his main "problem" as he described it was "with Islam, or radical Islam anyway," he also narrated an array of concerns around Britain "let[ting] too many people in." Like many of the pro-Brexit Facebook users, Carl spoke of a number of personal experiences that had contributed to or validated these views. He said his childhood had been very difficult, including being "abused as a kid" and "chucked out" when he was fifteen. Since then, Carl had "looked after meself," going from not having "a pot to piss in" to now owning his own home and successful business. He contrasted this with his perceptions of what was being offered to new arrivals, telling anecdotes from his job about moving "brand new" furniture and PlayStation consoles for "African" migrants who he claimed spoke no English and had received these and other expensive items for free. Although he described his current situation as "comfortable," Carl felt he worked long hours "to pay for migrants to come over here and get free benefits. Why can't *I* get benefits? [. . .] I'm working my fuckin' arse off here" (Carl's emphasis). By the time of the fieldwork, Carl's online research had driven him not only to become a frequent Public Sharer of material on Facebook and Twitter and occasional flat-Earth conspiracy theorist, but also a highly active (offline) member of UKIP in his local area. Carl used Facebook "just for politics," and the only Friend he had on there who he knew offline was his partner, who was similarly politically involved. Carl said he spent "all day" online keeping himself informed: "when I'm not working, I don't drink, I don't smoke, [. . .] I just relax and I just read politics and [. . .] educate meself on certain subjects."

Carl framed his claims about the benefits enjoyed by new arrivals in decidedly anti-multiculturalist and nativist terms, contrasting this alleged undeservingness with his own self-made success. Carl's everyday experiences, which played a primary role in his trajectory as he understood it, were made salient through an interpretation and articulation that became more likely within the social and political context of "new" or "cultural racism" in Britain (Barker 1981; Modood 2015).

Post-9/11 Securitized Islamophobia

Islamophobic frames, closely related to discourses of cultural racism but particularly salient in the context of the "war on terror" (Kundnani 2014), play a key role in Carl's directing of his attention toward Islam in particular. The pervasive circulation of these frames in British and other Western societies clearly influenced the way the pro-Brexit Facebook users interpreted their interactions with Muslims and facilitated their conflation of Islam with terror and violence.

This was a prominent theme in Beatrice's account. A retired special needs teacher in her sixties living in North Wales, Beatrice said she got "dragged into" signing up for Facebook around 2011 or 2012 as a way of staying in touch with friends in South Africa, where she and her husband had been spending several months each year since retirement. Beatrice's Facebook use became political after she joined a UKIP Facebook Group for her then local area in the Northwest of England in the lead-up to the EU referendum. Beatrice became a paid-up member of UKIP offline and "stood behind tables' for UKIP and Vote Leave in her local area because they were "meeting my needs in [terms of] Brexit." By the time of the fieldwork, she was spending several hours each day Posting dozens of items of content around Brexit and Islam. She felt so strongly about then-Prime Minister Theresa May "signing away the country" with the proposed exit deal that she had organized a minibus for herself and a number of similarly-minded people locally (whom she had only ever met online) to travel to an upcoming "Brexit Betrayal March" in London. Despite spending so much of her retirement engaging with content around Brexit and Islam on Facebook, Beatrice downplayed her knowledge of formal politics. With no little sense of irony she claimed, "I am not politically minded. [. . .] I really wasn't that interested in politics until this issue of Brexit came about, and it's only because of that that [. . .] I've started on this mission."

When asked what had sparked her interest in Brexit, Beatrice said it had probably been long-time UKIP leader Nigel Farage's television interviews and his stance on "immigration and getting the country back" that had appealed to her. She said there had been no particular "Eureka moment," but rather "a gradual process and listening to [Farage]." Farage's rhetoric appeared to speak to resentments that Beatrice had developed over many years. These stemmed from her perception of the changing demography of her local community and her interactions with students and parents at the school where she taught. For Beatrice, these resentments revolved around Muslim residents in particular. She replicated Islamophobic tropes about the perceived increasing unwillingness of Muslims to "integrate" since 9/11. She said she came to the view that "[Muslims] are the only people who have come over to our country and want to dominate. [. . .] They just want to install their way of life." The timing of this shift in Beatrice's perception is no coincidence, given the growth in negative attitudes toward Islam and Muslims that the "war on terror" prompted.

For Beatrice, this was also later compounded by media coverage of the "grooming gangs" scandal, cases of which she said were uncovered near her local area. This term was commonly used in the media—and subsequently in the pro-Brexit Facebook milieu—to refer to the alleged cover-up by local authorities in multiple British towns of cases of organized sexual exploitation of mostly White girls by groups of men of Asian Muslim heritage. The cases date back to the 1980s, but came to the public's attention through a series of prosecutions and official inquiries in the 2010s (Dearden 2019; Jay 2014). This scandal was exploited by right-wing populist politicians (Cockbain and Tufail 2020), which saw it become a flashpoint for Islamophobic sentiment.

Importantly, it was embroiled in accusations of "reverse racism" for the sake of "political correctness," and thus was implicated in loss of trust in authorities within these communities and used as justification for opposition to multiculturalism. Racialized reporting that focused on the ethnic background of the perpetrators created the conditions for Beatrice to interpret her local community's experience of this scandal as incriminating evidence against ethnic minorities and Muslims.

In this way, despite her claims not to be "politically minded," Beatrice's political sensibilities were developing long before she encountered UKIP's racist discourses on television and subsequently became engaged on Facebook. That Beatrice cited Farage's television appearances as particularly significant in transforming her latent resentments into support for Brexit and online and offline political action serves as a reminder that neither Eurosceptic nor anti-immigration discourses are new, and nor have they been confined to online platforms. Traditional media outlets have laid considerable groundwork for the anti-immigration and anti-establishment discourses that circulate online (van Dijk 2000), particularly with regard to reporting on EU immigration (Fox 2018).

The Impact of IS and the Syrian War

Islamophobia in Britain was further exacerbated by the emergence of IS following the failed Western occupation of Iraq and unrest in Syria. The terrorist attacks attributed to this group in Europe in the early 2010s had a clear impact on the attitudes of the pro-Brexit Facebook users toward Islam and Muslims, and contributed to their trajectories toward online political engagement.

The influence of these events and the Islamophobic frames they engendered feature in Jessica's account. Jessica was in her forties and had previously run a successful business in the removals and haulage industry. She lived with her Nigerian-British partner and their adolescent daughter in London. Like Beatrice, Jessica attested that she had not previously been "political," having only voted once in her life. Then a personal event (the details of which she preferred not to be recorded) turned her life upside down, leaving her lost and with little to do to fill her time. "Switching on the news" became Jessica's "escape" from her grief. This happened in 2016, and one of the first things Jessica began looking into was the issue of Brexit. She "stumbled across" Russian state-backed news outlet *RT* on television, whose subversive and conspiratorial narratives led her to question the content of British news outlets and the interests behind them. Later in the year, the terrorist attack in Nice occurred, which left her "absolutely devastated," particularly given that a truck, the symbol of the industry to which she had dedicated her life, had been used in the deadly assault. Whether or not she had already been engaging with Islamophobic material is unclear, but the event, as she narrated it, helped to cultivate her suspicion around Islam and Muslims: "I even had Muslim friends and I was like 'what on Earth is going on?' and they couldn't really tell me, you know, because they didn't really *want* to tell" (Jessica's emphasis). Jessica then moved from engaging with news on television to "literally put[ting] all my time" into investigating politics online.

As she continued to "dig deeper" into Islamophobia and conspiracy theories, Jessica experienced what she described as an awakening. Being "awake," she said, means "tuned in to what's going on, rather than just living in my own personal bubble of family and work life and stuff." Some of the claims that Jessica came to believe included that "one nation" politicians were secretly orchestrating a "new world order" by facilitating financial chaos and encouraging mass Muslim immigration to Europe. According to Jessica, during the Syrian War, the British government "bombed strategic places to allow the migration to take effect" which she thought prompted "imams in mosques all across Northern Africa and the Middle East" to begin an "emigration jihad." Jessica felt these and other conspiracy agendas were "very much" related to Brexit, because from within the EU it would not be possible to "take back control" of the way the "people at the top" were "doing commercial deals" for profit rather than "for the people."

Jessica's account demonstrates how the discourses of fear and suspicion created by certain geopolitical conditions can provide fertile ground for the uptake of Islamophobic and far-right conspiracy theories. More than a decade of post-9/11 securitized Islamophobia had laid the ground for Jessica to interpret her Muslim friends' refusal to account for the Nice attack as part of a conspiracy of silence. Disruptor news outlets like *RT* capitalize upon such suspicions (Hall 2022a). It is therefore not surprising that Jessica was keen in interviews to relay "truths" about Syria and the White Helmets group that closely matched the Russian strategic narrative of the conflict that *RT* had been promoting (Dajani, Gillespie, and Crilley 2019). Research with *RT*'s Facebook audiences has demonstrated how the appeal of this alternative, anti-Western narrative of the Syrian War is underpinned in the UK by the legacy that the Iraq invasion had on public confidence in British foreign policy (Hall 2022b). The "long shadow" cast by the UK's decision to participate in the invasion of Iraq in 2003 and the revelations that this was likely based on false intelligence (Alexander 2011; in Clements 2013, 121) combined with popular Islamophobia to create opportunities for the narrative that Western involvement in Syria was enabling IS. This narrative served to sow further seeds of doubt over whether we were being told the "whole story" about Britain's role in the complex geopolitical conditions unfolding at the time. The climate of distrust created by misgovernance in the years leading up to the EU referendum will continue to be addressed later in this chapter.

Racialization of Migrants During the "Migrant Crisis"

Another key aspect of the geopolitical conditions surrounding these users' trajectories was the so-called "migrant crisis." In 2015, more than 900,000 people arrived in Europe seeking migration or asylum (Spindler 2015[1]). These conditions were capitalized upon by right-wing actors to further fuel racism, nativism, and Islamophobia in Britain (Abbas 2019). This created the discursive opportunity for the deployment of Leave campaign material like the infamous UKIP "Breaking Point" poster, which depicted what was revealed to be a column of Syrian and Afghan refugees being escorted between Croatia and Slovenia, but contained the text "We must break free of the EU and take back control of our borders" (Faulkner, Guy, and Vis 2021).

The effect of racialized discourses around the migrant crisis is particularly stark in Eileen's trajectory. Eileen was a property entrepreneur in her early sixties, who spent most of her time at her home in rural Northwest England. She said she had once looked down on those who used Facebook. Even after her stepdaughter had created an account for her, she had only used it to connect with friends and colleagues she already knew offline. Eileen said, "I completely misunderstood what Facebook was about. [. . .] Up until probably prior to [the 2016 referendum on] Brexit, I just used it like anybody else." What Eileen, like many other pro-Brexit Facebook users, now saw Facebook to be "about" was finding and Sharing political information.

Eileen attested that in the past she was oblivious to issues like the "migrant crisis": "My husband said I lived in cloud cuckoo land, and I didn't know anything about politics." Her visceral experience of this crisis at the French port in Calais, she claimed, radically transformed her attitude towards politics and propelled her into full-time "blogging," as she called it, on Facebook. Eileen described how on two occasions driving back to the UK with her husband from their holiday home in Austria she witnessed what she interpreted as threatening behavior by "migrants" who she described as "African." "That was my epiphany," she said. Racist logic is apparent in Eileen's interpretation of the border chaos she witnessed as a polluting encroachment on peaceful and civilized Europe: "I said 'we can't live like this! [. . .] We shouldn't have this in our life. This is wrong.'"

Eileen began to research the issue online. She set up a Facebook Group to share "evidence" about stowaways and related dangers allegedly faced by drivers between Calais and Dover. Information about this, Eileen felt, was deliberately being withheld or hidden by the British government. Eileen said she gathered this information from and for truckers because as a truck driver's daughter the issue of safety on the motorway was particularly personal to her. She conducted deeper and deeper online research, and piece by piece "information" she discovered furnished sinister explanations for the "migrant crisis" and placed the EU at the heart of these. She heeded alleged warnings that enforced societal change, in Britain and across the Western world, would have dystopian consequences. Similar to Jessica's case, preexisting racist discourses coupled with online far-right ideas provided Eileen with ways to articulate her negative experiences. Racialized media depictions of the "migrant crisis" (De Genova 2018b) laid the ground for issues like Brexit to appeal to her sense of fear and bewilderment.

Then, Eileen said, "I had to do something. [. . .] The biggest thing I could do was explain what Brexit was really about, cos I didn't really know [either]. I knew once I did the research." In the lead up to the referendum, Eileen dedicated herself to "explaining" Brexit to others in an effort to garner support for Leave, primarily through Facebook Posts but also in person and over video calls. As she Posted more and more information and analyses on Facebook in her own self-described "funny" (humorous) style, she began building up a following there, something she claimed happened unwittingly. At the time of the fieldwork, she had become one of many small scale "alternative influencers" (Lewis 2020) in the pro-Brexit Facebook milieu, spending about five hours a day curating a Public Facebook Page with tens of thousands of Followers alongside Publicly Posting on her own Timeline to spread the word about Brexit and the post-referendum "breakdown of democracy."

Eileen's trajectory demonstrates how the border chaos engendered by the "migrant crisis" provided key discursive opportunities for the dissemination of far-right conspiracy theories about population replacement and imposed multiculturalism. Such conspiracies also feed on mistrust and resentment toward authority, a force I continue to explore in the next section.

Sociopolitical Opportunities

While discursive opportunities provided the frames with which to (re-)articulate experiences as motivations for engaging with Brexit and right-wing populist politics online, other sociopolitical conditions engulfing Britain at the time provided key opportunities for right-wing populist sensibilities to develop. The testimony of the pro-Brexit Facebook users reveals how indignation and contempt stemming from these conditions served as prime opportunities for right-wing populism's anti-establishment and anti-left ideas to become appealing.

Austerity and Indignation

At the time of the fieldwork, the economic context of life in the UK had been marred by the effects of the 2008 global financial crisis, policies of financial austerity implemented in its aftermath, and the huge consequences of this for poverty and homelessness (Adler 2018; National Audit Office 2017). The frustration and indignation engendered by these conditions was acutely described by the working-class pro-Brexit Facebook users in this study in particular.

Carl, whose story featured earlier in this chapter, expressed a palpable indignation and loss of trust in UK governance when describing his motivations for becoming involved with UKIP. He described his resentment at how the strength of the Labour Party vote in his local area had made the council complacent and neglectful. According to Carl, this manifested in potholes in local roads, missed bin collections, "kids on the street with no food," and local councilors "just sit[ing] in the pub all day." Carl too had voted Labour all his life, until he "educated" himself on what he now saw as "corruption" and a lack of motivation to look after the needs of the working class. In Carl's words, "how can you have them leading a working-class party? They all at the top are all millionaires."

Audrey, a care worker in her fifties living in Northwest England, said of Britain's politicians, "They are not good leaders. They're very self-centered, selfish people. [Politics is] money orientated." She lamented the lack of investment in social welfare and infrastructure in Britain and described how this had influenced her turn to using Facebook: "I have to look after old people who barely survive. [. . .] It's like a smack in the face, and it's wrong [. . .] We need help here. We've people here starving, there's kids starving, who . . . old people, the national health . . . You put the news on and sometimes it's so depressing. That's why I got Facebook, because it's not as depressing." Audrey, however, saw this deprivation as the product of spending on foreign aid and migrant arrivals, saying "you can't have everybody in the world living in our country" and "[migrants] seem to get everything, and yet when our older people try and apply for a bit of a benefit [. . .] and they don't get it, [. . .] how is that fair?" Audrey and Carl's interpretations illustrate how indignation engendered by misgovernance and neglect lays the foundations for racist and nativist right-wing populist logics to appeal.

Similar frustrations can be seen in Helen's case. In her 50s, Helen was a full-time caregiver for a family member and mother of two young adults in the Midlands. She first opened her Facebook account around 2012, as a way of keeping an eye on her children's social media use because of concerns over online safety. Helen mostly spent her time on the platform "looking at cat pictures and playing Scrabble" until she started to find information about a range of political issues, particularly Brexit. By the time of her participation in this study in 2018, her activity on the platform had shifted to "the political Posts, thick and fast." Though she attested, "I never thought I'd ever get into anything like that online," Helen did not see her concerns as new. "I think before [. . .] the word 'Brexit' [came about], [. . .] I was never comfortable with being in the EU," she said, "because I felt, I've always felt, our politicians have hidden behind the fact that 'oh we can't do this, we can't do that' because of the EU." In her second interview, she reiterated that, "I've learned so much over the last five or six years, but I was pretty much of this mind-set anyway with the limited knowledge I've got, cos it was a *feeling* inside me" (Helen's emphasis).

Helen described an array of experiences she had had over her lifetime that had contributed to this "feeling"—which further discussion revealed constituted a sense of unease about immigration and what Helen called "identity politics." These included occasions when her daughter had experienced gender-based harassment in what she called a "Muslim-heavy area" and bullying from left-wing "Corbynistas"[2] at school; the ill-fated romantic involvement of her niece with a Muslim boy; and her son's difficulty finding work as a "White, heterosexual male." For Helen, these culminated in a strong sense of White victimhood, a concern that "anything to do with the White population doesn't matter" in the political and media agenda and that "Whites" were constantly being told they were "bad." This interpretation was compounded by the visible (and in her eyes, exclusively White) poverty she regularly encountered on the streets of her hometown, "a crumbling NHS, a shortage of school places, massive potholes," alongside what she perceived to be the increasingly confident presence of Asian and Muslim cultures. Helen tried contacting her local MP but found the response unencouraging. Because of this, she said, "You get pushed toward social media, and try and speak to people that don't want to shut you down."

Despite Helen's long-held "feeling," she had in fact previously been a Labour voter. This was because, having caring responsibilities and coming from a working-class background, she was opposed to austerity policies. Her first experiences of Facebook-based political engagement were on the Left, but they were not positive: "I did find myself on a few Pages that were sort of quite left-wing, and I sort of came off those because I just found that they were very information-light, [. . .] name-calling and mudslinging, [. . .] and the more I listened to it, I thought 'God, why did I ever vote Labour?'" This prompted Helen to have an "about-face" in her party and political allegiances, turning instead to right-wing Facebook Pages, which she found "far more informative." At the time of her participation in this study, Helen was in the habit of having Facebook open "nearly all the time." Alongside Brexit, Helen's primary concerns were child protection, "grooming gangs," and gender politics, but also extended to things like race tensions in South Africa and minority representation in soap operas.

While much of Helen's account of her trajectory is framed in anti-multicultural and Islamophobic terms, her views were also strongly informed by her experiences of living through Britain's age of austerity and the concurrent neglect of working-class communities. This contributed to Helen's frustration at the Labour Party for having seemingly turned away from working-class politics in favor of a focus on social progressivism. Helen's long-held unease found articulation in the idea that her conservative social values were being ignored or ridiculed by the Left—her sense of White victimhood was accompanied by what I term "Right victimhood." This ultimately led to her change in party allegiance and evolved into a preoccupation with the politics of gender and minority recognition. Both Helen's negative attitude toward the left and her loss of trust in politicians formed fertile ground for her subsequent engagement with right-wing populism.

Content circulating in the pro-Brexit Facebook milieu exploited such frustrations over Britain's economic troubles, positing them as evidence not of domestic politics or wider global economic dynamics, but of the negative consequences of membership in the EU. For one user, Fred, this had particular resonance as a family member had been made redundant due to what he came to interpret as EU policy. Fred was a retired administrator in his sixties living in Northeast England. He recounted the following anecdote in both of his interviews:

> [The factory was] performing superbly. European Union came along and gave a bribe [. . .] to move the factory to Poland. [. . .] They made all the workers redundant. [. . .] The Polish workers insisted on more money, smashed the machinery up, so Twinings tea, having a 300-year-old history in Britain, now comes from China. [. . .] All because of Europe trying to move British industry to Europe, and they've been doing that for the last 40 years. More and more manufacturing has been taken away from Britain and put into Europe.

In his anecdote, Fred alludes to discontent at wider processes of globalization and their effect on local communities and national culture, but places the blame for this on deliberate interference. Fred came to the view that EU membership had "certainly not benefited Britain in any way, shape or form."

Highlighting the role played by policies of austerity and processes of deindustrialization is not necessarily to affirm economic theories of the rise of the radical right (cf. Gest, Reny, and Mayer 2018). Rather, the testimonies here illustrate how experiences of this policy context became salient in combination with the discursive opportunities discussed above, the technological opportunities provided by social media, and the crystallizing power of Brexit.

Memories of the 1970s and 1980s Left

Meanwhile, for some users it was experiences of the 1970s and 1980s—characterized by a tumultuous period of economic policy and the rise and subsequent suppression of the trade union movement in Britain—that contributed to their right-wing dispositions and openness to the appeals of right-wing populism. A number of users described the polarizing context of those years, in which disagreement over industrial action had created "so much bitterness" (Fred). Mark, a secondary teacher and single father in his fifties living in Yorkshire, recounted vivid memories of having, "lived through the 70s and 80s, where this country was run by people like [Labour Party leader Jeremy] Corbyn,[3] and it was a God-forsaken shithole of a place. Strikes every week, [. . .] power cuts. [. . .] I'm scared of going back to them days when this country was bloody, oof, horrible."

In Olivia's trajectory, disdain for left-wing politics cultivated in that era worked in combination with an intense Islamophobia. Olivia was in her fifties and living in Southeast England at the time of the project fieldwork. Throughout her two interviews, she repeatedly professed to place a high value on "academic education." As a young girl in the 1970s she and her parents had lived abroad, where Olivia attended private school, but upon returning to Britain during Olivia's adolescence, she said she was sent to public school, against her wishes. Olivia's family had moved to what she described cynically as "somewhat of a diverse town. [. . .] In other words, all nationalities, all colors, blah blah blah." In Olivia's eyes, "the majority of people, of course, we all got on, [. . .] but, already back then I have to say the ones that didn't so much get on, unfortunately, were the children that were being brainwashed with Islam."

Olivia also saw her school years as being formative of her party-political allegiances. She recounted how she had challenged the impartiality of her openly pro-Labour geography teacher, an incident which she said had "got me interested in politics." Olivia spoke positively of neoliberalist Prime Minister Margaret Thatcher, praising her record on education which she felt had later been deliberately decimated by Labour. She said that Thatcher inspired her to become a homeowner at eighteen years old, and start her own successful property business in her twenties. When she participated in this research, she said she had already been retired for almost two decades.

As an adult, Olivia continued to develop her discriminatory attitudes toward Islam and Muslims. She was a keen traveler, but for the past fifteen to twenty years had "boycotted Islamic countries" because of what she saw as repeated bad experiences with locals there. At the time of the fieldwork, Olivia was considering moving out of her current local area because she claimed it was unsafe—three times in the past few weeks alone she had come across armed police she assumed were a measure against "Muslim radicals."

For reasons like this, unlike Beatrice and Eileen, Olivia had long considered herself a political person. She described her opposition to Islam as having "gone on 44 years," during which time she had written multiple letters of complaint to the BBC and to her Member of Parliament. However, she had only shifted this political activity online recently. Despite owning a Facebook account since around 2006, when a friend had created it on her behalf, Olivia had taken no interest in what she back then had deemed "nonsense Posts" about things like holiday plans. It was not until she witnessed first-hand a street demonstration against the visit of President Donald Trump in London in the summer of 2018 that she "really started using" Facebook and other social media. She recounted her visceral reaction to the rally:

> I cannot tell you how disgusting it was. It was embarrassing to be British. [. . .] To think that some of the people had their children there! And the thing that irritated me all the more was the mainstream media, where they'd blown it out of proportion by saying goodness-knows-how-many people were there to protest against President Trump. It was absolute, complete lies. [. . .] Of course, I write to the mainstream media and I submit my complaint. Do they ever reply? No, of course they don't. [. . .] So then, [. . .] just out of curiosity I did a tremendous amount more research of Donald Trump, and that's when I started teaching myself [. . .] how to use Facebook [. . .] for the purpose of trying to educate other people.

Thus, despite repeatedly describing Islam as her "topic," Olivia's online engagement was ultimately triggered by an encounter that rekindled her antipathy toward the "shockingly badly behaved" Left. Olivia began by strategically joining left-wing Facebook Groups to Post "factual articles" there. At the time of her first interview, she was spending "about an hour" every day Posting several dozen items of content to her Timeline. Olivia's interest in Brexit was secondary, although like others she viewed it as the solution to her anxieties about immigration.

That Olivia held faith responsible for her negative experiences with certain individuals, rather than considering the social, political, and other factors that undoubtedly played a role, is reflective of contemporary Islamophobia. This assumes that "Muslims are the living bearers of an immutable 'Islamic culture,' which conditions their psychology, behaviour and actions in a fundamentally different way to members of other cultures" (Jackson 2018, 14). However, Islamophobia alone cannot fully account for Olivia's politicization. In her interpretation, her neoliberal, meritocratic, and anti-socialist views, developed from childhood, played a key role in propelling her from a political individual to an enthusiastic online activist in the struggle for cultural hegemony between the Left and Right. As we shall see in section II of this book, this concurrence between racism and an acute anti-leftism was a fundamental feature of the mobilization of the pro-Brexit Facebook milieu.

Declining Trust in Media

Another factor alluded to in Olivia's account was declining trust in traditional news media. Many of the pro-Brexit Facebook users attributed their move toward relying on social media for information to their disappointment or disillusionment with television and print news. This in turn was driven by a perception that these media no longer represented their views and interests, were biased against causes like Brexit, or in Fred's words "totally dishonest" about the effects of immigration and multicultural policies. Beatrice, whose account featured above, was emphatic about this:

> I've stopped watching television because I end up stressed and screaming at the television because of the lies and [. . .] the bias and, [sighs] [. . .] so that is why, really, I now use social media to keep up to date basically, [. . .] because at least with social media if somebody says something, [. . .] you can respond [. . .] and say "no I don't agree with this." [. . .] You can make your own mind up instead of being fed what [. . .] the mainstream media want you to know. So, that is why, basically, I use Facebook such a lot.

These are not only individual sentiments but reflect a broader trend among the British public and many other advanced democracies in which trust in news has been in decline (Bennett and Livingston 2018; Newman 2021). Low trust in traditional news media has, unsurprisingly, been found to correlate with a preference toward online news sources (Fletcher and Park 2017). But the direction of causality in this relationship should not be assumed to be unilateral—use of right-wing alternative online news sources, for example, may further degrade media trust because these sites explicitly challenge the journalistic authority of traditional media in order to construct their own legitimacy (Figenschou and Ihlebæk 2019). For the pro-Brexit Facebook users, while loss of trust in traditional media was interpreted as a motivation for their engagement, like many aspects of their political views it is not always possible to ascertain how much of their disdain toward so-called "mainstream media" was garnered from the content they consumed on social media *after* they began using it politically.

In Olivia's case above, her claim to have submitted complaints to the BBC many years prior to her online engagement is evidence that for some users such grievances were consciously developing, at least in some form, before anti-"mainstream media" narratives were consumed online. This is also the case in Mark's testimony. Mark, whose comments about living through the 1970s and 1980s featured above, also said that he did not "hold much stock with BBC News" since the 9/11 attacks, as he felt some of their programming at that time was "advocating or seemingly backing Muslim extremists." Mark thought "this is no way a reflection of any society I know" and even tried, unsuccessfully, to submit a complaint. He attested, "from that moment onwards, [. . .] every time I watched them, I just think, it's just biased." It was incidents like this that Mark said fed his frustration with "political correctness," which in his eyes had been "affecting this country for decades."

Within that context, the catalyst for Mark's interest in Brexit was not the EU referendum campaign, but rather the situation in the aftermath of the vote, "when people started mentioning things like [. . .] second referendums and things like that. I think the second referendum, mention of second referendum was the one that made me sit up and think 'what?' Because I don't think it takes a genius to work out that this could go on forever and ever and ever." Mark said he had never Posted about how he was planning to vote before the referendum itself, "and to be honest I had no reason to get involved until all the shenanigans and the scurrilous behavior that's started to go on to try and block the Brexit." Mark asserted that he and all of those around him "would have accepted it if the vote had been for Remain. We'd have just got on with life. [. . .] But there's so many things going wrong with this and it's so undemocratic, and this, it's terrible." From then on, Mark "started getting me teeth into all the Brexit stuff" on Facebook, and the number of users who Liked and Commented on his Posts gradually grew, reaffirming his sense that he was not alone in his views. In his interviews, Mark repeatedly stressed this, reflecting the people-centrism of the populist post-referendum discourse at the time in saying he had no doubt that the "normal folks" like himself, "the vast majority of people" "in the pubs at night," were "absolutely fed up." Mark's case points to the way in which, as shall be expounded throughout this book, distrust of and dissatisfaction with "mainstream media" not only represented a motivation for using social media, but was central to the sense of political marginalization or Right victimhood that drove engagement within the pro-Brexit Facebook milieu.

Technological Opportunities

In most of the trajectory accounts of the pro-Brexit Facebook users I spoke to, offline experiences took center stage and Facebook's influence was notably absent. However, this does not mean that aspects of Facebook's architecture did not play a role. That these individuals did not see the online environment as particularly significant to their trajectories can be considered a symptom of a more general lack of awareness of the power of Facebook's algorithmic suggestions among the group, which is uncovered in the analysis in chapter 2. Indeed, their political engagement would not have been possible in the same way if it were not for the affordances of Facebook for engaging in this style of politics, including the availability and searchability of vast amounts of transnational right-wing content. Reading between the lines of these individuals' accounts then, what part can we discern the architectures of social media playing in promoting right-wing populist engagement?

Social Media's Shifting Role

The broader shifting roles of social media in society—from social network to news and information platform, and from a platform for personal content to one for politics—were salient forces at play in these trajectories. Recall Helen's description of her Facebook use having transformed from "cat pictures" and "scrabble" to "political Posts, thick and fast." Soon after its launch as a nominally social platform, Facebook, like many other social media, evolved into "a contested space where private, public and corporate interests compete" (van Dijck 2012, 160). In 2021, half of adults in the UK (and a similar proportion in the United States, see Walker and Matsa 2021) used social media to keep up with the news. Facebook remains Britain's most popular social media platform for news consumption (Ofcom 2022), despite pledges by the company in 2015 and 2016 to tweak its algorithms such that users' Newsfeeds would pivot to displaying more content from their Friends than from news sites (Chaykowski 2016). Indeed, it has been suggested that by making official journalistic sources less visible, this algorithmic change—which, incidentally, occurred around the time the majority of the pro-Brexit Facebook users in this study became engaged—may have inadvertently resulted in the prioritization of less credible news and information sources (Grygiel 2019). As alluded to in the previous section, social media are also a prime arena for the dissemination of content from a burgeoning number of alternative right-wing news sites and blogs (Holt, Figenschou, and Frischlich 2019). Thus, at the same time as people were becoming disillusioned with traditional news media, Facebook was flourishing as an alternative space for seeking (and subsequently disseminating) political information.

Not all of the pro-Brexit Facebook users of this study mixed personal with political on Facebook. However, for some participants like Mark above, the positive reactions of friends and family to Facebook Posts reaffirmed their views. The significance of Facebook's mixing of personal and political can also be seen in Eileen's use of humor and charisma in her "blogging." Her informal, sarcastic style and occasional reference to her personal life drew Followers to her Page, engaging others at the same time as giving her a sense of purpose that motivated her own engagement. The fact that both news and entertainment coexist on Facebook adds to this potential for those who are not "political people" to stumble across political news content (Anspach 2017, 590), which may be perceived as particularly credible depending on which of their Friends has Shared it (Turcotte et al. 2015). In these ways and more,

Facebook's ability to politicize individuals goes far beyond the nature of the content it hosts.

Filter Bubbles

As noted at the start of this chapter, filter bubbles and echo chambers are two social media mechanisms that have been theorized as conducive to the hardening of right-wing political views. While the concepts are commonly used with considerable overlap, a filter bubble is the result of the tendency of algorithmically-derived social media "feeds" to *show* us more of what we L/like or agree with. Meanwhile, echo chambers on social media refer to forums whereby one's discussions and interactions are limited to likeminded individuals or content, which may include *active seeking out* of likeminded users made possible by the connected affordances of social media.

With regard to filter bubbles, the role of algorithmically-driven suggestions was most stark in Neil's account. Neil was a retired head teacher in his early seventies, living in South Wales. He had originally used Facebook to keep in touch with friends, particularly past pupils with whom he wanted to share old photographs he had taken at his school. He first became involved in information-seeking on social media around health and well-being "because I was concerned that I wanted to be healthy in my retirement." Through YouTube, he investigated "foods and vitamins and minerals and all the rest of it. And that's when I began to discover my concerns about the pharmaceutical industries and I started to see websites on the issues of vaccines." YouTube's algorithmically-driven "Recommended for you" function became what he described as a "rabbit hole," and eventually guided him toward the QAnon conspiracy theory and strong support for then US President Donald Trump. This conspiracy theory, originating in the United States but with large followings in the UK and other countries, claims that a far-reaching, evil, pedophilic "cabal" or "Deep State" is controlling US (and world) politics, and that Trump's secret mission during his presidency was to combat this (Argentino 2021). The theory effectively elevates Trump to the level of messiah and is said to have played a crucial role in rallying participation in the January 6 Capitol Hill insurrection in 2021 (Moskalenko and McCauley 2021).

This process for Neil began around late 2016 or early 2017. "Since then, of course, [the issue of] Brexit has come on board as well," Neil said. Upon hearing about Brexit, Neil said, "I went to find out more about the EU, how it was set up, how it's organized, how the political structure works, and I found myself very often looking at American YouTube presentations that were talking about Brexit, and I found that quite fascinating. And then finding European YouTube posts, which were talking about the American structure or even the Australian structure."

In this way, social media appealed to Neil as an avenue for information "not just from our own locality, but information from all around the world." Similar to Jessica, Neil's support for Brexit stemmed from his considering Britain's membership in the EU just one part of a complex global system of covert manipulation. According to Neil, "You suddenly realize that you can't look at issues like Brexit in isolation. All of these things are now interrelated on a global basis." Like Olivia, Neil said he had "always been interested in politics." This political curiosity, he claimed, was why YouTube's recommendations had "intrigued" him. However, he had not had particular concerns about the EU prior to beginning intense social media use, "because like most people I was ignorant about it. We only knew what we were told in the press." Compelled to share this new information with others, Neil moved from restricting his Facebook Posts to Friends (in particular, the local network of his own generation whom he felt were not interested in engaging with politics online) to Sharing his Posts Publicly. He felt that while at his age "it's a bit late now for me to actively get involved in [offline] politics" he could "be part of a change" by spreading the word on social media.

It is interesting to note the significance of the "rabbit hole" Neil went down via YouTube's "Recommended for You" content. Unlike for example Eileen whose experience in Calais led her to actively investigate the "migrant crisis," Neil's trajectory began with a seemingly harmless curiosity about health and well-being, somehow eventually ending at far-right conspiracy theory. In Neil's case, algorithmically-derived suggestions on social media provided an architecture through which to facilitate this cognitive move from wellness to conspiracy and all of the right-wing populist ideological baggage this encompassed. The popularization of the QAnon conspiracy theory in particular, of which Neil became a believer, was facilitated by the rise of Trumpism which coincided with Neil's retirement and with political attention to Brexit in the UK.

However, while the concept of filter bubbles focuses on the strengthening of views by continuously providing the user with ideologically-aligned content, Neil's experience demonstrates the consequences of how the reality of algorithmic suggestion goes one step further—it extrapolates from data about user preferences and machine learning from data on other users' activity, to identify new types of content one might be agreeable to. These algorithms have also been known to prioritize content that generates more user engagement, which is often inflammatory (Lima 2021). There is growing evidence that this results in providing users with content more extreme, violent, or hateful than that with which they were originally engaged (Little and Richards 2021). In Neil's case, searches for information on vitamins and natural remedies eventually led to him being recommended far-right conspiracy content.

As will be explored in chapter 2, once these users had become engaged, many of them were primarily passive information seekers, relying on these algorithmic suggestions. However, Neil's was the only account of *becoming* engaged in which these suggestions explicitly featured. The pro-Brexit Facebook users generally viewed their trajectories as active, agentic processes of information-seeking. This is significant as it points to the deliberate obfuscation of the algorithmic control embedded in the architectures of social media platforms. To create a seamless content experience and one which does not feel intrusive or controlling, Facebook seeks to draw attention away from the kinds of mechanisms described in Neil's case above. In this way, not only the presence of algorithmically-determined recommendations, but the way in which they (do not) appear in Facebook's interface is a salient force on trajectories toward right-wing populist online engagement. It facilitates some users to place trust in social media vis-à-vis traditional media as an arena for information consumption.

Echo Chambers

In line with some of the criticisms of the echo chambers hypothesis, trajectories like those of Helen and Olivia illustrate the role of contact with opposing views, rather than insulation from them, in processes of becoming engaged in right-wing populism online. In fact, almost all of the pro-Brexit Facebook users recounted negative experiences of interactions with the Left or Remain supporters, online and offline, that had impacted their perceptions of left-wing politics, describing these as "*vitriolic*" (Deborah, 50s, female, Northwest), "*aggressive*" (Olivia), or "*abusive*" (George, 70s, male, Northeast).

The role of conflict in these trajectories exemplifies the limitations of the specific concept of echo chambers to explain online right-wing populist engagement. This does not in itself negate the importance of online architectures, but raises the possibility that these platforms' propensity toward aggression in political discussion may be more of a salient force in solidifying political views (Hmielowski, Hutchens, and Cicchirillo 2014). Berry and Sobieraj (2013), for example, demonstrate how uncivil "outrage" media can bring individuals together in morally righteous in-groups against allegedly amoral outsiders. For the pro-Brexit Facebook users, the antagonism that is almost culturally endemic to Facebook appeared to contribute to a sense of shared identity and victimhood that empowered their online political engagement. While these altercations were described as leaving individuals feeling attacked and abused, their pride in being able to "rise above" conflict often transformed such encounters into moments of triumph or enhanced resolve that motivated their continued engagement.

The rise of online incivility is sometimes (rather reductively) attributed to an "online disinhibition effect" (Suler 2005). However, while social media logics and affordances certainly play a role in promoting conflict, these are not sufficient to explain conflict's prominence. The "outrage industry" examined by Berry and Sobieraj (2013), which includes both online and offline outlets, identifies a much more complex sociopolitical and economic system at play. In the context of Brexit, strong affective polarizations contributed to the hostile or tribal nature of contemporary British politics and political discourse at the time of this study, and these manifested both online and offline (Hobolt, Leeper, and Tilley 2020).

While the pro-Brexit Facebook users were not insulated from opposing views, Facebook did provide them with a wealth of opportunity to connect with a community of *likeminded* individuals, and to see this community's existence quantified through Likes, Follows, and Group members. This discovery of likeminded others did appear to contribute to a sense of affirmation, relief, or validation that was significant to the trajectories. As Helen described, "It was interesting to find out there were so many other people that thought the same. Because, from mainstream media you would think that everybody thinks the way they try and portray things. And I think the internet has brought people together and made us realize that more of us think the same than they try and make us believe."

That Facebook connected these users *across national borders* was particularly significant. Social media platforms bridge national boundaries to bring into dialogue individuals who may never otherwise encounter one another, and to draw parallels between issues that otherwise may not be drawn. The ability to link concerns about EU membership, migration, and Islam in Britain to similar experiences and sentiments in other parts of the world added to the validation and gratification experienced by the pro-Brexit Facebook users. Transnational logics of White victimhood and Right victimhood that Facebook's global connectivity made possible provided valuable resources for the justification of these individuals' resentments and anxieties. In their interviews and on their Timelines, anti-establishment "yellow vest"[4] protests in France were valorized and characterized as predictive of what could happen in Britain if frustrations over Brexit continued; accusations of "White genocide" in South Africa were given as evidence of global "reverse racism"; and parallels were drawn between the alleged negative consequences of immigration and diversity in continental Europe and the perceived situation in the UK. The actions of Trump and other right-wing populist politicians were supported in Posts within the pro-Brexit Facebook milieu regardless of whether they had any immediate bearing on British politics, demonstrating the strength of this transnational political affinity.

Lawrence's case demonstrates the significance of this. Having "traveled most of the world" as a young adult, Lawrence, a steelworker in his forties, moved from his hometown in East Anglia to the Midlands to be with his partner. He began using Facebook because it was "just the best way of keeping contact with all your friends and people you've met all over the world." However, he gradually came to use it to Post political content to "help educate people and open people's eyes to what's going on." Lawrence spoke of having fallen out with friends from his hometown who were not interested in his political Posts because, in his eyes, they did not understand what it was like to live with cultural diversity on their doorsteps. At the same time, however, he drew parallels with what he saw as fellow beleaguered citizens overseas: "It's a global invasion right now. America's got it, France has, France is overlogged [sic] with it, Greece is ruined, Italy's ruined, Germany's ruined. So many of the, I mean, even Australia, I see [on Facebook] the 'yellow vest' protests marching in on Australia because they're, everybody's just had enough." In this sense, even when one feels their political views isolate them from their local or national community, social media can provide international solidarity. This affordance of social media can help to explain the significant appeal of these transnational issues and their enigmatic link to nationalism.

The increasingly transnational nature of right-wing populist mobilization that is facilitated by online platforms is also capitalized upon at the organizational level of right-wing populist politics. This is seen, for example, in long-time UKIP leader Nigel Farage's collaborations with Donald Trump (Demianyk 2020) and the sharing of visual symbols between far-right groups across national and linguistic borders (Doerr 2017). Olivia and Neil's cases above demonstrate how the call to political engagement can be amplified by high-profile international causes like Trumpism. The incorporation of ideas drawn from globally-oriented conspiracy theories is also evidence of this, an important aspect that will be expounded in section II.

The transnationally shared sense of victimhood appreciated by the pro-Brexit Facebook users was also compounded by a narrative that has emerged in these online milieus regarding censorship. This narrative represents "the emergence of a novel techno-social victimology as an axis of far-right virtual community, wherein shared experiences or fears of being deplatformed facilitate a coalescing of assorted far-right tendencies online" (Jasser et al. 2021, 1). This sense of being persecuted by online left-wing censorship was embodied by the figure of "Tommy Robinson." His experience of online de-platforming and real incarceration generated support and outcry across the populist and nativist right at home and abroad (Allchorn 2018; Halliday and Barr 2018), and he was extremely popular in the pro-Brexit Facebook milieu at the time of the fieldwork.

In all of these ways, there were indeed multiple aspects of Facebook's architecture that contributed to the right-wing populist politicization of this study's participants. However, these were bound up with offline social and political conditions in complex ways that cannot be well-represented by concepts like echo chambers or filter bubbles.

The Crystallizing Power of Brexit

While all of the above-described discursive, sociopolitical, and technological conditions provided opportunities that were necessary in trajectories toward right-wing populist engagement online, the pro-Brexit Facebook users also owed their politicization to the issue of Brexit and its rise to prominence in British society. Though there was some variation in the emphasis each of them placed on support for Brexit, the referendum or its aftermath played a key triggering role in many cases, encouraging the users to transform their latent frustrations into active involvement in politics. For Mark it was calls for a "second referendum"; for Eileen it was the perceived need to "educate" others about the alleged harms of the EU; for Fred it was the attribution of blame for deindustrialization to the EU; and for Carl and Beatrice it was the forum provided by key Brexit advocates UKIP to get involved offline as well as online.

The EU referendum era was a unique moment in British politics, and the conditions engendered by this era provided their own set of opportunities that were central to right-wing populist mobilization. The emergence of Brexit as a dominant political issue was enabled by its advocates and by the amplification of their ideas and appeals in the media. As detailed in the introduction to this book, UKIP came to popularity in the 2000s, on the back of the ascension to the EU of Eastern European nations and using thinly veiled appeals to racism and xenophobia. Coverage of UKIP in prominent UK news outlets, while low in the 2000s, showed a marked increase from around 2013, the year before the party's breakthrough performance in the European Parliament Election (Deacon and Wring 2016). By the 2015 General Election campaign, UKIP accounted for between 8 and 11 percent of references to political parties in television news and newspapers (ibid.). The sensationalism of its leader Nigel Farage's populist rhetoric and nativist stances, and the way its racism cohered with the editorial agendas of many of Britain's tabloid newspapers, undoubtedly contributed to this coverage. By the time the 2016 referendum was scheduled, the EU was given as one of the top three important issues facing the nation by 20 percent of voters (Ipsos MORI 2022).

However, the rise of UKIP did not just bring the issue of Britain's EU membership into the public eye. The issue of Brexit represented an opportunity to express the frustrations, resentments, and anxieties discussed throughout this chapter in the arena of *mainstream* politics, and bring legitimacy to the racist and Islamophobic discourses that supported these grievances. As Mark contended, "It's only this Brexit issue and everything where people have actually had the balls to talk about immigration. [. . .] Up till recently you've not been able to say that without people saying you're racist."

Brexit thus became a key moment in the advancement of cultural racism, a decades-old force whose power lies in its ability to galvanize a range of seemingly disparate elements and invoke ideas of cultural and national differences to justify racial exclusion (Barker 1981; Gilroy 1987). Brexit brought together issues of nation, belonging, and entitlement, and bound them up with matters of sovereignty and control. It also provided economic and legal discourses to use as justification for isolationism and exclusion. Thus, for those who were to become pro-Brexit Facebook users, Brexit served as a powerful mechanism for crystallizing and articulating their grievances, and mobilizing them toward right-wing populism. Brexit became the object of these individuals' passion precisely because it offered to act as a vehicle for explaining, expressing, empowering, and legitimizing their discontent.

The result of the EU referendum added to this a populist discourse of democratic legitimacy. The "will of the people," it could be contended, was under threat from failed negotiations and Remain "second referendum" protests. In the face of this, the tangible, achievable goal of "getting Brexit done" provided an opportunity for agentic action. The frustration, anxiety, and indignation cultivated within the would-be pro-Brexit Facebook users in the ways described above left them with a desire to effect change. As will become clear throughout this book, engaging with pro-Brexit politics provided them an outlet for doing so and a concrete, within-reach goal that was imbued with tantalizing promises of reclaiming national glory.

The trajectories of pro-Brexit Facebook users, viewed in the context of the social and political life in which they were experienced, thus highlight the way in which certain mainstreamed political issues like Brexit can harness a particular power to explain and articulate, to extend and mobilize, right-wing populist discontents, through and around (both new and traditional) media. The emergence of Brexit as a salient right-wing populist issue within British politics marked a critical conjuncture at which the technological, discursive, and sociopolitical opportunities described above became ever more meaningful, and incited the active online political engagement of these individuals.

CONCLUSION: THE BREXIT-FACEBOOK NEXUS IN SOCIOPOLITICAL CONTEXT

Analyzing trajectories toward online right-wing populist engagement can no more produce a typology of such trajectories than can the complexity of the human experience be summarized into any analytical model. However, the insights gained from situating these trajectories within the lived experiences and sociopolitical contexts of individuals challenge the idea that mobilization of online support for right-wing populism can be explained by attending to social media architectures alone.

While the online environment undoubtedly plays a role in such mobilizations, this role is highly contingent. Architectural factors do not have the power to politicize individuals on their own, as they cannot become salient without an array of ideological and discursive opportunities found in the offline realm. Cultural racism, nativism, and Islamophobia, circulating discursively and structurally, are significant factors in these trajectories, and offline experiences are central to the operationalization of these discursive frames in individuals' new right-wing populist political interpretations of the world around them. These frames, although also encountered online, predate the advent of social media, their groundwork having been laid offline over many years, including in traditional media and (mainstream and contender) party-political discourse. Moreover, in the case of pro-Brexit Facebook users, it was when these converged with the crystallizing force of Brexit that individuals were provided with an empowering sense of legitimacy and the potential to work toward a tangible goal that promised to resolve all of their grievances at once. At this crucial conjuncture between sociopolitical factors like the "war on terror" and the "migrant crisis," the rise of right-wing populism on Facebook, and the emergence of Brexit as a right-wing populist issue, these individuals reinterpreted their prior experiences and found a unique populist legitimacy for their racist, nativist, and Islamophobic attitudes. As the testimonies of the pro-Brexit Facebook users in this study illustrate, the ability of this conjuncture to propel individuals into online political engagement around Brexit and related racist and right-wing populist politics was remarkable. The result was that individuals who had otherwise been largely politically disengaged were drawn to active engagement with politics.

Data scraping approaches to the study of political social media use may enable the identification of networks and trends in online communication, but they are less suited to understanding experiences, intentions, and subjective meaning-making, or to investigating the complexity of social phenomena that link online and offline lives. These lines of inquiry are crucial to understanding the role of social media and its consequences. Thus, to focus solely on platform affordances is not only to provide a superficial and fragmented account of the human, embedded experience of social media use. It severs this from offline lives and obscures the importance of forces like racism and their long history of interaction with politics. This complexity cannot be captured by theories like echo chambers or filter bubbles, and is not reducible to a singular process of net-based right-wing populist self-socialization. Nor are individuals passive targets of social media campaigns, as demonstrated by the pro-Brexit Facebook users' desire to understand themselves as having undergone active, agentic processes of research and discovery. We must look beyond a reductive focus on platform affordances and take into account these opportunities if we are to come to a meaningful understanding of the alarming potential for individuals to become so intensely engaged in right-wing populist politics.

Attention to the lived experiences of individuals and the social forces in which they are embroiled is not meant to validate claims that the EU referendum result was a protest cry of the "left behind," nor to in any way justify the racist and right-wing populist ideologies they engaged with. It is simply meant to demonstrate how no one factor, technological or otherwise, is sufficient to drive individuals to this sort of political engagement on its own. It is only by situating online practices within the context of online-offline lives and individual interpretations that we can begin to understand the reality of experiences of becoming engaged in right-wing populist politics online, and the significance of these processes to society.

When it comes to understanding engagement with right-wing populism on social media, processes of becoming engaged are only the first piece of the puzzle. The practices that pro-Brexit Facebook users went on to engage in on Facebook, and what these practices meant to them, are the subject of the next chapter.

NOTES

1. It should be noted that approximately 3,550 died attempting to do so (Spindler 2015), but arguably a humanitarian discursive frame was less prominent in the UK media, whose coverage of the migrant crisis was among the most aggressive in Europe (M. Berry, Garcia-Blanco, and Moore 2015).

2. A term used, sometimes derisively, to refer to dedicated supporters of Jeremy Corbyn, the UK Labour Party leader at the time (Smith 2016). A self-described socialist and passivist, Corbyn was portrayed in British media as a radical leftist (Cammaerts, DeCillia, and Magalhães 2020) and his character and politics were the target of much disdain in the pro-Brexit Facebook milieu.

3. See above note on the status of Jeremy Corbyn within the milieu.

4. The yellow vests, or *gilets jaunes*, was a French street protest movement that began in November 2018, at the height of the project fieldwork. It was sparked by opposition to fuel tax increases but developed into a broader anti-establishment movement, which saw it garner support in the pro-Brexit Facebook milieu and prompt small-scale copycat protests globally (Martin 2018b; Royall 2020).

Chapter 2

Meaningful Online Engagement Practices in the Pro-Brexit Facebook Milieu

In the previous chapter, I examined pathways to becoming engaged with Brexit and right-wing populism on Facebook. The critical conjuncture between Brexit, Facebook and social context prompted intense engagement that came to constitute an important part of individuals' daily lives. But what did this engagement entail? How did individuals actually use Facebook to engage with politics, and in what ways was this meaningful to them? This chapter examines the practices that comprised political engagement in the pro-Brexit Facebook milieu. Doing so elucidates the aspects of Facebook's architecture that made it a meaningful platform to individuals wishing to engage in this form of politics. The analysis thus contributes to the broader, important question of the role of social media in shaping practices of right-wing populist engagement.

Prior studies have quantified a range of observable interactions between users and online content, including Liking, Commenting, Sharing, Friending, and Following (e.g., Kalsnes, Larsson, and Enli 2017). The current study, however, revealed that most meaningful to pro-Brexit Facebook users were *finding* (which I use to mean both deliberately seeking and incidentally encountering) and *Posting*[1] (which I use to mean both Sharing existing and creating new) political content. These two types of practices were invariably interlinked and mutually reinforcing. Not only were both related to individuals' interests and political passions, but most content was encountered elsewhere on Facebook before it was Posted. Facebook's algorithmic logic means that data about what individuals Posted also undoubtedly fed back into decisions about which content was presented to them.

Determining which practices may be meaningful to others is not a straightforward task. The discussion in this chapter is based on an inductive, thematic analysis of interview accounts, alongside insights from immersive, qualitative observations on Facebook. Finding and Posting were practices that the pro-Brexit Facebook users most commonly spoke about and described as important, enjoyable, or worthwhile. In this chapter, the significance of each of these types of practices is explored in turn, particularly in terms of what they reveal about Facebook's role in right-wing populist engagement. The analysis reveals that aspects of the Facebook platform including its logics of automation, visuality, and Sharing, within the constraints of the attention economy and surveillance capitalism, contributed to shaping these practices. This is because they enabled as well as encouraged individuals to engage with right-wing populist politics in ways that made them feel valuable and in control.

SOCIAL MEDIA LOGIC AND AFFORDANCES

Although the previous chapter demonstrated the limitations of the ability of social media architectures to mobilize and motivate individuals to engage in politics in the absence of lived, offline opportunities, these architectures are neither arbitrary nor inconsequential for political engagement. They can enable, constrain, encourage and discourage different *forms* of participation. Wahl-Jorgensen (2019) has demonstrated, for example, how particular forms of emotional expression are structurally encouraged on social media platforms. Such studies demonstrate how "[i]ntent, agency, and affect [. . .] become to some extent contingent outcomes of the network itself rather than of human agency alone" (Hillis, Paasonen, and Petit 2015, 2).

A number of different concepts have been used to understand this phenomenon, including affordances (e.g., Davis and Chouinard 2016; Kim and Ellison 2021) and social media logic (e.g., Duguay 2018; Klinger and Svensson 2015). However, these concepts are defined and operationalized differently between scholars. This includes an ongoing debate over the scope of the affordances concept, in the face of criticisms that applications of the concept have been overly techno-deterministic and have thereby neglected questions of how individuals actually utilize technologies, the significance of individual motivations, and the way in which affordances are collectively constructed between social and technical realms (Pentzold and Bischof 2019). Social media logic (van Dijck and Poell 2013) aims to incorporate "the norms, strategies, mechanisms, and economies underpinning [social media] platforms' dynamics" (ibid., 2) and to acknowledge how aspects of social media have the power to appear as neutral "common sense" and be exported outside of those media to affect social relations and public life. However, this concept is also accused of singularity, leading some scholars to prefer "logics" in the plural (e.g., Klinger and Svensson 2015), and of being overly linear or fixed, thus ignoring the importance of the different processes and forms involved in social interaction (see Lundby 2009 re "media logic"). As Costa (2018) points out in her critique of social media logic's application, practices of social media use "are not predetermined outside of their situated everyday action and habits of usage" (ibid., 3,643).

An inductive, interpretive endeavor to understand the situated meaning-making of users does not lend itself to being bound by one predefined concept. My approach in the current study acknowledges the limitations of each of these concepts for understanding meaningful social media practices holistically and reflects the overlap between them. I incorporate both concepts, alongside discussion of the norms and cultures of social media use that they engender, to consider how they produced and interacted with the experiences and meaning-making of the individuals involved to contribute to online political engagement practices. For clarity, I employ a narrow definition of affordances, using the term to refer to aspects or structures of the Facebook platform that "enable or constrain potential behavioral outcomes in a particular context" (Evans et al. 2017, 36). Meanwhile, I use logic to mean "a set of principles or common sense rationality cultivated in and by media institutions" (Altheide and Snow 1979, 11).

FINDING CONTENT

Whether it be new evidence about European or domestic politics, or audio, visual or textual expressions of political outrage, *finding content* was a key practice that the pro-Brexit Facebook users found meaningful. Discovering the availability of such content on the platform had opened up new possibilities for these individuals, making Facebook a valuable resource for knowledge. As Neil (70s, male, South Wales) noted, "because of the internet and because of social media, we are finding information about things that in the past we never would have done. [. . .] Those things would have been hidden [from us] in the past." This was based on a broad distrust of and disdain for "mainstream media" that has been touched upon in chapter 1 and will be expounded in chapter 3. Deborah was a retiree in her fifties in Northwest England who had worked in various occupations and had been moving away from television and print news. In her view, Facebook provided "information that the general media don't put out," leaving citizens to inform themselves and each other online. Facebook was considered "quite a positive thing, especially with the media becoming more and more dishonest. Because people, other people do research and share the research they've found" (Fred, 60s, male, Northeast England). This made social media "the only fair way that you could actually [. . .] find out what was really going on in the world" (Beatrice, 60s, female, North Wales). But how did these individuals go about finding this content on Facebook? As we shall see below, these practices were characterized by the surrendering of a high level of control to Facebook's content algorithms.

Passivity: Content-Finds-Me and Facebook Reliance

Contrary perhaps to the sense of empowerment and agency that being able to find information on Facebook seemed to provide pro-Brexit Facebook users, their descriptions of their own practices revealed a high level of passivity. In studies of social media use, "passive" has generally been used to refer to a preference toward content *viewing* rather than active *communication* behaviors like Posting (e.g., Verduyn et al. 2015). However, I use the term here in a different sense. The passivity I refer to in relation to content finding practices is a content-finds-you approach, in which recommendations or nudges in the form of algorithmically-derived Newsfeed and Notifications are the dominant drivers of the content with which a user engages, as compared with actively visiting Pages or Groups in which one has a particular interest or utilizing search functions.

Most of the pro-Brexit Facebook users in this study found content passively; they tended to *encounter* rather than *seek* political content. They divulged in the interviews that to find content they primarily used their Newsfeed or Notifications, and many described a practice of "scrolling" through Facebook or encountering content that "comes up" (Beatrice). This was also the case with regard to Facebook Groups, of which most of the individuals were members. A handful were active in these Groups, but many only engaged with Group content when it appeared on their Newsfeed or in their Notifications. Mark (50s, male, Yorkshire), as a working single father, noted with regret that he "ain't got the time in the day" to explore everything he might like to on Facebook. Many pro-Brexit Facebook users in fact seemed to feel Facebook kept them busy enough already, which was unsurprising given the limitless nature of the Newsfeed portal. A user's Newsfeed is displayed on Facebook's homepage, and constantly loads new content as the user scrolls down, an affordance known as "the infinite scroll" (Jovicic 2020). Lupinacci (2020) argues that this experience of social media as a continuous and endless flow produces ambivalence, unsettledness and fatigue, accompanied by a sense that important happenings could be taking place that warrant one's immediate attention. This may very well have contributed to the passive ways in which these individuals used Facebook.

Indeed, for the same reasons of time constraints and ambivalence, some also admitted to not always reading the content of sites before Posting links to them on Facebook. This is not to say that they did not critically engage with information or at times attempt to verify or research further. In fact, as will be explored in chapter 5, these individuals claimed to place a high value on critical research. "Googling" topics that they wished to investigate further or corroborate elsewhere was described as a common practice. However, these investigations were usually prompted by content that had been passively encountered on the Facebook platform.

Many of the pro-Brexit Facebook users said they did not have favorite Pages or external websites, and generally the source of the information was less important than the content and the fact that it was "there." For example, when I asked Kirk, a Londoner in his sixties who owned his own long-running renovations business, about a particular online personality he had Shared content from, he replied, "Yeah, I'll Share anything. [. . .] I like her. [. . .] I would follow her. [. . .] I wouldn't sign up to anything, but if she's on there, I wanna know what she's saying." Although, as we will see in the next section, these individuals did *Post* content from a variety of sources within and outside Facebook, according to their interview accounts they were generally directed to these sources from their Newsfeed. Even when asked in interviews about the mainstream and alternative news sites and blogs I had seen them Post content from during the immersive observations, most said they did not visit these sites directly. This relative lack of interest in external sites illustrates the way Facebook acted as a centralized portal for information seeking. Because most of these individuals relied on Facebook for their information seeking, the content produced by other websites would have been unlikely to reach them without Facebook's mediation.

The general reliance on Facebook among the pro-Brexit Facebook users of this study can also be seen in the fact that very few were active on other social media platforms such as Twitter, Reddit, or Gab (a lack of crossover that is worthy of note by online political engagement studies researchers that have so neglected study of Facebook in favor of these platforms). For some this was because there was something about Facebook in particular that they preferred; Jessica (40s, female, London) described Twitter as "like tweeting into thin air" compared with a sense of community she enjoyed on Facebook. For others, however, this was simply because Facebook was the first social media platform they had been introduced to. Either the prospect of having to learn to use a new platform held little appeal, or as noted above, they felt Facebook on its own was as much as they could handle at once. Mark said he preferred to stick to Facebook because "it's the one I've always used and the one where I've built up [my Friends list]"; that is, the popular nature of Facebook meant that was where the network and audience was that made his Facebook use meaningful. He said he felt the difference between Facebook and other social media platforms was "much of a muchness [. . .] I think if you dilute it too much by using too many sites, then you lose the focus on that one site." Similarly, Deborah said she avoided joining multiple platforms because she did not want things to "get out of hand."

Carl (50s, male, Northwest England) was an exception to this, as he used both Twitter and Facebook. However, his method of finding content still demonstrated a high level of passivity. In practice, he did not differentiate between the two platforms. "I use em both the same," he told me, "I wouldn't know [which I use more]." Carl demonstrated in his interview, swiping to display the notifications on his smartphone's home screen, and describing in matter-of-fact terms: "What it is with me is, I'll just like sit on me phone now, and it comes [up on the screen], and I'll just go like that, and I'll see something here and I'll go, 'look.'" In other words, Carl did not "intentionally go on" Twitter or Facebook, but simply clicked on whichever content appeared in the Notifications on his mobile phone.

The only other user in this study who had diversified into other platforms was Olivia (50s, female, Southeast England). Perhaps because she had been using Facebook for a shorter period than others, she appeared to have little loyalty to it. Her use of platforms such as Gab, MeWe, and Wake Up UK was entirely instrumental, and was focused on her content Posting practices rather than her finding ones. She had two aims: having already incurred multiple temporary bans from Facebook, Olivia was future-proofing her online activity, but she was also deliberately broadening the reach of her messaging for what she saw as a fickle and simple-minded audience, something we will return to in the next section. She attested that she herself did not have a favorite platform, "but certain people will, cos people are habitual like that. [...] They're not prepared to take the time to learn how each and every one of these things work. *I am*. You know, so therefore I have to cover all elements of people, all elements of their brain capacity or lack of, and Post on all of these social sites" (Olivia's emphasis).

The Logic of Automation

Such exceptions notwithstanding, implicit in most of the pro-Brexit Facebook users' information-seeking practices was a passivity that belied the convenience of Facebook and the content-finds-me logic of the interface. The participants of this study would not be alone in this. The nudging of social media users toward certain content not only affords such passive content-seeking practices, but has engendered this as a norm of social media use. On Facebook, this is written into the architecture of the interface, with one's Newsfeed being the home page of the website or app, and the act of "scrolling" through this positioned as a central part of using the platform.

Notifications too, from their prime position at the top of the page, prompt urgent attention by indicating the number of unread items in red.

This passive approach to finding content is important because it means not the pro-Brexit Facebook users themselves but rather Facebook's algorithms were determining what content they viewed and therefore which issues they encountered and were subsequently engaged by. On Facebook, algorithms use information on user preferences—predicted and categorized based on, for example, what types of content they (and their Friends) have Liked, Followed, or interacted with, to rank content and determine whether and in which order to display it in that individual's Newsfeed or Notifications. This "algorithmic 'sorting out' has consequences for who is exposed to news and politics on Facebook" (Thorson et al. 2021, 184). A popular assumption that these algorithms are mechanically neutral underlies users' acceptance of the norm of passive content consumption (Gillespie 2014, 181). This assumption of course is erroneous. Facebook's corporate focus on generating profit from the sale of user data to advertisers necessitates frequent input from users, meaning there is a bias in these algorithms toward privileging content more likely to engender recordable actions or interactions (Bucher 2017; DeVito 2017; Thorson et al. 2021). In fact, leaked internal documents (known as the "Facebook Papers") have revealed that the company has on numerous occasions prioritized maximizing user engagement, even if that means giving more weight in its algorithms to harmful or violent content, or misinformation (Lima 2021).[2] That social media algorithms are popularly imagined as unbiased can be attributed to a "logic of automation" through which "social media platforms position themselves as neutral conduits of news information" (Duguay 2018, 22). In other words, Facebook's logic of automation can be identified as one important factor behind the content finding practices of those engaging in the pro-Brexit Facebook milieu.

Differing degrees of awareness of the presence and power of these algorithms among users may affect the way social media platforms are used (Bucher 2017). Such levels of awareness among the pro-Brexit Facebook users varied. For instance, Fred interpreted the increased volume of political content shown to him on Facebook in recent years as there being "so much [. . .] going on on Facebook," rather than considering the effects that his behaviors on the platform over time may have had on the types of content suggested to him. Similarly, when I raised the subject of Facebook's algorithmic filtering with Deborah, she reflected on her assumptions for what she admitted was the first time, saying that until that moment in our interview, "it never occurred to me how it, the system actually worked. [. . .] I just was under the naïve assumption that everything that came in worked its way through my Facebook [Newsfeed] at some stage." Lawrence (40s, male, West Midlands) also attributed the limited reactions to his Posts outside of "the same few" to the majority of his Friends not being "interested" in engaging with his content; he did not seem to consider that they may simply not have seen it due to their own algorithmically filtered Newsfeeds.

In contrast, Isaac—a home care employee and military veteran in Northwest England in his fifties—was aware that viewing certain content on the platform meant that he would be targeted by online advertisers seeking to sell particular products. He regarded this cynically, remarking that "I think that's just the progression of technology or AI. [. . .] [One day] they'll be pre-empting our thoughts." In reality, the tools of surveillance capitalism had already all but reached that level of progress. Mark too acknowledged that "if I happen across things it usually means that [. . .] you're more likely to happen across other things," and Eileen (60s, female, Northwest England) demonstrated awareness that "if you don't interact" with someone, you are likely to be shown less of their Posts.

This variation in degrees of awareness is in line with the results of prior studies (e.g., Eslami et al. 2015; Gran, Booth, and Bucher 2020; Rader and Gray 2015). What is interesting, however, is that even those who were somewhat aware of the existence of the influence of algorithms did not problematize this phenomenon in terms of the inherent political bias in the content they viewed and the routes they were prompted along in their information-seeking online. This was in contrast with their extremely critical stance toward mainstream media, and the criticisms of left-leaning bias they frequently directed toward Facebook's moderation policies. The inconsistency here seemed to be due to their assumption that the bias inherent in these media was invariably "left-wing," geared against them and the views they held—their Right victimhood worldview (see chapters 1 and 5). In this way, they viewed their information discovery as *despite* external control over information dissemination, rather than because of it. Encountering content about Brexit and related political issues on Facebook was understood by the pro-Brexit Facebook users as a product of their own agency and thus experienced as an empowering practice. It gave these individuals a means of discovering things they felt were otherwise hidden from them. That is, within the pro-Brexit Facebook milieu, the use of Facebook as a knowledge resource was a way of "taking back control," to borrow the infamous Leave campaign slogan. These individuals were unaware of the level of control they were in fact surrendering to algorithms when they relied on passive methods of content finding.

PRACTICES OF POSTING

For the pro-Brexit Facebook users, however, it was not enough to simply find content. As was touched upon in the trajectory narratives of those like Eileen and Beatrice in chapter 1, educating and informing others was an extremely important aspect of online political engagement in this milieu. Passing on information and other forms of content once it had been found was crucial. Deborah said, "The positives [of Facebook] I see are the fact that we constantly are passing on and exchanging information that we may not have been aware of, which only as far as I'm concerned bolsters whatever cause we might believe in."

In this way, in addition to encountering or being engaged *by* content, the pro-Brexit Facebook users also engaged *in* practices of publishing (Posting) content to their own Timeline. As noted in the introduction to this chapter, "Posting" here encapsulates both the use of the Share button to recirculate existing content (which may have been created by a Group, Page, another individual user or an external site), and authoring Posts of one's own. Although I differentiate between Posting and Sharing here for the sake of clarity, it should be noted that common vernacular often sees these used interchangeably, and this was sometimes reflected in descriptions by users in interviews.

On Facebook, one has the option of Posting either Publicly (visible to all Facebook users) or Privately (visible only to one's Friends, a selected group therein, or as far as Friends of Friends). The majority of the participants in this study had set their default Posting mode to Public. This proportion was of course a byproduct of the study's recruitment method, which necessarily targeted those who had Shared pro-Brexit Posts Publicly (see introduction to this book). However, to these individuals this setting was not arbitrary. It was meaningful, as it was often described as a conscious decision that reflected a passion for expressing their political views and informing others.

The above analysis of content finding practices necessarily relied on individuals' narratives of these practices. When it comes to Posting, on the other hand, I also benefited from being able to observe these practices as a member of their Facebook Friends during the immersive observations. This added useful insights to thicken the users' claims; there is always the potential for narratives about practices to be affected by potentially low degrees of awareness of these practices or by mindfulness of social desirability. It is worth reiterating, however, that the purpose of this approach was not to verify claims made by the participants about their behavior, but rather to add context to their meaning-making in order to form a richer understanding of it.

The ideological substance of the milieu will be examined in detail in section II of this book. In the current analysis, I focus not on the content of Posts, but on trends in content type and source, and what these reveal about the users' online practices. While it is not possible to discern whether the Posts observed during the immersive observations were representative of these individuals' Posts outside of this period, nor whether there was any degree of generalizability to the wider pro-Brexit Facebook milieu, some stark trends deserve analytical exploration. Figure 1 illustrates the proportion of different types of content that the pro-Brexit Facebook users were observed Posting to their Facebook Timelines.[3] The prominence of visual content is striking, and the implications of this will be explored below.

Visual Logic

As evidenced in figure 2.1, visual content in the form of images and video made up around 50 percent of the content that the pro-Brexit Facebook users were observed Posting. Social media are of course particularly visual arenas. In 2013 it was already estimated that over 200,000 images were uploaded to Facebook every minute (Horaczek 2012). This is engendered not only by technological advancement in terms of image and video creation and storage,

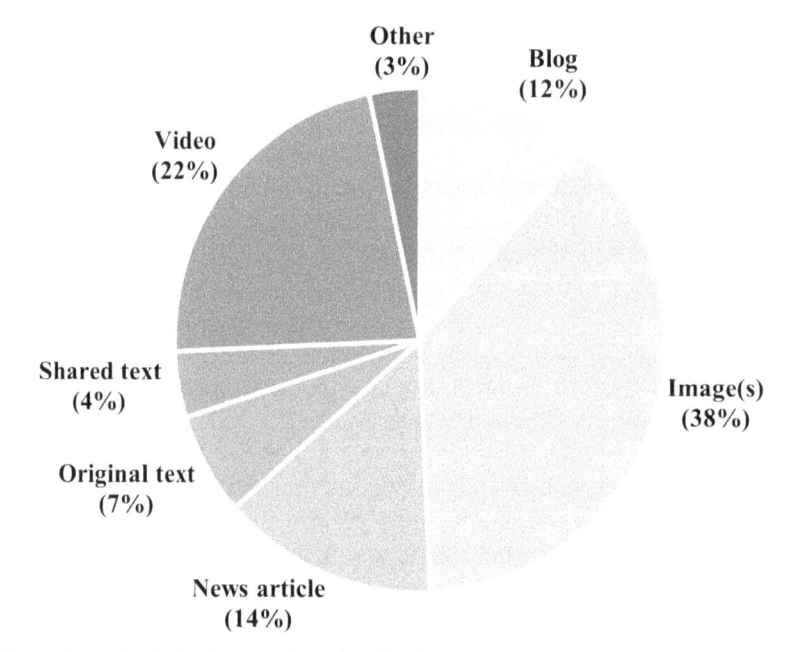

Figure 2.1. Posts by Content Type (n=3502).

Note: Posts including multiple types of content were classified based on the first displayed item. "Original text" refers to a text-only Post not Shared from another source (i.e., the study participant's self-authored text), while "Shared text" refers to text-only Posts Shared from other Facebook users, Pages or Groups. "News article" includes only conventional news websites; alternative news sites and all other unofficial information sites are classified as "Blogs." Posts including multiple "Images" or "Videos" were counted as a single Post. "Other" includes Facebook Memories, links to Facebook Events, Groups or Pages, tweets Shared directly from Twitter, and links to external websites that were not news or blog content (e.g. online quizzes). Any of the above could also be accompanied by a text-based Comment added by the study participant when they Published the Post. Source: Author's data.

but also by platform affordances. Videos stored externally can also be embedded in Facebook Posts such that viewers need not leave the Facebook page, and the default at the time of this study was for these to play automatically in one's Newsfeed, making them harder to ignore. These and other affordances for Posting and engaging with visual content on Facebook have contributed to an assumption of visuality within the culture and norms of Facebook's use—a visual logic.

Privileging of the visual is also endemic to the "economies of attention" in which Facebook plays a key role (Pedersen, Albris, and Seaver 2021). The multimodal nature of social media is one of the key aspects that makes them conducive to conveying and provoking emotional responses, and Posts that provoke such responses from users are desirable because they are more likely to retain users' attention on the platform and generate interactions with content that produce valuable user data (Cosentino 2020, 21; Kalpokas 2019, 5). McDonald (2018, 70–71) has demonstrated how online videos use music and visual aesthetics to create "moods" that draw users into radical ideologies. Information presented visually can also attract higher levels of trust as it can invoke a "realism heuristic" and therefore comes "with an implicit guarantee of being closer to the truth than other forms of communication" (Messaris and Abraham 2001, 217; in Dan et al. 2021, 641). This is despite the growing technological capacity for manipulation of visual content in order to mislead audiences (Dan et al. 2021).

The power of visuality has not escaped the attention of right-wing actors. An online handbook of German far-right activists for example recognized that "[p]eople respond to images in a stronger way than to text. By using images, we can do excellent memetic warfare and bring our narratives to the people" (Generation D. 2017, 2; in Bogerts and Fielitz 2019, 137). Indeed, "memes," while used throughout social media, have become a vital strategic tool in right-wing online milieus in particular (Bogerts and Fielitz 2019; DeCook 2018). These user-generated images constitute co-constructed discourses as they are constantly imitated, reinterpreted and revised. They can be used "to disseminate political arguments and ideologies" (Hakoköngäs, Halmesvaara, and Sakki 2020, 2) and are useful tools for mobilizing racist and nativist arguments, attracting new audiences, and arousing moral anger and hate to implore users to action against minoritized groups (ibid.).

The images Posted by the pro-Brexit Facebook users in this study were rarely memes in the narrow sense, in that they were not deliberate imitations that used intertextuality to mobilize irony or create subcultural shared understandings. However, these images very frequently borrowed the common meme format of an image overlaid with bold text. In this way they capitalized upon the ability of this format to be emotionally evocative while "crystalliz[ing] an argument in an easily shareable, concise, and often visual form" (Hakoköngäs, Halmesvaara, and Sakki 2020, 2)—a useful advantage within the attention economy of contemporary media.

The Logic of Sharing

Another important characteristic of Posts in the pro-Brexit Facebook milieu was the relative absence of original content authored by the Posting user. Figure 2.2 gives the type of immediate source of the Posts observed and logged during the fieldwork. Existing content internal to the Facebook platform was dominant, followed by content Shared from external sites, with original content authored by the user themselves being the least common type.

The majority of users engaging in this milieu were content consumers and redistributors, leaving content production to a select few. This included the "alternative influencers" (Lewis 2020) of the milieu, of which Eileen was one. In fact, Eileen said she rarely checked her Newsfeed: "I never get a chance to go on it cos I'm either writing something, Sharing something, checking something, or talking to somebody, or answering messages." Eileen relied on her own creativity and wit to produce self-authored text and video

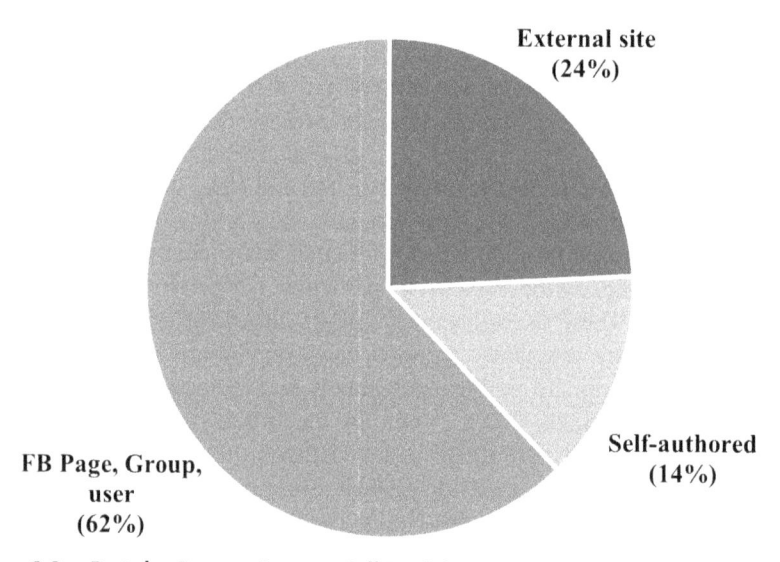

Figure 2.2. Posts by Content Source—Full Participant Group (n=3502).

Note: Content source was classified based on the direct source displayed on the Post itself. E.g., if a user Shared a Post from a Facebook Page such as "Get Britain Out," but the content of this Post was a link to an article on Breitbart.com, this was still classified as coming from a "Facebook Page, Group or user." Likewise, Sharing content from external sites does not preclude this content having been encountered as part of an internal Facebook Post before being Shared directly from the external site. Source: Author's data.

content for her avid Followers. If we exclude Eileen from the analysis, the proportion of self-authored Posts shrinks by more than half, to just 6 percent of all Posts observed (see figure 2.3). In other words, the Posting practices of most of the pro-Brexit Facebook users revolved heavily around Sharing existing content.

This trend reflects findings in the previous section about "passive" Facebook use. However, it also highlights the importance of "passing on" or Sharing of discovered information. "Redistribution" is one of the three types of "connected affordances" (Kalsnes, Larsson, and Enli 2017) within a "logic of distribution" specific to new media (Klinger and Svensson 2015). Although it is just one way in which users can "interact" with existing content (alongside Commenting on or Liking content, for example), Sharing is so central to Facebook use that it has been described as the basic premise of the platform (van Dijck 2013). Facebook "direct[s] users to share information with other users through purposefully designed interfaces" and this "ideology of sharing pretty much set the standard for other platforms" (van Dijck 2013, 46–47). This is supported by findings by Horsti (2017), who in her analysis of an Islamophobic image circulated online in Sweden noted that "mediated circulation through networks has become the dominant cultural logic that shapes social relations today" (ibid., 1447). Like Facebook's visuality and logic of automation, the logic of distribution that underlies the centrality of Sharing is

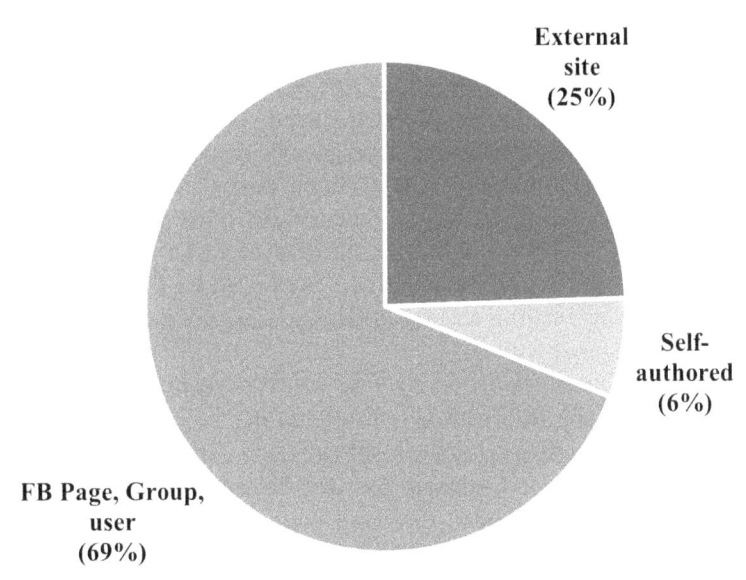

Figure 2.3. Posts by Content Source—Participant Group Excluding Eileen (n=3077).
Source: Author's data.

driven in part by the surveillance capitalism model (Zuboff 2019), whereby social media platforms can profit only by encouraging users to continue to engage and generate useful data to sell to advertisers.

However, what the pro-Brexit Facebook users chose to Share constituted only a portion of the content they encountered. Exploring the question of what made certain content Share-worthy is an important step toward unpacking what it was about Posting, and Sharing in particular, that these individuals valued. When asked in their follow-up interviews about specific content I had seen them Post, the pro-Brexit Facebook users often struggled to reflect coherently on their motivations. Sometimes this seemed attributable to a lack of conscious awareness around their own behaviors—Jessica claimed, "I Share from instinct," and Lawrence described "hitting the Share button" as having "almost become a natural thing about living." In other cases, it was simply that they did not see any complexity in this practice; if they "felt strongly" about content or felt it "need[ed] to be said" (Kirk), they would Share it. In Mark's words, the logic was simply "if I like it, I'll Share it." Some of the users played down the significance of choosing to Share, describing having Shared certain things merely because they found them humorous (Isaac, Jessica), thought they might be uplifting to others (Audrey, Deborah), or to support a friend or family member (Audrey, Mark). These ambivalent narratives point to the ordinariness of Sharing and its status as a practice central to Facebook use.

Despite such reported ambivalence regarding choosing when to Share content, these individuals were generally very passionate about the content they were Sharing. Much of what they Posted was emotionally provocative, and as alluded to above, "feeling" was frequently described as a factor in the decision to Share or to Comment. For instance, Kirk said he wouldn't interact with content "unless it really sort of gets in me throat." As Deborah put it, "it depends how I *feel* about the subject. Sometimes I'll just put a Like or a 'not like' or an 'angry,' or if I feel a little bit more involved I'll make a Comment. If I feel more involved, I will Share it with my Facebook Friends" (emphasis added). In this way, Sharing was for Posts that users felt more strongly about or that resonated most with them.

Indeed, for many of the users, Sharing was "the point" of Facebook and, alongside discovering information, constituted the main appeal of using it. Some were observed Sharing dozens of Posts each day. It was clear from the way they described their Facebook use that Sharing was valuable because it represented a way to spread the word or to educate others, which was considered crucial to regaining control over the current social and political predicament. This was also the reason these individuals gave for Posting Publicly. Many felt it imperative to make others aware of what they alleged was going on, "to inform each other" (Eileen) or to "warn everyone" (Olivia) in the face of a media and political system they felt was obscuring what they saw as important truths. Thus, the users also accounted for decisions about Sharing based on this being information "that people need to know" (Jessica). Lawrence summarized a sentiment commonly expressed in the milieu when he said, "you just wanna help educate people and open people's eyes to what's going on." As discussed in chapter 1, Beatrice took this on as her "mission," saying she felt that "having been [working] in education, it is one of my responsibilities to educate the young." Sharing was part of satisfying her compulsion to "get the message out," a desire which left her so frustrated she said, "sometimes I feel like stripping off naked and going standing in the street and [shouting] 'Why are you being so stupid? Why don't you listen to me!'"

Neil described his Sharing practice as "not necessarily to promote a particular message" but to encourage people not to "close your eyes and just ignore the things." In doing this, like many other users in this study, Neil hoped he could make a difference and "be part of a change." Sharing was sometimes described in altruistic terms, as though a form of volunteering one's time in service of their nation. Several of the users stressed that their Sharing and informing others was something they did for the sake of their children or grandchildren's future. This is encapsulated in an illustration that was Shared multiple times in the milieu during the fieldwork: a young, blond, pale-skinned girl looks up from a crowd of faceless, identical, full black veils. The girl at once appears on the verge of being swallowed up by a sea of black and brightly radiating from within it; the overlaid text reads "Britain 2050" and "Why didn't you stop them grandad?" Posts like this foreshadow the idea of an imperative to act, within which spreading the word on Facebook was part of a perceived duty to protect future generations and preserve the imagined Whiteness of the nation. This highlights how the pro-Brexit Facebook users saw their practices on Facebook as part of something greater than their individual networks. Sharing on Facebook afforded them the ability to contribute to an important political moment and thus gave them a meaningful sense of agency, which I explore next.

Sharing and Agency

As will become clear over the coming chapters, within the struggle in which the pro-Brexit Facebook milieu envisaged itself as embroiled, knowledge was power. Eileen, who dedicated herself full-time to researching, summarizing, and Posting information for her Followers, said, "I'm not interested in getting my way. I'm interested in other people making a choice from an informed platform." Eileen felt that the average person was too busy going about their lives and performing the duties of a good citizen to engage with anything other than the inadequate "mainstream media" news:

> If you don't follow social media [. . .] and you work in the Co-op [supermarket] and you're picking your grandkids up, [then prime minister negotiating Britain's exit deal] Theresa May is very plausible, and she's very convincing at telling you it's all gonna be ok, and you would be expected and you have the right to trust in that prime minister. [. . .] People jump on and off Facebook to suit their real lives which is "I'm picking me grandkids up, I've got to go to rumba or zoomba," whatever . . .

Thus, the pro-Brexit Facebook users felt it was their duty to provide these good citizens with information in a format they could understand. Echoing Olivia's reasons for using multiple platforms described in the previous section, these narratives were simultaneously valorizing and patronizing of the unenlightened who some of these individuals sought to serve. Mark described what he saw as a fatigue on the issue of Brexit, saying he felt Remainers were "trying to wear people down" and therefore "a lot of my motivation [to Post] is like 'let's keep going,' [. . .] cos these people'll [Remainers] get their own way."

To this end, comments in interviews also revealed instrumental and strategic elements to these individuals' practices aimed at attracting and maintaining audience attention. One of these strategies included Posting the same content multiple times. Although not all who I raised this with had clear recollections of their motivations for repeat Posting, Neil for example was aware that "when you go on [Facebook] there are so many Posts to look through [. . .] [that] people may not have seen what I Posted." Therefore, when they thought something was particularly important, some of the users were inclined to Post it again to "see whether Sharing it twice gets it out any further" (Lawrence). Beatrice's motivations for this were decidedly condescending. She showed me a gallery where she regularly saved images on her tablet in order to re-Post them "because people forget. [. . .] Unless you keep feeding people, [. . .] it's like a special educational needs kid. [. . .] Two sentences and they've forgotten."

Predictably, Eileen was especially clear about wanting to maintain audience interest, and curated both her personal Page and her interest Page accordingly. Regarding the interest Page she ran, which was Followed by tens of thousands of users, she said, "if I just stuck to Brexit, which is my passion, they'd get bored and they'd leave the Page, so I have to make it more general." On the Timeline of her personal Page she used humor to keep people interested, and on both Pages she described going to great lengths to present information in an accessible format. "People want to access information quickly. [. . .] Facebook Followers don't want to read [broadsheet newspaper] *The Guardian* and they don't want to read [broadsheet newspaper] *The Telegraph*. [. . .] So I'll bullet point a few things and then I'll do them on a Post and just quickly [Post] them."

Despite mostly Posting pre-existing content, some of the pro-Brexit Facebook users in this study also regularly included a Comment of their own when they Shared. For some, this added authenticity was seen as more likely to draw audience attention. When I asked Lawrence about this behavior in his second interview he said, "If you just Share something and you're not putting your own thoughts or your own feeling into it, people just look at what you're Sharing and just think 'they're off again.' [. . .] But I'd rather people know that I'm putting the effort in to have that tangent, and speak how I'm feeling." Olivia said she rarely wrote anything personal in this Comment, but rather tended to write "share share share" in order to "promote them to Share that video." This practice went both ways. As Deborah said, "quite often I'll re-Post [Share] something with no Comment, so that I'm not influencing anybody. I want to see what their reaction is."

These active and conscious curation practices used for customizing, adding authenticity to, and taking ownership of content, illustrate the empowering nature of some of Facebook's affordances for Sharing. Despite their mostly passive content finding practices and reliance on pre-existing content, these individuals sought to exercise agency in their Sharing, and Facebook facilitated this. According to Kirk, his political engagement on Facebook was about being able to express "my personal feelings. I wanna be able to say what I wanna say."

In Lawrence's case, social media gave him an opportunity to have a "voice" which the constraints of offline participation made difficult. The potential for expressing his political frustrations "offline" clearly excited Lawrence. In his second interview, he proudly described how he had placed a UKIP garden stake in front of his house in preparation for local elections because "I thought if I have my say it might make a few people think." He also enthusiastically showed me the "yellow vest" he recently had made with his own wording printed on it: "Brexit now: Destroy the corrupt." However, attending offline demonstrations where he could actually wear his new vest was still too difficult: "Unfortunately London's a hundred miles away and I have a lot of responsibility with my son." For Lawrence, this gap could be filled by Sharing content on Facebook: "I'm just trying to stand up for us at the minute. My voice is important while I still have it." Neil, too, appreciated the ease of Sharing content on Facebook, which afforded him the ability to make a contribution he felt his age might otherwise have prevented him from making. He said, "It's a bit late now for me to actively get involved in politics and things, you know, I'm 70 years old. [. . .] [But] I can work with other people on social media to promote the message."

In fact, some of the users said that they did not feel offline political activism was as worthwhile or effective as their political engagement on Facebook. As Fred told me, "I don't attend any [demonstrations] because I don't think there's a massive amount to be gained. I think the real danger is you're always gonna get agitators in there who will try to turn things around from what the original plan was." Meanwhile, finding and Sharing content online allowed individuals like Fred to focus on spreading the word in low-risk ways that were integrated into their daily routine, and which afforded them a variety of strategies for effectively seizing and maintaining people's attention.

Facebook was also valued by the users as "a place where we can speak" (Deborah), having been allegedly deprived of such an arena offline. Deborah was particularly explicit about the role that Facebook played in providing this sense of voice. She said she had a "general feeling that certain factions are just not listened to, that we're virtually gagged." Later, she divulged that she felt the issue of "racism against white people" was "not being acknowledged. [. . .] And this is where Facebook comes in. [. . .] We want our voice on Facebook for Brexit. Because, there again, we don't feel we've got much of a voice because we have been labelled in so many instances as ignorant, not really knowing what we're doing. [. . .] The only fight back that we have is on Facebook. Where else am I gonna tell people how I feel?"

This comment reflects a sentiment commonly expressed within the milieu that those who voted for Brexit were being wrongfully portrayed as not having known what they were doing or as "racist." As mentioned above, traditional media was seen to be failing to represent the views of Brexit supporters and those on the political right. This left users feeling "gagged." As Mark put it, "the majority of the mainstream people, they don't speak their minds, right? Because they're worried about consequences." In previous studies, this sense of political marginalization and "scepticism about the functioning of contemporary formal democracy" has been found to prompt individuals to engage in street activism (e.g., Pilkington 2016, 203). The users in the current study, however, found Facebook-based engagement to be a more appealing mode for expressing their frustrations and realizing empowerment.

Nonetheless, the affordances of Facebook had their limits. For example, there were also contexts in which the users described practicing caution in their Posting behavior. They were acutely aware of the potential for incurring a ban from the platform, often having learned from experience. Beatrice said she had become increasingly cautious because of the duty she felt she had to educate people: "If I get banned, who is left to put out that message?"

However, not only fear of incurring a ban, but also fear of social judgement and the users' own moral codes informed cautious Posting behavior. While some were keen to stress that they did not care what others thought of their views, Mark for example lamented that he was "too scared" to Publicly Post anything in support of "Tommy Robinson" because "I'd be fearful for people getting, you know, thinking I was a racist or whatever." Eileen said she was careful about Sharing content from certain websites or Pages, because despite her quite severe reservations about Islam, she did not want to encourage discussion on her Page to deteriorate into what she ironically called "Muzzie bashing." Deborah spoke of her reticence to join Gab—a "free speech" social media platform whose lack of moderation is said to allow far-right communities to thrive (Jasser et al. 2021)—and linked this to worries about how she might be seen by others. However, similar to Beatrice's fear of being banned from Facebook, Deborah's ultimate concern here was the ability to retain an impactful voice for the cause: "I do want to be careful. I don't want to be associated with extreme far-right. Not particularly because it bothers me what people say about me, but my views would not be listened to. [. . .] I'd be dismissed automatically. Almost like being a member of Ku Klux Klan."

The users also professed to exercise caution about Sharing Posts with photos of alleged vandals, pedophiles, or burglars. Such Posts rarely linked to the milieu's core political concerns, but were not uncommon. Many of the users in this study claimed they did not believe it was right to Share this unverified content given it could result in an innocent person being incriminated or targeted. These narratives did not always reflect the practices I observed, nor were these individuals' moral self-narratives necessarily consistent with the ideology revealed in other comments they made. However, such accounts reveal the pro-Brexit Facebook users' broader desire to understand their social media practices in moralistic terms. Not only did these individuals not wish to jeopardize their ability to have a voice on Facebook, but they were careful not to compromise their positive moral identities as "truth tellers." Their cautious behavior (or narratives about this in interviews) was another product of the righteous mission they saw themselves as being on, interacting with their awareness of negative perceptions of Brexit supporters and their desire to challenge these.

BURDENS, BURN-OUTS, AND THE QUESTION OF CONTINUITY

While aspects of Facebook's platform undoubtedly enabled or encouraged particular practices of right-wing populist political engagement, there were notable limits to the continuity or sustainability of these practices that were also shaped by Facebook. In addition to the threat of incurring a permanent ban within the context of Facebook's increasingly stringent application of its

Community Guidelines, several of the pro-Brexit Facebook users described the negative effects that their Facebook use was having on their emotional well-being and personal relationships.

Conflict and Relationship Strain

Brexit has been described as a particularly divisive political issue (Hobolt 2016), but research about how it is discussed and experienced within close personal relationships has challenged the power of this, highlighting the resilience of these relationships in the face of political disagreement (Davies 2022). In the current study, the online engagement of the pro-Brexit Facebook users *did* have an effect on their personal relationships. As will be explored in section II of this book, the ideologies that shaped what these individuals Posted mixed widespread forms of racism with more extreme illiberal views that attracted contention. The way that antagonism is culturally and architecturally embedded in Facebook use (see chapter 1) may also have contributed, alongside the way public social media's "context collapse" creates "context collisions" (Davis and Jurgenson 2014) and inhibits the tailoring of messages to one's audience or the placing of sensitive topics "off limits" to preserve social relationships (Chadwick, Vaccari, and Hall 2023).

Facebook blends political and personal arenas (e.g., Metz, Kruikemeier, and Lecheler 2020). Although some of the users in this study excluded face-to-face relations and personal connections from their Facebook activity altogether (either deliberately or because their peers did not use Facebook), others were connected on Facebook with a variety of friends, family, and other "offline" acquaintances, rendering the content they Posted visible to these ties. This sometimes resulted in conflict within these relationships.

For instance, Deborah described having "gotten into it with my son-in-law, big time" on Facebook. She said, "I felt he was attacking me and my political beliefs and I felt he had no right. I've got as much right [as he] to say what I want to say." Her strategy for dealing with this was to remove this site of conflict by "un-Friending" him on the platform. "I realize on certain political subjects we are never going to agree, [. . .] and I think it's better that we don't get into it, so I've decided I don't want him to see my Posts anymore." She assured me this was not meant to symbolize a severing of ties "offline" but was what she deemed necessary to avoid damaging their relationship or causing hurt to her daughter. In this way, Facebook was understood as an environment so inherently inclined toward hostility that family members who might otherwise find maintaining relationships unproblematic face-to-face could not be trusted to put political passions aside there.

Lawrence described a conflict that resulted in a severing of offline ties and caused him real hurt and disappointment. This occurred when one of his previously estranged stepsisters, to whom he had reached out on Facebook after the passing of his stepfather, strongly disagreed with his Posts regarding Brexit and eventually "removed herself from [his] Page." Although they had not known each other very well beforehand, Lawrence stressed that this altercation and rejection was significant to him given that he had felt they were grieving together as family members and that he had tried to "accept [his step-siblings] into my life to try and help them out a little bit." Lawrence described this as a "very sad" development.

In Neil's case it was sometimes closer relationships that appeared to be affected. Neil's online political engagement was particularly oriented toward conspiracy theories, and the content he Posted frequently received skeptical or critical responses from friends and relatives on Facebook. But he said that at a weekly social gathering he had with friends he regularly spoke about the information he had found online, eager to "keep them informed." He noticed these friends would sometimes lose interest or become fed up and, like those who reacted skeptically and dismissively to his Facebook Posts, he was aware that perhaps "some of them think I'm a sandwich short of a picnic." Neil had also had run-ins with a distant family member, who on Facebook had "accused [him] of being a lunatic" and whom he eventually had to "Unfriend." This, he admitted, had caused some tension with his wife, who was concerned about the way this conflict might affect their relationship with the rest of the family. Exactly how this had affected Neil's relationship with his wife was unclear. He mentioned she had also expressed unease at the amount of time Neil was spending researching alternative information online, but when asked about this in his interview he simply forced a smile and changed the subject. Neil was confident that his theories about the Deep State and globalism would be proven accurate in time, and so being able to continue his engagement on Facebook meant having to brush off the tensions that it was creating between him and his loved ones.

Emotional Well-being

In addition to impacting personal relationships, pro-Brexit and right-wing populist engagement on Facebook sometimes affected users' emotional well-being. As well as regularly being confronted with hostility, they were constantly bombarded with varying degrees of upsetting political content. Aware of the stress and frustration this was causing them, some of the users described dialing back their engagement, or certain aspects of it. Deborah said in her first interview,

> I have found myself changing about how I deal with Comments of things I don't agree with. I did get quite angry at one time, which I started to sense was

fruitless. [. . .] I didn't feel it would do any good, and now how I deal with it, usually, is I will either completely eradicate anything I've said, delete it, or I will on occasions, just agree to disagree. [. . .] If I feel there's a chance of maybe enlightening a person on some level, I will, but if I feel it's fruitless, I will not get into a rather nasty encounter. [. . .] I just find it leaves me very stressed, and that wasn't in my interest.

In her second interview, Deborah said she was now "taking a step back" from her engagement with news on Facebook because "if you allow yourself to constantly get bogged down with [the variety of opinions regarding Brexit], it's horrendous. [. . .] I'm trying now to focus on positive points, [. . .] and there's very few of those around."

Eileen too, by the time of her second interview, was alluding to the toll that spending around five hours a day curating her Pages was taking on her. She described her desire to "unclutter my Page from politics and go back to [. . .] just living me life, [. . .] go back to normal." Beatrice similarly said in her second interview that over the past week "I've tried to keep off Facebook because it just winds me up."

In Kirk's case, the content he was viewing on the platform was contributing to his engagement becoming a stressful and fatiguing experience. For the past two to three years Kirk had been using Facebook to engage with political content several times a week, for around two hours at a time. The immersive observations found that his Timeline was dominated by videos of violence at home and abroad, indicating the likelihood of the prominence of such content in his Newsfeed also. In his first interview, Kirk mentioned he felt his own Facebook Posts had become increasingly angry over the past few years. As we sat down to begin his second interview and I asked him how he had been since we last spoke, he divulged that he had been having trouble sleeping. Throughout the interview he alluded to the stress, anger, and anxiety that engaging with this upsetting content caused him. About politics, he said, "it's so much that's mucked up, so much. It's like, hundreds and hundreds of things that hit you every day."

Kirk contrasted this with how things used to be "before" when "we'll have a 5-minute discussion on that and forget about it." He also described how he now feared constantly for the safety of his family—safety from terrorist incidents out and about in London, as well as from violence or vandalism they might experience at home or in the car "because people read my Posts and they don't like me." However, he said he would not stop having his say on Facebook because of this; using Facebook to express himself and share the truth was too important. Kirk did not view the distressing content he engaged with as an outcome of his own algorithmically-derived Newsfeed; to him it represented "how the world is becoming." His attitude is also indicative of a feeling of hopelessness toward a perceived social decline that was expressed by the users, and the way in which finding and exchanging content on Facebook represented what felt like the sole means by which to combat this.

Lawrence also described fatigue. Already in his first interview he said, "When Brexit's over I hope my life will change to a little bit more of a happy side rather than all this political stuff." At the time of our second interview, he was excited about having started a new job which saw him take on more responsibility. The busy workload this brought had meant he had taken a step back from politics on Facebook. He said this had been "a good break" from sometimes getting "too enravelled [sic] in it if I've got too much time on my hands." This was puzzling in light of Lawrence's eagerness, outlined in the above section, to become more involved in political participation offline. Lawrence's experience highlights a contradiction between the pro-Brexit Facebook users' desire to exercise their political agency, and their simultaneous anticipation of the relief that stepping away from that participation could bring. It would be inaccurate to attribute the "social media fatigue" (Fielding 2011) observed here to simple "information overload" (e.g., Bright, Kleiser, and Grau 2015) or growing privacy concerns (Logan, Bright, and Grau 2018). These explanations fail to recognize the emotional toll that conflictual interactions and affective content take on those engaging in politics on Facebook. And for these individuals, their fatigue with political engagement was exacerbated all the more by their intense frustration over Brexit and the other political issues with which they were engaging.

The Threat of Censorship

In the context of Facebook imposing ever-stricter "Community Standards" upon its users, censorship was an additional threat to the sustainability of the political engagement in the pro-Brexit Facebook milieu. As noted above, Olivia was already prepared with user accounts on multiple other "free speech" oriented platforms and after being permanently banned from Facebook she did continue her activities there. Neil and Fred said they would consider using other platforms if they were banned too.

However, some of the other users were unsure about making the commitment required to learn how to use another platform, or whether there was a point in using a platform where they would not be able to interact with the audience they had now. For Eileen, perhaps it was the above-described fatigue she was experiencing at the time of our second interview that prompted her to say, "I can't see me doing this through another medium. [. . .] If I did get banned forever for some reason, [. . .] I don't think I'd start it up again. I think I'd just do something else. [. . .] I'd probably see it as a sign to shut up, get on with me own life, because I can still find out what's going on [through other means]." This was despite the strong dedication to the cause that Eileen's intense engagement appeared to reflect.

In other words, the site of their political engagement mattered to these individuals. It was Facebook that had drawn them to intense right-wing populist engagement, and afforded them the potential to do so. This finding has consequences for deplatforming agendas and their detractors (see Rogers 2020). While particularly tenacious individuals may be committed to continuing their engagement on alternative platforms, many of the users if permanently banned said they would use this opportunity to extricate themselves from the stresses that this engagement entails. Coming to use Facebook specifically to engage in politics was associated with discovering their passion for Brexit and uncovering what they saw as vital knowledge. As Deborah aptly summarized, "You know, we just, we want out. We want to be able to have our own sovereignty back, and Facebook gives us an outlet for that. [. . .] Is it absolutely perfect? Does it solve, is it the answer to everything? Is it going to replace the media, which I wouldn't trust as far as I can throw? No. But it's an alternative, and it's an alternative that I'd hate to lose."

CONCLUSION: "FOR WHAT I'M DOING IT'S BEEN INVALUABLE"

Engaging with politics on Facebook was a very important part of the daily lives of pro-Brexit Facebook users. As the above analysis has demonstrated, however, the significance of political engagement practices to them was contingent on the form these practices took. In the context of their political frustrations, encountering suggested content and Sharing this with others provided these individuals with a sense of agency and control over their political destiny. Each of these practices were enabled by the affordances of Facebook. However, they were also *encouraged* by the platform's logics, norms and cultures that these affordances played a part in engendering. Becoming part of Facebook's media logic meant that aspects of the platform like automation, visuality, the impetus to Share, and conflict were able to appear as neutral "common sense," engendering new norms for what was considered ordinary or natural behavior on social media platforms.

Despite the control that the pro-Brexit Facebook users actually surrendered to Facebook's algorithms and logics in the content they encountered and ultimately Shared, these practices were seen as a way of exercising agency and control. They provided these individuals with an opportunity to garner forms of knowledge that they felt they otherwise did not have access to, and express themselves in ways they otherwise felt they were unable.

As we saw in the previous chapters, the populist discourses of Brexit in the post-referendum era constructed both an imperative to act and a tangible goal to work toward. In this context, Facebook represented an unprecedented tool with which to take such action. It afforded opportunities and benefits that offline participation could not. As Eileen said, "Now we've got this wonderful opportunity to find out information and Share it with massive numbers. [. . .] You've got the facility, in your pocket, to find anything out, [. . .] [and] send it to someone. [. . .] It's powerful. [. . .] For what I'm doing it's been invaluable. Absolutely invaluable."

To the pro-Brexit Facebook users, contributing to this crucial political moment through finding and Sharing content on Facebook was empowering. Having already exhausted their democratic avenue via a referendum result they felt was being deliberately sidelined by those in control, these practices represented perhaps the only remaining means for taking action toward finally having their "concerns" addressed.

However, the sustainability of these practices was limited. The threat of censorship sometimes constrained these individuals' practices, which were also taking a toll on their relationships and mental well-being. In the system of surveillance capitalism (Zuboff 2019), social media business models rely on the monetization of user data, which in turn necessitates encouraging users to continue to engage and generate useful data to sell to advertisers. Within the attention economy, the content and interactions that generate the most user engagement are often those that provoke strong emotional reactions, particularly anger, frustration, hate, and fear (Wahl-Jorgensen 2019). Promoting such content ultimately creates stress and fatigue for users, whose emotional burden has limits. This highlights the paradox of social media in which its necessary profit-generation mechanism can harm its users and ultimately drive them away.

In short, the way right-wing populist political engagement is practiced online is affected by the system of surveillance capitalism in which contemporary societies find themselves ensnared. This system underpinned all of the logics that were found to shape online engagement practices in the pro-Brexit Facebook milieu. Recognizing this means acknowledging the need for the study of online political engagement to look beyond platform affordances to the structural conditions that produce them and give them dominance over other affordances.

Finally, the above analysis highlights the way that the practices engendered by these affordances and logics became meaningful to the individuals in question in the context of their social and political experiences. As well as being able to reclaim a sense of agency, the pro-Brexit Facebook users were able to take back a sense of value or validity through their engagement with Brexit and other right-wing politics on Facebook. The following section turns to the ideologies at the heart of these online political engagements, which shed further light on the relationships between these online practices, the content of the politics with which these individuals engaged, and their wider motivations and worldviews.

NOTES

1. A reminder that capitalization of the first letter is used in this book to identify a function of the Facebook platform and avoid confusion with broader terms, for example, to Share a Post with one's Facebook Friends versus share one's thoughts with a friend via a letter in the post.

2. Meta has publicly denied this, saying that the leaked documents have been taken out of context (Lima 2021).

3. The content I observed Olivia Posting is excluded from figures 2.1 through 2.3 (see introduction, note 3).

SECTION II

Ideology

Chapter 3

The Pro-Brexit Facebook Metanarrative

In examining what the experience of being engaged in pro-Brexit and right-wing populist politics on Facebook meant to users, the previous section has already made reference to the ideologies that motivated them to become engaged and to find and Share content online. A meaningful understanding of this engagement, however, also requires a focused, critical interrogation of the substance of the ideologies being promoted in the pro-Brexit Facebook milieu. Uncovering this ideological substance allows us to situate this milieu within broader transnational right-wing populism. At the same time, it provides clues as to the role of social media in connecting Brexit with relevant causes and movements around the world. The three chapters in section II uncover this ideological substance through the lens of narratives. First, the current chapter identifies the overarching metanarrative of the milieu and the implications of this for understanding pro-Brexit and right-wing populist engagement online, before chapters 4 and 5 bring the focus to the two main elements of the milieu's ideology: racism and anti-leftism.

SUPPORT FOR BREXIT AND ITS IDEOLOGICAL FOUNDATIONS

While British Euroscepticism has been a subject of study in political science over a number of decades (e.g., George 2000; Evans 1998), the rise of UKIP and the attribution of certain social meanings to support for the UK's departure from the EU has seen this phenomenon become an object of broader social inquiry. This body of research, both before and after the 2016 referendum, has drawn on media and campaign analysis (Fox 2018; Rone 2021; Zappettini 2019), quantitative surveys (H. Clarke et al. 2016; Antonucci et al. 2017; Henderson et al. 2017), theoretical discussions (Bhambra 2017;

Outhwaite 2017), and a small number of interviews and ethnographies (Patel and Connelly 2019; McKenzie 2017; Walkerdine 2020), to demonstrate how the political issue of Brexit has become a key mobilizer of nationalism, racism, and isolationism, as well as a vehicle for frustration with socio-economic conditions.

The emergence and normalization of political social media use, however, has opened up the potential for Brexit and its supporters to be connected with a range of international movements and issues, meaning support for Brexit online may not ideologically mirror that offline. Existing studies into social media-based support for Brexit have tended to neglect the substance of ideologies being espoused in these milieus in favor of a focus on the emotional form these pro-Brexit expressions take (Bouko and Garcia 2020; Lilleker and Bonacci 2017; Rosa and Ruiz 2020) or the networks of influence in the online Leave campaign (Bastos and Mercea 2019; Bossetta, Segesten, and Trenz 2018; Del Vicario et al. 2017; Gorodnichenko, Pham, and Talavera 2018; Howard and Kollanyi 2016). Those studies that do attend to ideological content are narrow in their focus. Bonacchi et al. (2018), for example, specifically examined the role of the pre-modern past in the construction of identities on pro-Brexit Facebook Pages, and Dobreva et al. (2019) focused their inquiry on "soft facts" in social media-based discussion of the murder of Labour MP Jo Cox in the lead-up to the referendum.

Furthermore, these and many other studies into social media engagement rely solely on data from social media Posts, without engaging with user interpretations. I contend that to understand the ideologies of online milieus and their social consequences we must attend to meaning-making; that is, what meanings do the individuals participating in these online milieus attribute to the ideas they consume and reproduce there. This cannot be done through observation alone, but must involve eliciting interpretations from social actors themselves. Online trace data such as Posts, Likes, Follows, or Shares are not windows into social reality, because they are constructed at the intersection of affordances, platform cultures, norms, and social relationships (Hall 2022c). For this reason, analysis of social media content cannot on its own reveal the meanings attributed to this content, or elucidate the role played by Facebook in engagement with the ideologies at play. Based on interviews with pro-Brexit Facebook users that were augmented and "thickened" with insights from observing their Posts, the chapters in this section aim to provide a critical analysis of the ideologies that were engaged with in the pro-Brexit Facebook milieu. The findings point to the role of Facebook in facilitating global connection and promoting and extending harmful ideologies.

NARRATIVES AND METANARRATIVES IN THE PRO-BREXIT FACEBOOK MILIEU

In this book, I use the lens of the narrative to illuminate the content of the ideologies being promoted and developed in the pro-Brexit Facebook milieu. Political narratives are key to meaning-making—they provide structured ways of understanding the world that play an important role in ideological identification (Haidt, Graham, and Joseph 2009). The type of narrative I examine here comprises cultural scripts and shared sets of meaningful assumptions, rather than singular texts that constitute whole coherent stories (as in individual life histories, for example). This definition of narratives resembles Page's (2018) concept of "shared stories" on social media, which are "collectively produced, consumed and reproduced" (ibid., 2). Social media have been described as "an emergent territory for digital storytelling," through their integration of text, videos, images, and audio (Venditti, Piredda, and Mattana 2017, S274). Features like those explored in chapter 2 that deliberately encourage Sharing enable the co-creation and co-telling of narratives on a vast scale, and facilitate feelings of engagement that reenergize users politically (Page 2018; Papacharissi 2015), making narratives integral to social media-based political engagement.

Narratives can play a particularly important role for those who, like the pro-Brexit Facebook users studied here, do not feel their views and agendas are reflected in mainstream media (Hackett 2016, 14). They can act as a form of resistance and reclamation by challenging or disrupting dominant or official narratives, as in the "counter-narratives" identified by Hewitt (2005, 57–58) or the "affective publics" proposed by Papacharissi (2015) and elaborated by Papacharissi and Trevey (2018, 93). The pro-Brexit Facebook users recited a shared set of narratives when accounting for their political stances, and these narratives also echoed content observed in Facebook Posts in their milieu. In the same way that these individuals bonded over mutual beliefs and values online, "shared stories" provided them with a common ground that they not only Shared via Facebook Posts but also *shared in* as a collective milieu.

Narratives come into being between and around texts, but although discourses are the building blocks of narratives, narratives are distinct from discourses in that they cohere around a temporal dimension (Miskimmon, O'Loughlin, and Roselle 2013, 7). That is, they are stories that include "an initial situation or order, a problem that disrupts that order, and a resolution that reestablishes order" (ibid., 5). In this way, narratives facilitate the connection of seemingly unconnected events and phenomena around a "causal transformation" (ibid.).

In this chapter I reveal how the narratives in the pro-Brexit Facebook milieu cohered around one overarching *metanarrative*, which I argue is integral not only to understanding the ideological nucleus of this milieu, but also the networked nature of transnational right-wing populism more broadly. A metanarrative is "an informal collective belief that rationalises a people's worldview, aspirations, institutions and practices" (de Oliver 2011, 977). Sometimes used interchangeably with "grand narratives," metanarratives act as "symbolic modes of communication" among groups of people, around which group identities are constructed (ibid.). Designating villains, heroes, and victims assigns moral value to groups, which also serves to legitimate deservingness and group privilege. Metanarratives deviate, however, from myths in that at their core is not a past founding moment but a future to be realized (Lyotard 1993, 18). Metanarratives represent "epic dramas" that locate the present within a "teleological unfolding" and embed us as "contemporary actors in history" (Somers 1994, 619). Illustrative examples in Western society include the metanarratives of capitalism versus communism (ibid.), or "Manifest Destiny" (de Oliver 2011).

The interview accounts of the pro-Brexit Facebook users suggested that they were observing and making sense of the world in this teleological sense, locating their perceived predicament within a broader historical drama or struggle. In fact, it was this sense of wider history-making implications—a chance to be part of something bigger than themselves or the moment in which they lived—that motivated many of them to become politically engaged online, and separated them from less passionate or less committed Brexit supporters. Below, I identify the basic elements of the pro-Brexit Facebook metanarrative, including plot, cast of characters, and evaluative criteria. Doing so reveals how seemingly disparate political concerns were understood by pro-Brexit Facebook users as interrelated. It illuminates the integration of ideas from far-right conspiracy theories into the metanarrative fabric, evidence of the power of social media and Brexit to extend the reach of the transnational far and populist right. Dissecting the pro-Brexit Facebook metanarrative also highlights the role of populist configurations in its composition, and thus the compatibility of post-referendum support for Brexit with transnational right-wing populist appeals.

THE PRO-BREXIT FACEBOOK METANARRATIVE

Although a variety of narratives were operating in the pro-Brexit Facebook milieu about a multitude of topics—including EU governance, migration, Islam, domestic and international politicians, and the media—these narratives overlapped with one another and were frequently employed in combination.

Indeed, the concerns underlying them were understood as all being connected to one another. In Neil's (70s, male, South Wales) words, "you can't look at issues like Brexit in isolation. All of these things are now interrelated on a global basis." As I demonstrate, an overarching metanarrative can be identified that links the array of accounts employed and grants them a greater meaning than the sum of their parts. I call this the *pro-Brexit Facebook metanarrative*. This metanarrative represents the overall raison d'etre of the milieu itself—the broader motivational force behind engagement with pro-Brexit and right-wing populist politics on Facebook that brought this milieu into being.

Synopsis and Cast of Characters: "Everything's Geared Against Us"

The metanarrative around which accounts in the milieu cohered was a story of an agenda from above to facilitate or force "left-wing" change to the detriment of real, common, or ordinary people like the pro-Brexit Facebook users. The agenda in question was depicted as global and all-encompassing, including but extending far beyond the institutions of the EU. Key to the plot were that this agenda was *deliberate* (being imposed from above), *deceitful* (orchestrated behind closed doors and actively hidden), and that the imposed change represented a clear *decline* (an ongoing change for the worse).

At the core of the metanarrative was a struggle for control over the direction of society. The villains, heroes, and victims identified were purportedly engaged in a clash between good and evil, the outcome of which would determine the fate of Britain and indeed the Western world. The way the users constantly constructed insidious links, both explicit and implicit, between things like gender rights and multiculturalism; political correctness and "open borders"; Islamization and "Cultural Marxism"; or European integration and media bias, demonstrates how the metanarrative thread was woven through all of their political concerns, which were brought together via Facebook. Whether this sinister agenda was to strip Britain of its sovereignty by subordinating it to a dictatorial master, impose communist social engineering, supplant Britain's White population with non-White inhabitants, or replace their culture with Islam, the key was that something was being taken away which was rightly "theirs." The pro-Brexit Facebook users and the White majority they saw themselves as representing were allegedly being robbed of control over their destiny.

In the villains' role, the EU was joined by a range of political, media, and organizational actors who, it was claimed, were intent on imposing this undesired social change. These included the UN and other so-called "globalist" organizations and individuals, outspoken members of the Labour Party and left-leaning media commentators, Remainers, the biased or deliberately brainwashing "mainstream media," and immigrants, particularly a transnational community of Muslims. Each of these was depicted in the metanarrative as having ill-intent, as power-hungry, scheming, and sinister. Those who facilitated or collaborated with this group's agenda were deemed "traitors," reinforcing the villains' malevolence and the zero-sum nature of the struggle. Whether or not concrete collusion was taking place between these villains was not important. What mattered was the broader sense that what each of these actors was trying to do to the victims of the metanarrative, and take from them, was driving things in the same leftward direction, the final destination of which was understood to be subordination.

Facing up against these villains were the heroes of the metanarrative. These individuals were depicted as stoically fighting to protect the victims by standing up to the aforementioned actors in the face of persecution (which simultaneously rendered these heroes victims too). They included right-wing populist leaders like then-U.S. President Donald Trump, online "truth" tellers like "Tommy Robinson," and prominent pro-Brexit politicians like Nigel Farage and Conservative MP Jacob Rees-Mogg. The heroes were even compared with emancipatory historical figures, implying history would judge them (and those whom they were defending) as righteous heroes in due course. In Jessica's (40s, female, London) evaluation, "Look at Gandhi, [. . .] and um Nelson Mandela. They were criminals before they became heroes, because people didn't agree. They tried to stop them from saying what they were saying, but then when the movements realized these people are telling the truth, that's when people start to wake up." In this quote, Jessica's indecisive shifting between past and present tense alludes to the strength of the parallel she draws between historical happenings and present events. She clearly locates the struggle of "truth tellers" like "Robinson" (who for part of the fieldwork was imprisoned for contempt of court over his illegal online coverage of a "grooming gangs" related trial) in an imagined historic moment. Right-wing actors with their criticisms of Islam and "political correctness" are cast as virtuous, and the completeness of the "brainwashing" agenda of the "left" is exposed through the accusation that it has inverted right and wrong in an epic injustice.

The victims in the pro-Brexit Facebook metanarrative were a broad category of "the majority" who, it was assumed, widely shared allegedly legitimate concerns about immigration, diversity, and moral relativism that they were not permitted to voice. The pro-Brexit Facebook users maintained their role of virtuous victim through ontological narratives (Somers 1994, 618) in which they made (often unconvincing) claims to their own nature as "not racist" or discriminatory, or as hardworking and noble-hearted individuals. They also constructed themselves within the shared "us" by asserting that they "knew" or "had the feeling"—based on what they had seen on Facebook or sometimes the conversations they had been having offline—that their views were representative of the majority of Britons. These individuals' use of "us" and "our" to refer to the victims of the metanarrative also alluded to the racialized categories of belonging employed by this metanarrative; the imagined victims simultaneously represented "ordinary Britons" and White (culturally Christian) citizens, problematically rendering these synonymous with one another.

The Manichean binary between actors in the metanarrative draws on the populism that was so prominent in the Leave campaign (J. Clarke and Newman 2017; Norris and Inglehart 2019). This people-centrism is a central tenet of populism (Mudde 2004; 2007). In populist discourse, as in the metanarrative, "the people" are presented as virtuous and their will self-evident, authentic, and homogeneous. The latter character of the people prompts populism, and right-wing populism in particular, to pay close attention to national belonging, which in turn leads to its compatibility with the kind of nativist racism that chapter 4 will demonstrate was prominent in this milieu. The content of the category of "the people" in the metanarrative remained largely undefined or an "empty signifier" (Laclau 2005, 67–128). In populism, this contributes to the category's "illusory appeal," in that it is at once universal and exclusionary, creating legitimacy as a democratic populace while simultaneously constructing enemies in elites and outsiders (De Genova 2018a, 360).

The anti-elitism that is also crucial to populism was a key part of the construction of the metanarrative villains. At its heart, the metanarrative was a story of an imagined collective under siege from above, and villains were seen as encompassing actors in national and supranational government without citizens' interests at heart. But in the metanarrative, the populist discourse of the Leave campaign was extended, adapted, and distorted beyond anti-elitist and racist conceptions of malevolence. The broadly construed category of the Left were key villains in the plot. As we shall see in chapter 5, while these groups were sometimes characterized as powerful or pompous, the threat they posed was not merely an elitist threat to a democratic referendum mandate. It was portrayed as a threat to conservative values in the form of (forced) societal change, a threat to White Christian cultural dominance, to definitions of gender and gender roles, and to the traditional family model.

Deliberate and Deceitful: The Role of Far-Right Conspiracy Theories

The pro-Brexit Facebook metanarrative wove together diverse sets of events and actors into an overarching and inter-connected plot focused on power and control, that was *deliberate* and *deceitful*. The idea of a hidden agenda was alluded to in narratives around a number of issues, such as the EU's role in immigration flows, the mainstream media's subtle pushing of "diversity," or the alleged Islamization of law and cultural practices. This deliberate imposition of change is important as it renders the metanarrative villains ever more sinister. That the agenda was being orchestrated and carried out covertly made it a greater threat to democratic virtues, and added to the alleged helplessness of the victims in the metanarrative.

While the pro-Brexit Facebook metanarrative did not constitute a single conspiracy theory in and of itself, and support for Brexit by no means necessitates belief in a conspiracy, it drew upon ideas from a number of transnational far-right conspiracy theories. Few of the pro-Brexit Facebook users in this study had good knowledge of the ins and outs of these theories, despite sometimes using their names. Instead, they incorporated the theories they had come across online when this was useful to justify their pro-Brexit, culturally conservative, and anti-immigration stances. The level of orchestration that each of them purported was involved in the agenda also varied greatly, or even fluctuated within individual accounts, depending on the narrative being employed.

A popular group of theories drawn upon by the metanarrative was the "Great Replacement," whose varieties include "White Genocide," "New World Order," and the "Kalergi Plan." This group of White nationalist, anti-Semitic conspiracy theories claims that there is a plan for White Christian populations in Western countries to be replaced with non-White and/or Muslim immigrants, to promote not only demographic but cultural and religious change (Cosentino 2020, 78; de Bruin 2017). Great Replacement theories were identified in the manifestos of White supremacist terror attacks in Oslo, El Paso, and Christchurch, highlighting the dangers of these theories' appropriation and inversion of the concept of "genocide" as justification for acts of extreme violence (Cosentino 2020; Fekete 2012).

Ideas drawn from these theories can be seen in the pro-Brexit Facebook metanarrative's claims about covertly planned demographic and cultural change, particularly the preoccupation of many of the users with "Islamization." In Lawrence's (40s, male, West Midlands) second interview, I asked him about some Posts he had Shared from a Facebook Page called "Exposing the New World Order." He summarized what this theory meant to him: "I find these Groups cos of the interests I have. [. . .] New World Order is, the political elites, the banks, war, oil, you know, it's all governed by one world force really. And I do honestly believe that the EU is trying to create one, one European solid state, with no democracy, everybody being controlled like they're just ants, um, all currencies being the same, et cetera, et cetera." Lawrence's description of the New World Order clearly paints this as a global conspiracy theory, but importantly, this is relevant to him in that it is seen as somehow directly linked to the EU's nefarious "superstate" aims.

The Kalergi Plan variety of the Great Replacement theory was particularly popular in the pro-Brexit Facebook milieu. It was commonly associated by the users with then-German Chancellor Angela Merkel, perhaps because of Germany's extension of its asylum program during the Syrian conflict. This conspiracy theory is particularly relevant to support for Brexit, as it centers around a plan for enforced ethnic mixing said to be the real reason behind the European project (de Bruin 2022; Gaston 2018). The theory posits that a passage in a 1925 book by a European politician named Richard von Coudenhove-Kalergi, who was instrumental to European integration, is evidence of a covert plot for enforced racial mixing as it predicts that "the man of the future will be of mixed race" (ibid.; see Coudenhove-Kalergi 1925). This theory was particularly popular in Alt-Right spheres during the post-referendum negotiation period, as this movement gained new proponents among far-right politicians in Europe (de Bruin 2022).

The Kalergi Plan theory caught the attention of Beatrice (60s, female, North Wales) for a period during the fieldwork. In 2018, she Posted a link to a blog post entitled "Angela Merkel and the Kalergi Plan—The Destruction of the White Race" with the Comment "This is where we are at." Several days later, Beatrice Shared an image from a Brexit-related Facebook Group that included a mockup picture of the front cover of Coudenhove-Kalergi's manuscript, alongside text reading, "To bring out a new breed of people as a result of careful and general racial confusion. The peoples of Europe must mix with Asians and other non-white races to create a multi-racial community that does not have a clear understanding of traditions and identity and therefore easily controlled by the ruling elite [*sic*]. This is what Remainers Voted for."

The Kalergi Plan theory was also particularly important to Eileen (60s, female, Northwest England), who mentioned this as part of her trajectory toward becoming politically engaged:

> I dug some more, found out what was really going on with the migrants and basically that it was a plan, it wasn't, this isn't some crisis. [. . .] Angela Merkel knows exactly what she's doing. [. . .] Then you start going deeper and deeper into these things and you find out that someone like [left-wing philanthropist George] Soros [. . .] has got a vested interest in this and, and it's all about basically keeping society poorer so that they depend on the World Bank to borrow money. [. . .] So, there'll be this parasitic elite of Europe, [. . .] while the working classes of these countries are going to be forgotten. [. . .] So I got highly suspicious of the root requirements of the EU. And you look at the disguises, yeah, the disguises are all the financial add-ons that they sell us, and then when you look into it, all the money that we get back in rebates we send it to them anyway. It's our money coming back, except it's only half of it.

Here, Eileen's narrative reflects not only the power of the Kalergi Plan conspiracy to capture the attention of Brexit supporters on Facebook, but also its ability to flow into and blend with other far-right conspiracy theories and with more everyday Eurosceptic arguments within the metanarrative. Eileen referenced a number of far-right conspiracy theories in her interviews, dipping and diving into their ideas. In fact, when acquainting me with this theory, she mistakenly described its protagonist as "Coudenaf-Calgarian." Those theories, or pieces thereof, that best explained or justified the imperative to leave the EU were selectively gathered and rearranged in the pro-Brexit Facebook milieu to form the metanarrative.

A second conspiracy theory that was a major influence for the pro-Brexit Facebook metanarrative was the theory of Cultural Marxism. This idea has its roots in post-Cold War anti-socialism, having been employed in rhetoric by neo-Nazi groups for decades (Jamin 2014). As the narrative goes, Gramsci's Prison Notebooks were written to urge Marxists to gain control of education and other institutions of cultural production in order to brainwash the masses toward socialism. According to the theory, this strategy was brought to the United States by the Frankfurt School scholars, and it subsequently influenced generations of Americans and contributed to the left-wing social movements that followed, including feminism, Black power, and environmentalism. Importantly, and contrary to the reality of post-1980 neoliberal hegemony (Harvey 2007), the theory of Cultural Marxism "represents the New Left as history's victor," and it is this socialist hegemony which the Alt-Right sees itself as engaged in a battle against (Mirrlees 2018, 54).

Cultural Marxism was mentioned multiple times in the pro-Brexit Facebook milieu during the fieldwork. Deborah (50s, female, Northwest England), for example, Shared a Breitbart article via a nationalist Facebook Page in 2018, about how unconscious bias training at UK universities was allegedly targeting older, White, male professors. A Comment that came with the original Post (i.e., authored by the Facebook Page that Deborah had Shared from) read "[. . .] cultural Marxists are now in full control of academia in the UK."

When Helen (50s, female, West Midlands) mentioned the term "Cultural Marxism" in her initial interview, I asked her what the term meant to her, prompting the following exchange:

> Helen: It's the um deconstruction of everything that held, holds society together. The smashing of the nuclear family, the pushing down our throats of the LGBT-XYZ whatever uh, group, groups. If they wanna be that way that's how they are. Yes, let them get on with it, but why do we need to be fed it for breakfast, lunch and dinner? Why do our children need to know about it so early? Their childhood is being robbed. [. . .]

Interviewer: So, this is all like part of this, what they're calling "Cultural Marxism"?

Helen: Yeah, I think it came from the um Frankfurt School, about smashing societies. Uh, but, getting rid of the patriarchy—I'd rather live in the patriarchy than in an Islamic society.

Interviewer: Okay. So, do you mean you feel like one is being replaced by the other?

Helen: Oh, definitely. You can see it everywhere. You can see everywhere um in um adverts, in soap operas, in films, everywhere. Once you start seeing it you can't unsee it. [. . .] They push everything on you, to make things that aren't that normal normal. [. . .] Then you can go onto feminism. Oh! Don't get me started!

Here again we see how popular far-right conspiracy theories are drawn upon by the pro-Brexit Facebook metanarrative, incorporated in piecemeal and combined ways and intermingled with racist ideas. In the milieu, terms like "Cultural Marxism" and "communism" were often used interchangeably, acting as vehicles for users' interpretations of elitism, control, and social engineering.

More importantly, even when it was not referenced explicitly, the central concept of the theory of Cultural Marxism—the idea of secretly and gradually orchestrated left-wing cultural change—was key to the plot of the metanarrative. The theory was already well on its way to becoming extremely popular within the global Alt-Right during the post-referendum negotiation period. The way in which tenets of this theory and of Great Replacement theories were directly imported to the metanarrative reflects the pro-Brexit Facebook milieu's transnational linkages to the far-right and other right-wing populist causes. These linkages were made possible through global social media, where these connections were made via both Newsfeed-determining algorithms and deliberate dissemination.

Evaluative Criteria

Evaluative criteria are a set of fundamental principles and values that order and give meaning to the elements of a metanarrative (Somers 1994, 617). These criteria underpin the identification of the crisis in the plot that seeks resolution, and the designation of the metanarrative's victims, villains, and heroes. To identify the evaluative criteria of a metanarrative is thus to illuminate its ideological core.

The evaluative criteria of the pro-Brexit Facebook metanarrative were primarily conservative values, such as traditional family and gender roles and patriotism, alongside nebulous universal (or Western) values such as democracy and freedom. The primacy of conservative values can be seen in the designation of the Left as villains identified above, and depictions of "loony leftie" pushes to normalize deviant or depraved behaviors, which will be explored in depth in chapter 5. In the pro-Brexit Facebook milieu, this demonization of the Left was linked to the values of democracy and freedom through the narrative that socialism and communism were being used by the EU to rob individuals of their democratic freedoms.

In the metanarrative, democracy was constantly depicted as under threat, in crisis, having been polluted, or in need of saving. This strong focus on the value of democracy is enabled by the populist people-centrism described above. Moralistic discourses about democratic values are consistently and strategically employed in populist rhetoric to invoke "the people" that populism purports to defend. As De Genova (2018a, 359–361) notes, the category of "the people" is "enshrined with a certain unquestionable halo of integrity as an essential premise of all democratic politics."

Eurosceptic discourses prior to the referendum which brought the democratic credentials of the EU into question (Goodwin and Milazzo 2015) further facilitated the creation of Brexit as a pro-democratic, populist cause. In the pro-Brexit Facebook milieu, the "bureaucrats in Brussels" were portrayed as "unelected" and "unaccountable" (Neil) in their extravagant spending on office buildings and travel. In Kirk's (60s, male, London) words, "When you read about what the EU are giving politicians and all this sort of stuff, [. . .] they're nothing more for me than a load of gangsters that are just lining their own pockets."

However, the threat to democracy in the metanarrative was depicted as primarily centering around the UK's exit from the EU being "undermined" by calls for a second referendum from Remainers, and by delays caused by the inability of the UK parliament and then-Prime Minister Theresa May to conclude (or walk away from) negotiations with the EU. In this context, the enemy was "anybody that's giving up democracy and things like that, or [. . .] sovereignty" (Mark, 50s, male, Yorkshire); that is, those "going against the will of the people" (Lawrence). This demonstrates how the political and discursive struggles between Leave and Remain camps during the post-referendum negotiation period provided newly fertile ground for moralized populist appeals to take hold. Framing the metanarrative struggle as a fight for democracy served to normalize the milieu's views and demands while negating and delegitimizing criticisms and counterarguments by condemning them as "undemocratic."

In the case of Brexit, the seductive populist "fantasies" with which the Leave campaign was injected—promises of "freedom, liberation, subjectivity and agency" (Browning 2019, 223)—could not be fulfilled by leaving the EU. This is because, as Browning contends, they rely on nostalgia for a forgone time, and their inherently contradictory nature generates continued anxiety, disillusionment, and alienation. Browning could not have predicted the pandemic crisis that would overshadow (or perhaps redraw the lines of) such alienations in the aftermath of Britain's eventual exit from the EU in 2020. However, in the post-referendum negotiation period, these insecurities were exacerbated by the unfulfilled populist promises of the referendum result. That result represented, in the pro-Brexit Facebook milieu's account, the democratic will of "the people," and the failing of the Brexit negotiations to enact that manifest will was prompting an intense disillusionment with the functioning of democracy.

Temporality: Decline and the Opportunity for Redemption

Part of the power of Brexit's populist fantasies, according to Browning's analysis, lies in the way in which they are predicated on an "if only" style of "identification of obstacles to be overcome," which has imbibed them with drama and enabled them to "perform a sense of crisis" (Browning 2019, 222–223). The frustration that the pro-Brexit Facebook users expressed at the perceived injustice for democracy was also accompanied by this sense of crisis or impending doom. Eileen captured this foreboding emphatically as she connected threats to democracy from the EU with those from Remainers:

> If this [the blocking or watering down of Brexit] happens, you're witnessing the breakdown of democracy. That is a tragic state of events, because the future without democracy is grim, because there's only autocracy, which is a dictatorial rule, which is what I feel the EU is. [. . .] So, this isn't about Brexit anymore really. It's about the breakdown of democracy and the fight is about upholding democracy, because without it we're sunk.

Eileen's quote embodies the way in which the fight for Brexit was depicted as an historic moment, embedded in a much broader struggle of the highest significance. Painting the potential impending triumph of Remainers and the EU as a tragedy, she adds dramaturgy and a sense of temporality that transforms current events into plot points within the metanarrative.

This temporality in the plot represented a consistent allusion to where we had come from and where we were going. It was characterized by a trajectory of *decline*, particularly within British society. Nostalgia was mobilized to depict the past as a more positive time than the present, and the future as inevitably worse, unless Leavers acted now. Representations of societal decline were littered throughout users' narratives. This is encapsulated in a quote from Beatrice: "It is this thing about family and looking after your own. [. . .] You've fought for your own, you know, and now suddenly they want to give it all away. But why? Why give it away?! [. . .] And then you're wondering why the whole country's going to the dogs, because they can't get into schools, they sit on the motorway for hours on end, [. . .] and yet, 'let's invite more people' [cynical laughter]. It doesn't work!" Here Beatrice's use of the continuous present tense in her claim the country is "going to the dogs" alludes to an ongoing process. Beatrice's use of "they" to refer to those who "want to give it all away" is tellingly vague, acting as a placeholder for multiple metanarrative villains. She also alludes to the key idea explored above that this decline was not happening by accident but was being done to the victims deliberately.

Fred's (60s, male, Northeast England) depiction of an alleged assault on free speech—an issue of major concern within the milieu, which will be elaborated in chapter 5—provides another useful exemplar:

> I think political correctness should never have been introduced into this country. It's a way of molding people's minds into . . . and controlling what they say. [. . .] We've had our free speech revoked, without us being aware of it. [. . .] At one time you'd be able to speak out quite clearly and not be condemned for it. [. . .] Now if you do, you're shot down as being an extremist. [. . .] Political correctness allows that agenda, and it's a very dangerous thing. If you look at the history of political correctness, it gets all the more alarming. [. . .] Its intention was exactly what's happened: to take away free speech, to control the minds of people, [. . .] but it's been lauded as something that's wonderful and fair and equal, which it isn't.

Fred identifies a trajectory of decline in his contrast between the freedom we once had at an imagined time when people were reasonable and respectful of each other's views, and the persecution allegedly faced now by those who dare voice a dissenting opinion. In Fred's account, the advent of "political correctness" was an intentional "agenda," which had been quietly executed for some time, and which extended beyond controlling speech to controlling minds. The agenda had allegedly been so successful that people had come to believe it emancipatory rather than oppressive.

The prominence of declinism in the metanarrative was consistent with the nostalgia deployed in the Leave campaign (Campanella and Dassù 2019), but also with a much older state of postcolonial melancholia in Britain identified by Gilroy (1987, 46). However, the pro-Brexit Facebook metanarrative builds on these, focusing the blame for this decline not only on "the dilution of once homogeneous and continuous national stock by alien strains" (ibid.), but also the "breakdown of democracy" and the incursion of progressive social values.

Meanwhile, the story was not over. This decline was ongoing, with the worst potentially yet to come. In Lawrence's assessment, "Great Britain'll turn into bedlam. It'll turn into a hell hole. It's already getting that way anyway cos we've got a lack of control, lack of care." But it did not have to be this way. A coming climax to the plot represented a crucial juncture at which "we" would either triumph over evil or all would be lost. At one point in the fieldwork, this climax was imagined as the December 2018 House of Commons vote on the EU Withdrawal Bill; later it became the European Elections of May 2019; at times it was represented by the Article 50 deadline—originally 29 March 2019, extended to 31 January 2020—by which a deal between Britain and the EU must be agreed or Britain would automatically leave the EU with no deal. Whenever the promised crescendo was not reached on each date, the climax was reconfigured or redefined, and this was reflected in the ever-evolving content of the Facebook Posts circulating in the milieu. Within the metanarrative these were not simply milestones but judgment days upon which the fate of the struggle rested. The imperative to "fight" or "act" before it was too late—by finding and Sharing information on social media—afforded the alleged victims the potential to take back control from the villains and save the plot from its imagined dire conclusion.

According to the metanarrative, this discontent could spill over into a "rebellion" (Eileen) if things continued the way they were going. The victims were "fed up" (Mark; Beatrice). As Eileen put it, "People are rejecting globalism." "Things could erupt in this country" (Deborah), or in Carl's (50s, male, Northwest England) words, "there is gunna be a big overthrow soon." The French "yellow vest" (see chapter 1, note 4) protests that coincided with the project fieldwork were employed in users' accounts to symbolize the consequences of allowing such sentiments to boil over. As Lawrence put it, "It's all I can see happening here if we don't get out." This was particularly resonant as French President Emmanuel Macron, a prime target of the protests, was understood in the pro-Brexit Facebook milieu as one of Europe's foremost symbols of EU-led "globalism." Like the "yellow vest" protestors, victims in Britain and around the (Western) world could rise up to reclaim control. Neil described a global awakening in which people would no longer abide their suppression: "They're standing up and saying 'No. No, no, no, no! We're not having this [i.e., putting up with this] anymore." And that will spread, it's already spreading. [. . .] That is the awakening." The game was up for those working against us, as people were armed with revolutionary social media platforms with which to inform themselves. Social media had "completely changed the face of political information [and] information structure" (Neil). "Everybody is waking up now" (Jessica) to what was being done "outside our knowledge and without our permission. [. . .] Politicians can't hide anymore" (Neil).

This significant turning point was a fundamental element of the dramaturgy of the metanarrative plot. This dramaturgy was fueled by frequent use of terms like "fight" to describe the struggle in which the milieu was engaged. Facebook content the users Shared used this same terminology alongside militaristic imagery of soldiers and embattled flags to portray the situation as a war. References were also made to World War II, not only as a symbol of lost patriotism and glory or as a reminder of the sinister potential of Germany, but to draw parallels that emphasized the critical nature of our current historic moment. Deborah emphasized this link at the end of our follow-up interview when she lamented the contemporary divisions within British society: "That is how we won the war—because we were all on the same side, which we no longer are. And this in a way is a war."

Wartime rationing was an object of romantic nostalgia. In Deborah's mind, now just as then, solidarity and sacrifice were required to win. Leaving the EU, particularly without having agreed to a trade deal, may bring economic hardship, but this hardship was necessary, temporary, and even welcome for its assumed ability to bring people together. Britain would "bounce back" and any disruption caused mattered little compared with the freedom that would be achieved. Mark's comments summarized this, while highlighting the way in which the metanarrative constantly assumed the will of the victims as a collective: "I haven't spoken to any person that wants to leave that's not willing to take a little bit of a hit at first. [. . .] Yeah, we might struggle a bit for the first couple of years, but so what? We're willing to do that. Crikey, we've overcome more adversity than this before as a country."

Several users described a sense of being personally engaged in or having a stake in this battle. Beatrice likened herself to a soldier when she spoke of the inevitability of facing conflict through her Facebook activity: "If you put your head above the parapet you have to expect to be shot at. [. . .] If they want to shoot at me, they can shoot at me. I don't have a problem with that, but they will have to fight me." In this way, the scenario of a battlefield afforded the potential to transform the users from victims of the metanarrative plot into members of the hero category they revered.

Thus, this was not just a story of victimization but one of opportunity—a call to action. Agency over this undesired societal change could be reclaimed only if action was taken now. The online political engagement practices of the pro-Brexit Facebook users, as discussed in chapter 2, took on a special significance because they afforded them the ability to fight back. The vision of victory was at times vague, and what was at stake was constructed mostly through ominous and symbolic references to destruction of values and culture. But what was clear to these individuals was that they were participating in a critical moment in British and global history, and by doing so they could be part of determining the legacy they left to their "children and grandchildren" (Beatrice).

CONCLUSION: "THIS ISN'T ABOUT BREXIT ANYMORE REALLY"

Narratives in the pro-Brexit Facebook milieu were often incoherent; their targets and logic shifted in ways that were at times even conflicting. However, in essence, the moral of the story was the same: that "the people" were being victimized, and that this was wrong and had to stop. According to the metanarrative around which these stories cohered, a legendary conflict was underway between the morally virtuous majority of White Britain or the Western world and sinister forces who sought to impose left-wing cultural change and a multiculturalist takeover. The promise of redemption in the metanarrative reflected the Leave campaign's call to "take back control." However, the metanarrative was about much more than Britain's membership in the EU; as Eileen put it, "This isn't about Brexit anymore, really." Membership in the EU was conceptualized as a product, and producer, of a variety of negative social changes, and the EU as just one actor in a wider agenda to facilitate or deliberately orchestrate change. In this sense, leaving or standing up to the EU was merely one, albeit very important, step toward mitigating that change and reclaiming control over the direction of British society.

A Manichean or "good versus evil" worldview structured the metanarrative and its designation of heroes, villains and victims. This move to "simplif[y] complex developments by looking for a culprit" (Pelinka 2013, 8) provides a degree of ontological security (Kinnvall 2015; Nefes 2013; in Ylä-Anttila 2018, 362). Like conspiracy theories and populism, the metanarrative was a way of organizing and affording certainty to what was seen to be disorder and insecurity, both personal and collective. Centering on the orchestration of oppression from above, the co-construction of this metanarrative in the pro-Brexit Facebook milieu can be understood as a product of users' feelings of being out of control of their own destiny, an expression of will to agency. It provided them with a (comparatively low-cost and low-risk) opportunity, even an imperative, to take back control by using social media.

The metanarrative's powerful appeal lay in this invocation of a sense of loss, impending doom, and potential reclamation through online action. A clear sense of past, present, and future in the metanarrative located Brexit as a key moment within a dramatic, historically significant struggle. It mobilized nostalgia for a past time in which Britain was in control of our own laws and social destiny. The vision for this social destiny was governed by conservative values and the control sought was symbolized by the idea of democracy.

In the pro-Brexit Facebook milieu, it is no coincidence that the EU was accused of being an undemocratic organization that impeded Britain's sovereign democracy through the imposition of EU law, at the same time as elected British MPs were accused of failure to implement the "will of the people" by approving an adequate Withdrawal Bill by the promised deadline. Both share a preoccupation with democracy that has its foundations in populism.

The pro-Brexit Facebook metanarrative also drew its conception of victims from populism's people-centrism. However, thanks to its integration of ideas from conspiracy theories popular in the far-right online sphere at the time, the metanarrative's conception of villains was more complex than the anti-elitism at the core of populist appeals. The pro-Brexit Facebook metanarrative brought together a range of seemingly disparate threats, villains, and political causes into a unique assemblage. It represented a loose coagulation of conspiracy theories, populism, racism, and Euroscepticism, selectively combined to account for users' political motivations and make sense of their everyday experiences.

The shape-shifting ability of the metanarrative afforded it a capacity to appeal to a variety of discontented individuals. Most concerningly, it provided far-right ideas with new audiences—Facebook users who had mostly become politicized around the issue of the EU referendum. Not only local concerns but global and civilizational ones were woven into the metanarrative plot and its cast of characters, sometimes in ways that were far removed from the issue of Britain's membership in the EU. These connections are evidence of the strength of the reach of the transnational far and populist right today, enabled by the connectivity of social media. They prompt the question of where the plot of this metanarrative originates and for whose benefit. Cultural Marxism and the Great Replacement can act as important vehicles of transnational sense-making as well as transnational solidarity. That ideas drawn from these far-right conspiracy theories featured so prominently in the pro-Brexit Facebook metanarrative indicates the possibility that extreme right actors deliberately capitalized upon the unique combination of the technological and ideological opportunities of the Brexit-Facebook conjuncture to disseminate their ideology to a new audience.

Over the next two chapters, I delve deeper into two central ideologies of the pro-Brexit Facebook milieu that separate it from narrower forms of Eurosceptic populism that focus on ire toward Europe and sources of elite authority. These two ideologies—racism and anti-leftism—hold the key to the appeal of pro-Brexit engagement on Facebook. They generated the two forms of indignation which drove engagement in the milieu: the White victimhood which has already been well-documented in studies of the far- and populist right, and what I term "Right victimhood," or the misplaced idea that those who do not conform to left-wing values are the victims of wrongful oppression.

Chapter 4

Racisms and White Victimhood in Pro-Brexit Engagement on Facebook

The previous chapter showed how immigrants and ethno-cultural-religious minorities, particularly a transnational community of Muslims, were constructed as one of many villains in the pro-Brexit Facebook milieu. The increasing presence and influence of these groups in British society was deemed problematic, and an integral part of undesirable social change that should be stopped. That racialized groups should be demonized in the pro-Brexit Facebook milieu may come as no surprise—since the rise of UKIP and the focus on immigration in its electoral campaigns, support for Brexit has been characterized as an expression of racist attitudes. As Virdee and McGeever (2018, 1,804, 1,807) claim, the Leave campaign "carefully activated long-standing racialized structures of feeling about immigration and national belonging" or "a reservoir of latent racism."

This chapter explores the role of racism—or more accurately, racisms—in the milieu. Research into support for Brexit and related right-wing populist causes on social media has tended to focus on measures of contemporary phenomena such as a "post-truth era" or "disinformation age." The analysis presented here provides a much-needed re-centering of racism in the study of this form of online politics. Connecting online content with the real individuals who consume it, their worldviews, motivations, and interpretations, reveals that racist ideologies play a much more prominent role than is accorded in many accounts. Indeed, the linkages facilitated by social media between transnational far-right and right-wing populist spheres meant that these racisms were likely nurtured and emboldened there. In the pro-Brexit Facebook milieu, racism engendered a White victimhood that constituted a key form of indignation sustaining political engagement.

THE CONTESTED PLACE OF RACISM IN BREXIT ONLINE AND OFFLINE

While undoubtedly not all of those who voted to Leave in 2016 were primarily motivated by racist attitudes, quantitative research has demonstrated a link between Euroscepticism and opposition to immigration (Ashcroft 2016; Goodwin and Milazzo 2017; Patel and Connelly 2019). Studies of Euroscepticism, the Leave campaign, and Leave voters have highlighted the role of a perceived threat to national identity, racialized conceptions of national belonging, and nostalgia for a lost imperial glory (Clarke and Newman 2017; Virdee and McGeever 2018; Campanella and Dassù 2019). While migration from continental Europe was particularly demonized in tabloid news in the 2000s and early 2010s (Fox, Moroşanu, and Szilassy 2012), non-European immigration also became the target of UKIP and the Leave campaign, with highly racialized undertones (Gupta and Virdee 2018). The significance of antipathy toward these groups is supported by the experiences of racialized communities in the lead-up to and aftermath of the referendum (Abranches et al. 2021; Rzepnikowska 2019; Tyler, Degnen, and Blamire 2022; Williams et al. 2022).

Meanwhile, the importance of racism to support for Brexit is contested by some ethnographic studies with White working-class communities whose members claim immigration is not their primary concern (Balthazar 2017; Koch 2017; McKenzie 2017; Walkerdine 2020). However, as Mintchev (2021, 136) points out, awareness of the strong connotations of illegitimacy attached to accusations of racism in social discourse mean that conscious deflections of such accusations are not unlikely. That Brexit supporters deny racism does not preclude the potential role of racist ideology in that support, as denials of racism are a feature of post-racial racisms (Lentin 2014; 2018). Furthermore, these ethnographies' privileging of explanations surrounding White working-class marginalization is unhelpful considering that a larger number of Leave voters were middle class, and that the most economically disadvantaged in society are often not White (Bhambra 2017).

In the months following the referendum, one survey found that anti-immigrant attitudes had softened in the UK, calling into question the role of racism in pro-Brexit mobilizations during this period (Schwartz et al. 2020). Indeed the issue of Brexit at that time, as we have already seen throughout this book, was marked by particular populist appeals to democracy, nationalism, and isolationism, with rhetoric targeting the EU bureaucracy and Remainers seen as trying to overturn the referendum result. Did these overshadow the role of racism after the referendum? The abovementioned survey found that a greater sense of control provided by the result is what mediated this effect of softening anti-immigrant attitudes. If this was the case, it could not have lasted long, at least not in the realm of social media. In the pro-Brexit Facebook milieu, a sense of disempowerment, of being ridiculed and ignored, and of being plotted against by nefarious forces, was strong in the post-referendum negotiation period—"control" continued to be sought after. Furthermore, events like the publication of Boris Johnson's infamous column in August 2018 in the *Telegraph* comparing veiled Muslim women to "letterboxes" (Allen 2020), and racialized coverage of the "grooming gangs" scandal and of the rising numbers of migrants attempting to reach Britain via the English Channel (Cockbain and Tufail 2020; Parker et al. 2022), are just some of the stark reminders of the continuing political capital of racism in British society in this period.

The importance of White victimhood to the far and populist right has been well-documented (e.g., Bonilla-Silva 2006; Sengul 2021), as have the racist ideas and rhetoric disseminated on social media by the online far-right, particularly in terms of "White supremacism" (e.g., Greene 2019; Duvall 2020; Froio 2018; Holt, Freilich, and Chermak 2022). But research into support for Brexit on social media, unlike its counterpart offline, has tended to overlook the role of racism. Studies in this field have more often focused on phenomena that are alleged to be consequences of the technology itself, such as bots, other networked influence, echo chambers, misinformation, or social media's privileging of emotive content (e.g., Bastos and Mercea 2019; Bossetta, Segesten, and Trenz 2018; Bouko and Garcia 2020; Del Vicario et al. 2017; Dobreva, Grinnell, and Innes 2019; Hänska and Bauchowitz 2017). The way the newly politicized categories of Leavers and Remainers play out on social media has also been a subject of study (Meredith and Richardson 2019; Brändle, Galpin, and Trenz 2022; North, Piwek, and Joinson 2021). Important though all of these novel phenomena may be, the neglect of the study of racism in the online pro-Brexit sphere is puzzling and represents a crucial oversight.

In the post-referendum pro-Brexit Facebook milieu studied here, narratives about migrants and diversity featured prominently. These narratives, reflected both in interviews and in the Posts observed on Facebook, drew on a variety of racist ideas and tropes that were by no means new, including those associated with differentialist racism, cultural racism, nativism, and Islamophobia. These varieties of racism are certainly not separate phenomena; they overlap, intersect and work in tandem. However, in the below analysis, I use these categories as analytic tools in order to dissect the multitude of racist logics that operated within the milieu. Uncovering how racist appeals were made and legitimated in the pro-Brexit Facebook milieu offers a stark reminder of the ability of "mainstream" political issues to promote, extend, and embolden existing racist logics, and connect users to transnational right-wing populist and far-right ideas.

DIFFERENTIALIST RACISM: GETTING ALONG AS IMPOSSIBLE

In the pro-Brexit Facebook milieu, narratives underpinned by "differentialist racism" were commonly used to justify opposition to immigration—or "too much" of the "wrong sort" of immigration. Differentialist racism is built on the idea that different races should live separately because it is impossible for diverse societies to peacefully cohere (Balibar 1991). The pro-Brexit Facebook users claimed to speak for the majority of Britons when they described a supposedly natural frustration, discomfort or alienation caused by increasing diversity. Such narratives of inter-group antagonism as human nature have returned to the spotlight in the racialist logic promoted by highly criticized public intellectuals like David Goodhart and Eric Kaufmann (for analysis see Lentin 2018; Saini 2017). They have also been promoted by Alt-Right founder Richard Spencer in his quest for a White ethnostate (Hartzell 2018).

According to the pro-Brexit Facebook users, the EU was a major source of this allegedly problematic immigration as it was "forcing us to take more and more people" (Lawrence, 40s, male, West Midlands), particularly from outside Europe. Kirk (60s, male, London) told a story he had seen on social media claiming that then Home Secretary Sajid Javid had let in 400,000 migrants "through the back door," but Kirk blamed this on EU membership "because being in there [the EU] you feel that in the back rooms of some place they're saying you must take a quota in." According to one narrative in the milieu, informed by the Kalergi Plan conspiracy theory (see chapter 3), this was part of an agenda to force racial mixing and multiculturalism and supplant Europe's White heritage. Less sinister versions of this narrative simply viewed the EU as a key driver of multiculturalism through its unspoken left-wing ideology. As epitomized in UKIP's "Breaking Point" poster and its depiction of a menacing column of Middle Eastern-looking migrants, such sentiments were not limited to those engaging with Brexit on social media (S. Faulkner, Guy, and Vis 2021; see also Stockemer et al. 2020). Gupta and Virdee (2018, 1750) aptly observed in 2018 that the EU was "increasingly held to be an apparatus for supporting immigration and the accommodation of difference," partly exacerbated by the context of the "migrant crisis."

One user who was especially preoccupied with demographic change, which she felt had happened "almost overnight," was Deborah (50s, female, Northwest England). She spoke of her concerns over the ability of British society to adapt to such rapid change: "It takes time to integrate people into society. There isn't the time. Suddenly you look around and there's so many, for example, women in burkas, that a lot of us are not comfortable with." Deborah spoke about pictures of London in the 1950s and 1960s that she had seen on Facebook, describing how the city was now "unrecognizable," and that a "massive influx" had "just upset the whole thing." Combining this with perceptions of change in her local community, she referenced Enoch Powell's infamous 1968 "Rivers of Blood" speech (perhaps the epitome of differentialist racist discourse in post-war Britain, see Hickson 2018), saying, "maybe he [Powell] didn't couch things very well, but he was right. He warned about the overdoing of immigration. And this is what's happened."

Eileen (60s, female, Northwest England) used the integration policy of Austria, where she spent time holidaying every year, as an example with which to contrast Britain's perceived dysfunction:

> Austrian values come first, [. . .] [it's] safe, prosperous, everybody has a job, everybody's polite, everything's shut on a Sunday. (. . .) The society's working, and it's not because they're cruel and austere. It's because they're sensible. [. . .] And you have to speak German. What's wrong with that? That's gonna make the society work. They've got people there from Syria who are doctors, they've got people there who are in the construction business, because they fitted in.

In Eileen's comment, accommodation of the wrong sort of diversity is not a "sensible" path for society. Implicit in this comparison with Austria is the idea that British society is not "working" in this way, as immigrants here are not "fitting in." Thus in Eileen's view, "good" immigrants are distinguished from "bad" ones by their ability to conform to an imagined set of static, homogeneous British values—including Christian traditions like closing shops on Sundays. This distinction between "good" and "bad" immigrants is not novel and has commonly been employed to justify exclusion (Hackl 2022). Notably, Britain's failure to take a firm stance against multicultural values is not attributed in Eileen's narrative to its membership in the EU, with allegedly anti-multiculturalist Austria also being a member. Narratives in the milieu were malleable and inconsistent in this way. Particularly in racist narratives that demonized ethno-cultural-religious minorities, the status of continental European countries shifted to ally. This was in stark contrast to many of the milieu's Eurosceptic narratives that constructed opposition between Britain and "Europe," seen for example in Fred's account in chapter 1 of "Europe trying to move British industry to Europe." In those narratives, Britain's geographic status as part of the European continent (and the prominent decision-making role it played in the Union) was ignored in favor of an idea of British exceptionalism. However, in the racist logic of the milieu, this enmity disappeared, demonstrating the unique significance of Whiteness to the milieu.

This contradiction is also illustrated by a "clash of civilizations" narrative that sometimes featured in the milieu. In this narrative, Britain and the West more broadly were represented as essentially Christian and thus fundamentally at odds with Islam. While this form of civilizationalism has been identified as a feature of recent European right-wing populism (Brubaker 2017a), it has also informed Islamophobia since at least the 1990s (Haynes 2019). Jessica (40s, female, London) reproduced this narrative, painting Islam as a cruel and (ironically) intolerant religion: "Most of the migrants are from Muslim countries, and Islam is virtually the opposite to Christianity. [. . .] At the end of the day, the European continent is a predominantly Christian culture, where we don't agree with, you know, child marriage, and we don't agree with killing people because they don't believe in something that you believe in." In this way, differentialist racism was inextricably linked with Islamophobia in the ideology of the milieu. As Jessica's comment alludes, Muslims were seen as the most problematic group within British society. Their alleged innate inability or inherent unwillingness to "integrate" has already been highlighted in comments by Beatrice and Olivia in chapter 1. Islamophobia played its own important role in the milieu and will be addressed in depth in a later section of this chapter.

Some users suggested that disharmony between religious and cultural groups was being deliberately facilitated for sinister purposes. This agenda was represented by the United Nations Global Compact for Migration, which was finalized in July 2018, signed in December 2018, and known in the milieu as the "UN Migration Pact." This Compact, which aims to tackle irregular migration and agree on human rights protections for migrants, is voluntary and non-binding (Vera Espinoza, Hadj-Abdou, and Brumat 2018). However, it was being mobilized against transnational far-right spheres precisely at the time of the fieldwork (Rone 2022) in what has been described as a disinformation campaign (Guhl 2019). The artifacts of this disinformation campaign were evident in the Facebook Posts observed for this project, with the Compact mentioned multiple times. Jessica echoed the Cultural Marxism conspiracy theory propagated by far-right groups (see chapter 3) when she claimed the Compact was evidence of a "Marxist" plot to increase immigration in order to divide communities and ultimately "bring down Europe." Here again, the same "Europe" that was portrayed as the enemy in anti-EU narratives was presented as somewhat of an ally of Britain, sharing a common cultural-religious heritage as one White Western civilization.

These differentialist racist narratives portrayed Britain as a country on the brink of civil unrest because of ethnic and cultural diversity. Kirk was particularly concerned about this: "some of the stuff that's happening, with the gang raping [. . .] and all that, [. . .] we ain't got quite to the place where it's like a tinder box that's gunna blow up, [. . .] fighting in the street and . . . it ain't got to that yet, but I can see it in the next couple of years, [. . .] like France with 'yellow jackets'" (see chapter 1, note 4). The apparently out-of-control situation in some continental European countries that the pro-Brexit Facebook users saw depicted on social media, was where the UK was supposedly headed if it remained in the EU. Kirk's mention of "gang raping" as part of the catalyst for this unrest extends the differentialist racist narrative beyond a failure of people from other cultural backgrounds to integrate into British society, to the idea that they are fundamentally deviant. This will be explored next.

CULTURAL AND POST-RACIAL RACISMS: MIGRANTS AS DEVIANT

In their interviews, the pro-Brexit Facebook users were keen to assure me that they were not "racist" and used a variety of discursive strategies to absolve themselves of this accusation. We have already seen this above in Deborah's qualification of her assessment of Enoch Powell—that "maybe he didn't couch things very well, but [. . .]." Her comment reflects a common practice within the milieu to preemptively deflect attributions of racism, such as those associated with Powell and his inflammatory rhetoric, and portray anti-immigration sentiments as based on logical reasoning or observable evidence. This "credentialing" practice is key to cultural racism (Barker 1981; Miles and Brown 2003; for empirical evidence see Flemmen and Savage 2017; Mann and Fenton 2009; Martin 2013; Millington 2010; Wells and Watson 2005) and has been documented in the anti-immigration narratives of Leave voters (Patel and Connelly 2019).

Such denials of racism within the milieu were undermined by the way the role of the villain in the narratives often noticeably shifted from those at the top seen as responsible for immigration levels to migrants themselves. These ideas are endemic to an enduring culturally racist trope in which "culture" is used as a "synonym for 'race'" (Garner 2010, 134) and cultural deviance is attributed to ethnic and racial minorities in order to legitimize their exclusion (ibid., 137). Eastern Europeans were sometimes the object of racialization, echoing broader discursive trends that have underpinned Eurosceptic responses to the enlargement of the union and freedom of movement within it (Fox, Moroşanu, and Szilassy 2012). Eileen, who received dozens of private messages weekly from her Facebook Followers, recounted the stories of two elderly individuals who had contacted her about no longer feeling safe in their neighborhoods, and said that it was sympathy for such situations that motivated her to continue spending so much time Posting about Brexit and immigration. One of these individuals felt she could no longer sun herself on her front porch because, "the Bulgarians come out at night, and they all sit in the street, and they have wrestling matches and quite often they're drunk and they fight properly and draw knives on each other. [. . .] That's why I believe in Brexit. We should control who's coming." Eileen's comment reproduces negative stereotypes of Eastern European migrants as being violent and barbaric. In this way, the users sometimes explicitly linked their opposition to (certain types of) immigration with their support for leaving the EU and ending freedom of movement of EU nationals to the UK.

A separate individual who had also allegedly contacted Eileen via direct message complained that she was now, in Eileen's words, the "only White woman in this street" where she had lived fifty-five years and would no longer leave her house after dark. This reflected the way in which, more frequently than Eastern Europeans, it was non-White racialized individuals who were associated with criminality and deviance in the milieu, particularly Muslim or allegedly undocumented African migrants. This is in line with Gupta and Virdee's (2018, 1756) analysis of UKIP and other Eurosceptic party manifestos, in which "'criminals' were predominantly 'foreign,' and 'terrorists' were invariably 'foreign' and 'Islamic,' and were imposing upon and corrupting (infiltrating) the authentic citizenry."

Among the pro-Brexit Facebook users, certain continental countries like France, Germany, or Italy were painted as already being in chaos thanks to Muslim and African immigration. Videos that I observed the users Sharing on Facebook depicted large groups of African-looking males running, yelling or generally causing havoc, and the users frequently referred to anecdotal "evidence" from social media content they had seen to demonstrate how letting in too many of these people had led to a breakdown in law, order, and public safety. The users' reference to videos and imagery in these narratives illustrates the power of Facebook's visual logics, discussed in chapter 2, to inject dramaturgy and realism into anecdotes about the alleged impact of immigration.

Eileen said that one business in Italy, according to a video on Facebook, had, "been vandalized 52 times by hordes of migrants. [. . .] This shop's full of cakes. [. . .] It's a beautiful little place, and these maybe 20 Africans come in with sticks, [. . .] nick some food, go in the till, [. . .] smash everything and run out again. You can't live like that [. . .] We're not at war." The "beautiful little" patisserie described here is quintessential of an idealized Western Europe—innocent, traditional, and stoic in the face of repeated vandalism. Its desecration is symbolic of the assumption that these Western nations were once safe and civilized before their pollution by uncivilized non-Western immigrants. This echoes Eileen's account of her experience at the Calais border that prompted her trajectory toward engaging with politics online. In Eileen's narratives, the presence of "African" migrants brings chaos, violence, and criminality. These attitudes were also reflected in Eileen's provocative description of an alleged German government document that she had found online "showing migrants how to ask for sex, cos of all the sex crimes, raping people cos they don't respect women and they think it's their right and all the rest of it."

In another example, Kirk was scrolling through his Facebook Newsfeed during his first interview and found an amateur video of an incident at a railway station in South London. In the video, which Kirk later Shared to his Timeline, a man was roaming the platform brandishing a machete before being tasered by the British Transport Police. Kirk said, "He's obviously a migrant. [. . .] I guarantee he's African, because there's certain looks, and the way they dress and everything else. [. . .] You think to yourself, 'what's he doing in this country?' [. . .] You can't let everybody in because first thing they do is throw away, they've got no identification, you know?"

Alongside the association being made here between violent criminality and African heritage, Kirk's comment reveals the racialization of the category of migrant seen in public discourse around the "migrant crisis" in Europe (De Genova 2018b). In the pro-Brexit Facebook milieu, "African" migrants were understood as undocumented young men, part of a broader category of asylum seekers and migrants who were portrayed as opportunistic, ruthless, and criminal. The issue of "illegal immigration" (George, 70s, male, Northeast England) and particularly "immigrants going across the Channel" (Isaac, 50s, Northwest England) was mentioned by a number of users as an issue of particular concern, reflecting the rise in English Channel crossings at the time and their portrayal in the British media as a "major crisis" (Parker et al. 2022). This dehumanizing "border spectacle" (Maggs 2020) engendered in large part by UK politicians is not inextricably bound to the issue of Brexit, as demonstrated in the way it has been repeatedly reinvoked by disingenuous actors following Britain's departure from the EU (e.g., D. Faulkner and Watson 2023; BBC News 2022; 2020a). Asking "what's he doing in this country?" Kirk's blatantly exclusionary discourse also points to the troubling resilience of racialized national belonging.

Meanwhile, for Kirk this encroachment of deviant migrant figures was strongly linked to the idea of societal decline. Kirk recounted his experience growing up free and fearless in London and contrasted this with what he now saw as the constant threat of violent terror. He claimed that the only warning his father ever gave him when he went out to play was "mind the road," but nowadays he was forced to worry about the safety of his wife, children, and grandchildren out and about in London because of the risk of terrorism: "And that ain't right, really, in your own country, is it? [. . .] Outside agencies from foreign countries, making you feel unsafe. [. . .] And she [my wife] goes 'oh, you're paranoid,' but that's how it . . . It makes you paranoid."

Such declinism, as demonstrated in chapter 3, was a fundamental aspect of the pro-Brexit Facebook metanarrative. In Eurosceptic discourse since well before the referendum, "Europe" has been portrayed as "the ultimate institutional expression of British and English decline" (Wellings 2012, 2). But the idea of societal deterioration or desecration through "the dilution of once homogeneous and continuous national stock by alien strains" has been a symptom of Britain's "post-colonial melancholia" since the 1960s (Gilroy 1987, 46). In this way, the cultural racism exhibited in the pro-Brexit Facebook milieu reflected long-enduring narratives and ideologies within British society.

NATIVISM: BELONGING AND ENTITLEMENT

Another prominent narrative used to justify opposition to immigration in the milieu was that high levels of immigration were placing an unsustainable burden on social infrastructure at a time when Britain could ill afford it. While social services were being cut and poverty and homelessness were evidently on the rise, the pro-Brexit Facebook users invoked the idea of "charity begins at home" (Audrey, 50s, female, Northwest England) and argued that the British government should be "looking after its own" first. Nativist logic is at play here (e.g., Sanchez 1997). Nativism is a concept that acknowledges contemporary racism's focus on antipathy toward "foreign" groups who are perceived to be a danger or threat to the nation (Ward 2014, 268). This threat is to national identity from linguistic and cultural diversity, as well as the threat posed by an alleged propensity of immigrants to take undue advantage of limited welfare, education, and health system benefits, of which they are deemed to be less deserving than natives (Sanchez 1997). In nativist ideology, "states should be inhabited exclusively by members of the native group" (Mudde 2007, 19).

Nativism is not simply a who-was-there-first hierarchy of "fairness," but functions as a system of racist oppression of those deemed non-native for the purpose of justifying the superiority and dominance of the native (Huber et al. 2008; Lippard 2011). Nativism has even been described as the element that separates right-wing populism from other forms of populism; right-wing populists are nativists, claims Mudde (2007), and invoke "natives" of the nation to fulfill the populist category of the true or pure "people." Unsurprisingly given the well-evidenced link between support for Brexit and opposition to immigration discussed above, one UK survey study, which categorized responses as either high or low in nativism, found that high nativist sentiment correlated with support for leaving the EU, but anti-elite sentiment only showed a relationship with support for the EU among those who reported high nativist sentiment (Iakhnis et al. 2018).

According to the narratives of pro-Brexit Facebook users in their interviews and in the content they Shared on Facebook, new migrants were being unfairly prioritized in the distribution of social welfare, thereby unfairly depriving the majority. As seen in chapter 1, echoing decades-old narratives (e.g., Hewitt 2005), the pro-Brexit Facebook users rehearsed rumors about new migrants receiving vast amounts of financial assistance from the British government. In Deborah's words, "I can't understand why suddenly all these immigrants have got council housing, when British people that have been here for generations can't get it." Carl (50s, male, Northwest England) contrasted his perceptions of what "African" migrants received for free with his own experience of financial struggle: "I'm not jealous—I think we should just be fair. [. . .] If I see kids on the street with no food, fucking feed 'em! Don't give all our money away and then say you've got nought [nothing] to give me." Lawrence, Mark (50s, male, Yorkshire), Audrey, and Helen (50s, female, West Midlands) also spoke of their frustration at levels of homelessness and hunger they had witnessed in person as well as on social media when justifying their opposition to immigration.

Narratives about pressures on the National Health Service (NHS), schools, housing, and other essential infrastructure featured prominently. Several users drew on what they saw as common-sense logic to describe how a system such as the NHS was designed to be used by those who had spent their lives paying in, and the idea that there was rampant exploitation of this by undeserving new arrivals. George, a retired civil servant in his seventies from the Northeast of England, attested that his reasons for supporting Brexit were related to the UK's allegedly disproportionate contribution to the welfare of "poor countries" such as Greece and Poland, and not to immigration. However, he went on to say,

> I think you have to be able to bring something to the country. You can't just come to the country and sort of go on benefits straight away, you know? That's one of my main things. [. . .] I mean they go on about NHS needing all these foreign workers. Well, that's fine, that's great, cos they come across and they bring skills. [. . .] It's when you get people coming over who just want to come over in a rubber dingy and just land on the beach and just get taken straight to the nearest Job Centre, you know?

In Britain, the NHS is a highly politicized resource. It was cannily but misleadingly used in Leave campaign messaging that suggested money "we send the EU" could be used to "fund the NHS instead." Fitzgerald et al. (2020,

1161) argue that this is no coincidence. They describe attitudes toward the NHS in the context of Brexit as embroiled in a "cultural politics of heredity," at which nationalism intersects with racialized and heredity-based welfare structures. Heredity is a central category in nativism's construction of deservingness and was mobilized in narratives about social welfare and immigration in the milieu. This can be seen for example in Carl's comment touched upon in chapter 1 that "migrants [. . .] come over here and get free benefits. Why can't I get benefits? [. . .] I'm literally *born* here" (emphasis added).

Although, as noted in chapter 1, Britain's economic policies of austerity were part of the significant context behind these users' engagement with pro-Brexit and right-wing populist politics on Facebook, it is notable that they did not attribute their grievances around the availability of public services and welfare to these policies. Rather, immigration and multiculturalism were blamed. Helen drew on the nativist distinction between "deserving" Brits and "undeserving" new arrivals when recounting an anecdote in her follow-up interview:

> We are paying for people that are now retired that have come to this country that have hardly ever worked. [. . .] I see it every day. [. . .] I got kicked out of a bloomin' consulting room at the hospital, cos it was the only consulting room that had got a special telephone where they could get hold of an interpreter to bring this little woman in a sari with her entourage. [. . .] I was going in for a procedure. I was quite nervous about it. [. . .] Just gets me so angry! And I mean, that costs us a fortune.

Helen's account implies that her nervousness over the procedure she was about to undergo should have taken precedence over the language needs of the other woman; in the consulting room and in Britain, she was there first. The cost of her own procedure was of no consequence, as she was understood as entitled to the provision of universal health care as a native Brit. Meanwhile, the interpreting service required by the other woman to receive the health care she needed was perceived as an illegitimate expense, one which costs "us"—a group of taxpayers with which this racialized woman was not associated. The woman's visible ethnicity and inadequate linguistic competence meant her status as an undeserving new arrival who had not contributed to National Insurance was assumed a priori. Being "native" here becomes an all-important criterion for deservingness, while the fact that Helen herself was not currently working seems to have been deemed irrelevant. This anecdote was representative of the highly racialized nativism that was so prominent in the interviews and Facebook Posts of the pro-Brexit Facebook users.

ISLAMOPHOBIA: DEVIANT MUSLIMS AND ISLAMIZATION

Muslims were the racialized group problematized the most often within the pro-Brexit Facebook milieu, and concerns about immigration were often code for concerns about Muslim immigration. Analyzing the Leave campaign, Virdee and McGeever (2018) highlight the significance of Islamophobia. They argue that although the Farage-led Leave.EU campaign constructed migrants as an *economic* threat to give traction to the notion that the campaign's target was White Europeans and deflect accusations of racism, this campaign simultaneously constructed migrants as a *security* threat. Against the backdrop of terrorist incidents in continental Europe, the latter representation was an effective tool in that it "dovetailed so neatly" with repertoires of Islamophobia that had long been a feature of British society (Virdee and McGeever 2018, 1,807). Although leaving the EU technically promised only to end freedom of movement within Europe, as noted above, for many Brexit supporters it represented an opportunity to limit Muslim immigration, seen as incompatible with British society and concepts of British nationhood (ibid.).

This reflects the way that anti-immigration politics in Britain and beyond increasingly center on the figure of the "Muslim" (Rhodes and Hall 2020). In political discourse, Muslims are blamed for a supposed lack of societal cohesion, positioned as a threat to national security, and held individually responsible for challenging violent extremism (Kundnani 2007; Matthews 2015). Thus, the relationship between the Leave campaign and antipathy toward Muslims or Islam should be understood within the context of the "intensification and banalization of Islamophobic sentiment, policy and practice in Britain, alongside the increased targeting, both violent and mundane, of British Muslims" (Alexander 2017, 13). As we saw in chapter 1, this is not a new phenomenon (Kundnani 2012, 156), but has arguably intensified since the Syrian conflict, the "migrant (or refugee) crisis" and Isis-attributed terrorist incidents in continental Europe in the mid-2010s (De Genova 2018b).

In the pro-Brexit Facebook milieu, essentialist and racialized depictions were employed alongside familiar Islamophobic tropes to construct Islam and Muslims as problematic and unwelcome. One of Carl's comments was illustrative of a position expressed by many of the participants: "I'm not racist, but [. . .] I have got a problem with Islam, or radical Islam anyway, and Islamists. I have got a problem with that." Although many Islamophobic groups have sought to decouple Islam from Muslims, disavowing racism by contending that they are opposed to a religion or ideology rather than a group of people (e.g., Allen 2011; Burke 2018; Pilkington 2016), as Alexander argues, Islam cannot be separated from Muslims, nor can the notion of "Muslims" be separated "from the black and brown bodies who form the largest proportion of Muslims in Britain, and globally" (Alexander 2017, 15).

In the pro-Brexit Facebook milieu, the beliefs and practices of Muslims themselves were not simply problematized. A prominent narrative claimed that Muslims were intent on imposing those beliefs and practices on British society in order to "Islamize" it. According to the narrative, this was wrong because it was "them" who should be changing to suit "us," demonstrating the overlap between this Islamophobia and a nativist perspective on cultural integration. Audrey drew on an analogy that has become a familiar trope in justifying nativist and Islamophobic claims (see Jackson 2018): the delineation of "guests" from those who have a right to claim a country as their own and make decisions about social norms: "Everybody, when they live in this country, they agree to our laws. But they seem to bring a lot of theirs over, and we're having to agree to theirs, and that's wrong. [. . .] When I go in somebody else's house, I don't say to them, 'you have to do what I want.' [. . .] I have to be respectful. When they come to live in your country, they're not."

Audrey made scant explicit reference to Islam or Muslims, but this comment was in the context of comments about a rumor she had heard that someone who exposed "a gang that were [. . .] grooming and raping girls" had gone to prison while the perpetrators had walked free, connecting it to the racialized Islamophobic discourse about the "grooming gangs" scandal (see chapter 1). The normalization of public discourses around the alleged encroachment of Sharia law also makes it clear which group she was likely referring to. This is demonstrated by a similar comment made by Neil (70s, male, South Wales):

> You have to control immigration. [. . .] There are places like Leicester which have become virtually a Muslim enclave, and they want to have Sharia law. I mean you can't have that. You can't have people coming in and saying "well you come here to live because it's free and it's safe but we're gunna change the rules." [. . .] If you want to live under Sharia law there are countries that have Sharia law and you can go and live there. If you want to live here you've got to abide by our rules. And you've got to be part of our culture. You can come and join us, but you can't dictate and change things just to suit you. Doesn't work that way.

Lawrence lamented this alleged phenomenon, saying with palpable frustration, "Why? Why are we having Islam forced down our throats? Why is everything about the Western world having to change right now to suit everybody else?"

Implicit in such Islamization narratives are intensely negative attitudes toward Islam and Muslims, but also a construction of Islam as a threat to

Western cultural values (Fekete 2009). As noted above, in the pro-Brexit Facebook milieu this was portrayed not only as an issue facing Britain, but as a global civilizational issue in which a struggle was underway between the West and the rest. This focus on Islamization acted as a link between the pro-Brexit Facebook milieu and transnational right-wing populist mobilizations online (Bhatt 2012). Particularly in Europe, these mobilizations have portrayed such alleged Islamization as deliberately orchestrated, or as a byproduct of naïve promotion of multiculturalism by the Left (Fekete 2012; Swami et al. 2018).

In fact, the Islamophobic narratives of the pro-Brexit Facebook users mirrored those of broader right-wing populist spheres in a number of ways. They drew upon femonationalist and homonationalist logics (Farris 2017; Puar 2013); that is, they framed their anti-Muslim stances as a righteous defense of secular liberal values by positioning Islam as a threat to the rights of women, sexual minorities, and animals (Rhodes and Hall 2020, 288). Of course, this purported progressiveness by right-wing groups is "strikingly contradictory" given that its form of "liberalism" is also "deeply illiberal" (Brubaker 2017a, 1,210). Indeed, as will be discussed in chapter 5, anti-feminist and anti-LGBTQ attitudes were regularly espoused by the pro-Brexit Facebook users. Nonetheless, femonationalist and homonationalist logics were appealing and popular discursive moves within the pro-Brexit Facebook milieu.

The same went for the issue of animal rights, with Halal slaughter being a common topic. Pro-Brexit Facebook users spoke of it in interviews, and were observed Sharing on Facebook, content "exposing" the alleged sale of unmarked Halal meat in mainstream supermarkets, the serving of it in restaurants and schools, and ritual slaughters in local backyards. The authors of these Posts purported to be nobly protecting the welfare of animals, but these were all-too-conveniently compatible with the milieu's preoccupation with Muslim deviance.

As Deborah expressed, "There is a very strong feeling on Facebook, and it won't go away, that this is an extremely backward culture, and we will not accept it. And we feel that we have had to lower our sights with Christianity in order to accommodate it." A narrative was employed in these Posts that non-Muslim consumers and school children were being forced to specify their requirement for non-Halal meat, where Halal should be the special requirement that deviated from the norm. Such narratives of imposition by Muslims allowed the users to go beyond simple critiques of Islamic practices (e.g., on the basis of animal rights or gender equality) and employ logics of fairness, a "right to choose," and the forced degradation of assumed superior cultural practices. They also contributed to suspicions of covert Sharia imposition that construct Muslims as the transnational enemy within (Hussein 2015).

Femonationalist logic was seen in the strong focus on Islam's purported treatment of women, primarily among the female users in this study. Practices of veiling and female genital mutilation were of particular concern, and reference was made to the comments by Boris Johnson about veiled women looking like "letterboxes" noted above. These comments, which were made during the project fieldwork and became a major news issue, were thinly disguised in rhetoric about the freedom of women to choose what they wear and couched as humor. However, they were widely condemned as inciting Islamophobia (Allen 2020) and indeed led to an increase in reports of hate crimes experienced by Muslim women (Dearden 2018). The pro-Brexit Facebook users supported Johnson and condemned the anti-racist criticisms that had been directed at him, saying for example, "These women are suffering. [. . .] As a civilized country we should be giving these women an excuse to take [the veil] off" (Eileen). Eileen's use of the term "civilized" echoes representations of Muslims as uncivilized and Islam as barbaric which are a key feature of Islamophobia.

Deborah attested that "backward" Muslim attitudes were having an undesired effect on "our" country and culture: "There's a huge dichotomy now on women trying to still gain equality, not to be sexually assaulted or abused, and then we look around and we see women coming into the country that we feel cover up because [. . .] that's [. . .] what they've been led into. They don't have freedom of choice, which a lot of us don't feel comfortable with. [. . .] [Like] female genital mutilation, we don't want that sort of thing here, but we have no choice." The sincerity of Deborah's alleged concern for women's rights and freedom of choice was thrown into doubt by other comments she made in her interviews deriding progressive social change surrounding gender and feminism. Her comment can be characterized as a deployment of femonationalist logic to suit an Islamophobic agenda.

Both Helen and Olivia (50s, female, Southeast England) repeatedly referenced a narrative of Muslim men as a danger to Western women, and they used multiple examples from their personal experience and experiences of their daughters in attempts to illustrate this. In her follow-up interview, Helen argued that Muslims in her local area were luring White women to take them as "trophy wives" who they could control. She described how her young niece moved in with the family of a Muslim boyfriend:

> She's a strawberry blonde, pale, blue eyes, freckles . . . [. . .] Next thing we knew she was wearing their type of clothing, not the black stuff but the sari type stuff, that's heading in that direction. Dark brown hair. She'd even darkened her eyebrows. Thank God we got her out of it. [. . .] He used to take her to college, he used to come and meet her at the lunch time, and he used to pick her up at the night, and I think that got a bit much eventually. [. . .] And I said to my

sister-in-law [. . .] "for God's sake, get her down to a family planning clinic and get her an implant," I said, "because [if] she has a baby with him, that's her tied to him for the rest of her life." [. . .] Thank God she did. [. . .] [Now] she's got a nice White boyfriend [chuckles] and she's passed college. [. . .] He didn't want her to go into education you see.

In this anecdote, the young girl is a naïve, agentless victim who must be protected from capture by the Muslim community and found a White partner before her contamination and brainwashing reaches the point of no return. To save her from control, the girl's family had to paradoxically claim authority over her reproductive agency. This idea of Muslim men as a danger to White women and girls was promoted by right-wing media in Britain around the "grooming gangs" scandal and subsequently legitimated by actors claiming to have feminist interests at heart (Cockbain and Tufail 2020). However, it draws on much older orientalist stereotypes about the sexual appetites, deviance, and misogyny of Muslim men (Bhattacharyya 2008).

Helen's narrative painted Muslim men as involved in a sinister plot to capture White girls, "so many" of whom, she alleged, had "disappeared from their families." Kirk too was suspicious of the motivations of Muslims in Britain. He was concerned about the number of mosques that he heard on Facebook had been built in London in recent years. He recounted the same anecdote in both his interviews about a video he had seen on Facebook of a congregation in a mosque claiming to be "moderate" but all raising their hands in support of violent and radical practices. Thus, Kirk's horror and outrage at the building of "hundreds" of new mosques in London—not only Britain's capital but his home city—can be linked to his subscription to a narrative that mosques are breeding grounds for extremists and alludes to the symbolic significance of this in terms of a perceived eclipse of Britain's predominantly Christian culture. He described how his concerns had been affirmed by content that had appeared in his Facebook feed:

> They all go to one area. [. . .] I feel like it's a cancer. [. . .] They get on the council [. . .] and they start running it and then they get more Muslims . . . [. . .] I was thinking that and then low and behold, a thing on social media pops up with a Imam [. . .] and he's saying to another guy, [. . .] "we've gotta get more Muslims in here. They've gotta have loads of children, populate the area." [. . .] It's a hidden agenda behind what they're doing. [. . .] In my head a lot of [my motivation] was that sort of thought that, in years to come, my grandchildren . . . so, you know, I've gotta stand up and say something now, to try and stop it.

With the comparison between Muslim immigration and "cancer," Kirk's disgust is laid bare, along with a troubling indifference to the bounds of social acceptability with regard to open expression of racist attitudes. In line with existing analyses of Islamophobia (e.g., Kundnani 2007), Kirk's comment explicitly links Islam and Muslims with national security threats and violent extremism. However, a more prominent concern in the milieu, as seen in Kirk's comment about protecting his grandchildren's future, was the threat of cultural change and domination posed by Muslims—an "Islamization" that in Kirk's mind and the minds of many other pro-Brexit Facebook users was being coordinated covertly.

The urgency in Kirk's comment reflects how language and imagery in this narrative seamlessly shifted from that of cultural imposition to that of an invasion. Olivia, for example, described "the *allowed* Islamic takeover" as her "biggest concern" and asserted—using an equally troubling analogy as Kirk's and one which reflects racist stereotypes about the size of Muslim families—that, "Islam *will* dominate. [. . .] They breed like rats anyway" (Olivia's emphasis). Beatrice (50s, female, North Wales), who also gave Islam as one of the primary concerns motivating her political engagement, said that "tak[ing] over the world" was Muslims' "whole intention," and "we're letting it happen." The progression of representations of Muslims from terrorist sympathizers and refusers of cultural integration to sinister invaders is evidence of the absorption of increasingly extreme forms of racism from the far and populist right via social media.

CONCLUSION

The pro-Brexit Facebook milieu was ostensibly mobilized around opposition to Britain's membership in the EU. However, true to studies of Leave voters and analysis of the Leave campaign, racist ideology was revealed to be a significant feature. In their interviews, the pro-Brexit Facebook users spoke at length about their frustrations and anxieties around immigration and ethno-cultural-religious diversity in Britain. They drew on the logics of differentialist racism, cultural racism, nativism, and Islamophobia that long predate the rise to prominence of Brexit and the advent of social media.

Despite their proven link with Brexit, the significance of these racisms to engagement with Brexit on social media has yet to be explored. Phenomena like affective polarization between Leaver and Remainer identities, and the influence of dis- and misinformation online may be of interest to scholars attempting to distill the effects of social media on democracy and on the health of British society. However, racism too poses a threat to both of these while at the same time causing immeasurable and sustained harm to racialized individuals. Its consequences include economic disadvantage, physical, mental, and emotional harm, and even death (whether this may be the result of racially motivated violence or neglect by those meant to serve, protect, and care for us). It is therefore of crucial importance to continue to acknowledge how and why racism is sustained in online right-wing populist spheres, and to do so beyond those political movements that are most explicitly connected to issues of race, such as the far-right, Alt-Right, and other White supremacist groups.

In fact, dissecting the variegated facets of the racisms being perpetuated by pro-Brexit Facebook users revealed that this milieu was digitally connected to and influenced by these more extreme transnational mobilizations. As demonstrated in narratives and Facebook Posts about the pollution and desecration of Europe by violent and chaotic non-White immigration, and civilizational narratives pitting the West against Islam, a shared White victimhood united this milieu with right-wing populist causes around the world. The prominence of Great Replacement narratives, ideas of a deliberate Muslim takeover, and the taking up of causes like opposing the United Nations Compact for Migration is evidence of the way the far-right's influence permeated the pro-Brexit Facebook milieu through the connected affordances of social media. These phenomena also illustrate the ability of supposedly legitimate and mainstream political issues like Brexit to embolden racist logics and connect social media users to more extreme racist ideologies that appear as the natural extension of those that pervade British society.

In this way, White victimhood constituted one of two key varieties of indignation that galvanized the pro-Brexit Facebook milieu. Key facilitators of this claimed White oppression were the Left, through their allegedly naïve promotion of immigration and multiculturalism. The link between racism and antipathy toward the Left is expounded in the following chapter, which also reveals the second form of indignation that drove this political engagement, a sensibility I term "Right victimhood."

Chapter 5

Anti-Leftism and Right Victimhood in Pro-Brexit Engagement on Facebook

In the pro-Brexit Facebook milieu, growing ethnic diversity and the perceived incorporation of the cultural demands of minorities were not the sole social changes portrayed as concerning. In fact, these were often understood as merely symptoms of a broader, undesirable left-ward push. As outlined in chapter 3, the Left were constructed in the milieu as villains orchestrating this change, to the detriment of British society. In these narratives, the Left were frequently assumed synonymous with the milieu's Brexit adversaries—Remainers. Negative representations of these groups were used to advance claims of a plot to mold society to the Left's not only multiculturalist but also socialist or "Marxist" vision—a vision allegedly shared by the EU.

While the relationship between racism and support for Brexit has been the subject of much public and scholarly discussion, the role of anti-leftism has not previously been illuminated. In this chapter I explore this anti-leftist ideology and its operationalization in support for Brexit on Facebook. I reveal how this facet of the milieu's ideological basis is at once an extension of anti-leftist narratives that have been advanced by right-wing media and politicians in Britain since at least the 1980s, *and* a product of the absorption of ideas from the transnational far-right. The pro-Brexit Facebook users' preoccupation with the allegedly sinister nature of the Left demonstrates the reach and appeal of these ideas and their compatibility with right-wing populist causes like Brexit. Importantly, the advancement of this form of anti-leftism in the pro-Brexit Facebook milieu was made possible by the Leave-Remain divide that so prominently structured British identity and social relations in the post-referendum negotiation period. These conditions meant that, alongside the White victimhood engendered by the racist ideologies described in chapter 4, the pro-Brexit Facebook milieu was also driven by a strong sense of what I term "Right victimhood." This phantom victimhood posits the Left as history's illegitimate victors, based on a construction of their deviant ideological agenda as far-reaching, totalitarian, and silencing of dissent through the oppressive device of "political correctness."

THE "LOONY LEFT" AND CULTURAL MARXISM

In British society, the demonization of the Left is neither new nor confined to extreme groups. Petley (2018b, 58) contends that "attempts by right-wing British newspapers to demonise sections of the Left are as old as the Left itself." This includes representing socialism as "deranged and psychotic" and a danger to society (ibid.). Being born before 1980, the pro-Brexit Facebook users in this study lived through not only the Cold War alarm over the communist "enemy within," but also a particularly concerted construction of the "loony left" folk devil during the Thatcher era.

In the 1980s, amid a value conflict between those who grew up in the culturally disruptive 1960s and older generations who wanted to preserve conservative notions of authority and respect, what came to be known as the "new urban left" emerged in metropolitan centers like London and Manchester (Curran 2018). This group brought their progressive and liberationist ideas to local government and community organizing, promoting the rights and representation of women, lesbians, gay people, and ethnic minorities. A moral panic (Cohen 1972; Hall et al. 1978) ensued over gay liberation in particular, with the "loony left's" agenda portrayed as harmful, dangerous, and not simply allowing but celebrating and promoting homosexuality (Curran 2018; Smith 1994). This was spearheaded by the Conservative Party-aligned popular British press, who also took aim at left-controlled London councils' allegedly favorable treatment of ethnic minorities and other anti-racist endeavors (Petley 2018b). Before "political correctness" entered the common vernacular, gross distortions reported in right-wing tabloids alleged "loony left" London boroughs like Hackney, Islington, and Brent were banning words like "manhole" and nursery rhymes like "Baa Baa Black Sheep" (ibid.). The way in which Thatcher's neoliberal project famously took aim at striking miners also provided grounds for the Labour Party to be thoroughly delegitimized within British politics, and the Left's socialist project along with it (Steber 2018).

This toxification of the Left in Britain was an outcome "significantly different from the fragmentary identity politics that took shape in the United States" (Curran 2018, 15). After the end of the Cold War, however, it was in the United States that these demonizations of the Left were extended to construct a new conspiracy theory called Cultural Marxism. With the "red menace" no longer a tangible threat, American neo-conservatives developed this theory in its place via a number of books and alternative magazine articles (Jamin 2014). As noted in chapter 3, Cultural Marxism is an agenda said to have been brought to the United States by the scholars of the Frankfurt School. According to the theory, this covert agenda is a Gramscian move for cultural hegemony; with the failure of economic Marxism, Cultural Marxists are said to have designated women, foreigners, homosexuals, non-Christians, and other minorities as the "new proletariat," and the alleged strategy to advance these groups is through accusations of sexism, racism, homophobia, anti-Semitism, and so forth, and the enforcement of "political correctness." The ultimate goal of the conspirators is said to be the discrediting of institutions such as the nation, the family, authority, Christianity and morality, and to build a multicultural, ultra-egalitarian world that was incompatible with values like democracy and freedom (ibid.).

The Cultural Marxism conspiracy theory was cited many times by U.S. Republican figure Pat Buchanan in the 2000s, but little attention was paid it outside of the most extreme spheres until the terrorist attack by Anders Breivik in Norway (Jamin 2014). The term was used over one hundred times in Breivik's manifesto, in which he broadened and developed the alleged threat to include a heavy focus on Islamization (discussed in chapter 4 of this book) (ibid.). The ideas of Cultural Marxism gained further prominence since the rise of the Alt-Right movement, where the theory was popularized with the aim of "exposing" the left-wing ideological forces this movement claims are controlling society. Since then, as Mirrlees (2018, 49) aptly notes, Cultural Marxism has become, among the online transnational far and populist right, "shorthand for an anti-American bogeyman, a symbol for every liberal or left-leaning group the right defines itself against, and an epithet for progressive identities, values, ideas, and practices that reactionaries believe have made America worse than before." The theory's transnational popularization has seen its ideas used, for example, by the far-right in Australia (Busbridge, Moffitt, and Thorburn 2020), and by European far-right and right-wing populist politicians such as Viktor Orban in Hungary and Thierry Baudet in the Netherlands (de Bruin 2022). The term has also appeared, if infrequently, in material published by UK-based far-right movements the British National Party (BNP) and the English Defence League (EDL), and by key Brexit campaigners the United Kingdom Independence Party (UKIP) (Jamin 2014; Richardson 2015). The stage was set for the extreme ideas of the Cultural Marxism theory to permeate the pro-Brexit sphere online. As I demonstrate below, the anti-leftism of the pro-Brexit Facebook milieu under investigation here combined Thatcher-era "loony left" moral panic narratives with sinister representations of the Left found in the narratives of Cultural Marxism that circulate on social media.

REMAINERS AND THE LEFT: IMMATURE, IMMORAL, AND HYPOCRITICAL

While negative attitudes toward Remainers were significant among the Leave voting contingent of the British population during the post-referendum period, the pro-Brexit Facebook milieu's preoccupation with demonizing the Left set it apart from this broader group. I contend, however, that in the context of the urban left's prominent role in Remain campaigning, the bitter Leaver-Remainer social divide during this period opened the door for the logic of Cultural Marxism and its demonization of the Left to take hold in this online milieu, effectively facilitating the dissemination of these far-right ideas to a new audience.

The 2016 EU referendum is said to have exposed as well as inflamed divisions in British society. In the post-referendum negotiation period studied in this book, the categories of Leaver and Remainer had become salient new identities that structured the way people in Britain understood social relations, deemed a new form of "affective polarization" (Hobolt, Leeper, and Tilley 2020; see also Meredith and Richardson 2019; North, Piwek, and Joinson 2021). However, little has been made of the effect this has had on the social meaning attributed to the categories of Left and Right. It is no secret that a greater proportion of those who identify as left-wing voted Remain than Leave. Many more of those who backed Labour, the Liberal Democrats, and the Greens in 2015 chose Remain, in contrast to the 58 percent majority of Conservative voters who chose Leave (Ashcroft 2016). Remain voters were also greatly overrepresented among those who supported left-wing causes like multiculturalism, immigration, feminism, and the environment (ibid.). It could be argued that this is partly the product of the focus in the Leave campaign on demonizing immigration and the Left's focus on anti-racism. Thus, despite the fact that many on what could be termed the "economic" Right (vis-à-vis the "cultural" Right) opposed Britain's exit from the EU (including Conservative Prime Ministers David Cameron and Theresa May), and despite the existence of a leftist faction that supported Brexit (known as "Lexit") in opposition to the neoliberal policies of the Union (Worth 2017), Remain has come to be associated more with the Left than the Right of British politics.

After the referendum, the derogatory term "Remoaner" entered the right-wing tabloid press vernacular to describe Remain supporters who were allegedly attempting to overturn the result. These attempts included the High Court case brought by London-based financier Gina Miller that forced the referendum result to be ratified by parliament before it could be recognized as binding (Binns, Bateman, and Mair 2018), and the campaign for a "People's Vote" on the outcome of the Brexit negotiations (Bosotti 2018). Remoaner has been mobilized in widely the same way as the epithet "snowflake" that is used to depict the young Left as easily-offended tantrum-throwers. Remoaners are also depicted in the right-wing tabloid press as out-of-touch metropolitan elites (e.g., O'Neill 2020), much like the 1980s demonizations of the new urban left discussed above. The emergence of such terminology is evidence that the same sorts of discursive tactics that have been used to delegitimize the Left have also been employed with regard to Remain voters, and this was made possible by the fact of Leave's victory in the referendum.

In Posts observed in the pro-Brexit Facebook milieu and interviews with the users engaging there, categories like Remainer and "leftie" were used interchangeably, demonstrating the way these were seen as mapping onto each other. Both groups were depicted as morally bankrupt, deviant, and vindictive individuals, as well as irrational and oversensitive. This was juxtaposed with Leavers, centrists, or right-wingers who were represented as moral, rational, evidence-based, and the victims of online harassment. As noted in chapter 1, almost all of the users in this study recounted a personal experience of having received abuse from "lefties" or "Remainers" on Facebook, in response to something they had Posted that was condemned as "racist" or similar. These left-wing individuals were portrayed as instigators, who (unlike the pro-Brexit Facebook users, it was alleged) commonly used "vile" language in hysterical tirades of abuse. As Deborah (50s, female, Northwest England) described, "I mostly communicate with likeminded people, because I don't mind having a discussion on Facebook, but I'm not in the market for a stand-up fight, because some people can be absolutely vitriolic."

Anecdotes of offline personal experiences were also used to support these narratives. For example, Helen (50s, female, West Midlands) told of how her daughter was bullied at school after it became known that she supported UKIP. She derided the primary culprit, describing her with palpable disdain as, "[Her] mummy and daddy have split up, [. . .] always going on about how she hates men, [. . .] lives in a gated house. [. . .] Daddy bought [her] a car but she hates men." This is demonstrative of a representation of the Left and Remainers as hypocritical, intent simply on criticizing others, while themselves being spoiled and privileged. To Helen, the fact that the girl's parents were separated was significant, either because it represented the idea that the Left's progressive values were incompatible with functional family life, or that left-wing and Remainer "snowflakes" were simply maladjusted children lashing out. The issue of class is also at play. From Helen's perspective as a working-class woman, the Left and Remainers belonged to the middle class and had never experienced hardship. According to the pro-Brexit Facebook users, these people were disingenuous "do-gooders" (Audrey, 50s, female, Northwest England) who simply wanted to "take the moral high-ground" (Eileen, 60s, female, Northwest England).

This poor character was also portrayed as extending to violent tendencies, particularly when it came to street protests. In this narrative, balaclava-clad "Antifa" members and their extreme tactics were representative of the Left in general: prone to temper tantrums and willing to stop at nothing to have their way. Olivia (50s, female, Southeast England) said at protests she had been warned by police not to approach counter-protesters because they were known to be "aggressive" and "violent." She also spoke of a video she had seen on Facebook in which a young American boy on a school trip wearing a MAGA (short for "Make America Great Again," Trump's popular campaign slogan) cap was verbally abused by an older man: "My gosh, he was vile toward this child. I mean it was just shocking. But, this young boy, he just stood there. He said nothing. [. . .] He just looked at this abhorrent left wing . . . " She went on to describe the Comments on this video: "I mean the things they were saying online! 'shoot the kid,' 'kill the kid,' 'cut the kid's head off,' 'put him through a shredding machine. . . . ' It was just vile!" This description was emblematic of narratives in the milieu about the depravity of those on the Left, in contrast with the dignity and superior moral character of those on the Right. Olivia's use of an anecdote from a video about Trump supporters is a reflection of the transnational nature of these anti-left representations, which have even been capitalized upon by Trump himself in his designation of far-left "Antifa" (in reality more of an international coalition of individuals than one organized group) as a "terrorist organization" (Wilson 2020).

"Lefties" and Remainers were also commonly portrayed by these users as unwilling to accept facts that did not support their political stances, and as far more emotional than rational. As I demonstrate in chapter 6, the constructions of these groups were part of an effort to reclaim the milieu's own epistemic capital, experienced as revoked by delegitimizing discourses about Brexit supporters. In addition to being sore losers when it came to the referendum result, Remainers and the Left were depicted in the pro-Brexit Facebook milieu as arrogant, automatically condemning as wrong, racist, or ignorant any stance that challenged their own. For example, Mark (50s, male, Yorkshire) described his frustration at feeling talked down to by this group: "I can't believe how people can be so outrageously pompous. [. . .] It's not their opinion so it can't be the right opinion." After describing online right-wing populist personalities like Ezra Levant and Candace Owens as "calm and measured," Helen contrasted this with the "rude" behavior of those on the Left: "They'll just revert to name-calling, i.e., racist, bigot, homophobe, transphobe—you name it, they've got a 'phobe' for it."

Anti-Brexit and left-wing commentators and politicians were all the targets of disdain in the milieu, with terms like "treasonous" and "traitor" commonly used to describe them. Then-leader of the Labour Party Jeremy Corbyn and Shadow Home Secretary Diane Abbott were particular targets. Diane Abbott, a Black British woman, appeared in Facebook Posts and interview narratives as a bumbling buffoon and typical bleeding-heart agitator. The thinly-veiled misogynistic and racist narratives about Abbott in the milieu reflect and extend those to which she has been subjected in the news media (Gabriel 2017). Representations of Corbyn too echoed the vociferous campaign against him by the British press at the time, in which "loony left" representations had been reignited to quell grass-roots support of this self-professed socialist leader (Cammaerts, DeCillia, and Magalhães 2020; Piazza and Lashmar 2017). Corbyn was portrayed in the milieu as a terrorist sympathizer, a dishonest man, and a conniving communist, including in images Posted on Facebook during the fieldwork that commonly depicted him as shriveled and grotesque. The general consensus among interviewees and in their Facebook timelines was that a socialist Corbyn government would be a dystopian outcome for Britain.

These representations in a pro-Brexit context are intriguing because Corbyn is known for his long-term critical stance toward the EU, albeit from a left-wing, anti-neoliberalist perspective (Hertner 2016). He became leader of the Labour Party during the EU referendum campaign, and subsequently softened his criticisms to satisfy the strong Remain contingent within Labour and its voter base (ibid.). However, these were widely deemed unconvincing, an idea that haunted Corbyn's tenure (Watts 2018). In the pro-Brexit Facebook milieu, while Corbyn's inconsistency was indeed used against him and his party, this was far less prominent than critique of his socialist principles. The particular resonance of the anti-leftist demonization of Corbyn points to the significance of the operationalization of anti-leftism within the pro-Brexit Facebook milieu: at times this ideology could trump even animosity toward the EU.

LEFT-WING AGENDAS AND THE NORMALIZATION OF DEVIANCE

Alongside these depictions of the poor character of Remainers and left-wing individuals, a prominent narrative in the milieu was that left-wing agendas were deliberately normalizing deviant aspects of society. This narrative drew on moral panic logic to position this as ludicrous and as a harbinger of a broader collapse of the proper moral basis of society. For example, Carl (50s, male, Northwest England) expressed his frustration and bemusement regarding "diversity" agendas:

> All this gender crap [. . .] is just totally rubbish. [. . .] Before, a man was a man and a girl was a girl. It's annoying me when you see, like that video I saw

[on Facebook] what I told you about before with the children all dressed up in yellow. [. . .] I've just been to Citizens Advice Bureau, and there was four pages asking me name, me gender, date of birth, me address. And then, the next paragraph, the ethnicity. I didn't fill 'em in. [. . .] I don't think it's got ought [nothing] to do with anything.

Here, Carl alludes to a perceived connection between left-wing agendas around gender rights and those around monitoring ethnic diversity. He invokes "common-sense" logic to justify his confusion at and opposition to these agendas and the progressive social change they represent. The ridiculous ideas presumed to be inherent in these are portrayed as having infiltrated arenas of public life where they do not belong; they are alleged to represent an attempt at social control. This suspicious narrative resonated with Carl to the point where he perceived even simple questions about his identifying characteristics as insidious.

Feminism was also objected to in the milieu as a facet of this left-wing agenda, and deemed representative of a class of raging, patronizing snowflakes (despite claims made by the users, as discussed in chapter 4, to be defending women from illiberal Islam). In Fred's (60s, male, Northeast England) words, today's young feminists were "absolutely ridiculous. How can anybody who's standing there [at feminist demonstrations] expect people to want to support them?" What was being articulated in the pro-Brexit Facebook milieu, however, extended beyond a "backlash" to perceived victimization of men by feminist agendas. Feminism was seen as part of a vile movement to deliberately normalize unnatural and unwanted societal change. In Deborah's follow-up interview, I presented her with a Post she had Shared about lace boxer shorts for men. She described this as "utter madness" and went on to say, "I sometimes think there are certain factions in this world that want to turn us all into asexual worker ants, you know? No! I like the division between men and women. [. . .] And they're eroding that. I don't see why men can't be masculine and women feminine. [. . .] Let's applaud the difference. Absolutely. I don't want my men in lace drawers [laughs]." In this narrative, the issue of effeminate underwear was not a private decision of individual attire, but rather was symbolic of the perceived erosion of masculinity within society. Importantly, divisions were not "eroding" on their own, but "certain factions" were instigating this erosion deliberately. Deborah's comment reflects how feminist movements were seen as bound up with issues of gender fluidity and thus transgender and gender non-binary rights movements. In this way, feminism was understood as seeking not to improve opportunities for gender equality but to erase all gender differences and, ironically, limit men and women's ability to choose to be masculine and feminine, respectively. With "asexual worker ants," Deborah also equates this perceived phenomenon with the communist intentions claimed in the theory of Cultural Marxism.

In a similar vein, those seeking to promote transgender rights were also portrayed as nefarious. Reference was frequently made to the notion that the acceptability of gender fluidity was being wrongfully taught to young children in schools. The idea was that these minority concerns were being "pushed" or forced onto children from too young an age, in a way that was unnatural or posed a threat to their welfare. The issue of gender-neutral toilets was frequently raised as a concrete example of what was represented in the milieu as lunacy. Controversy over such facilities was topical in the transnational right-wing populist sphere at the time due to then-U.S. President Trump's revoking of school guidelines that had been introduced by Barack Obama (Trotta 2017). While similar moralized discourses have been invoked in the UK context, none of their proponents matched the high profile of Trump in the online right-wing populist sphere. Trump's policies on the transgender issue, and the way he disseminated them on social media, have been described by Pepin-Neff and Cohen (2021) as engendering a moral panic that advanced the assumption that transgender people were invalid, deviant, and a burden on U.S. society. In Posts in the pro-Brexit Facebook milieu, such recriminations were given alongside depictions of transgender individuals as unattractive, middle-aged men in drag, either leering over children or making fools of themselves in public. For example, George Posted a photo to his Facebook Timeline of a Remain demonstration with a transgender woman in the foreground; it was overlain with the text "I don't know about you . . . but this pic makes me want Brexit even more." This was representative of the ridicule that was directed at transgender people in the pro-Brexit Facebook milieu, and of the clear overlap in these narratives between issues of gender recognition and leaving the EU.

In many ways, this contemporary transgender moral panic mirrors that of the gay rights movement that was seen in the 1980s, which in the UK led to legislation outlawing the "promotion" of homosexuality by local authorities and in state schools at the time (Petley 2018a). Homosexuality and transgenderism—and the politics of minority rights that surround them—were sometimes confused or conflated in the pro-Brexit Facebook milieu, understood as two sides of the same coin. This was partly underpinned by an awareness among these users of the shared advocate base for these issues on the Left. In fact, in the pro-Brexit Facebook milieu, there were not only newer anxieties over the promotion of transgenderism but also enduring concerns about the alleged promotion of homosexuality. As Helen put it, "We shouldn't be having these conversations with children until they start asking the questions themselves. [. . .] I didn't wanna know about that stuff when I was 7, 8, 9, 10. They're shoving it down bloody primary school children's [throats] now.

I don't want some gay pride birthday cakes and stuff like that, putting ideas into their head." While most of the pro-Brexit Facebook users claimed to accept homosexuality, their angst over the perceived potential to go beyond simple acceptance and into the promotion of alternative sexualities exposes an implicit negative value judgment, underpinned by an unspoken homophobia. This is despite homonationalist claims by, for instance, Olivia, to sympathize with gay Islamic apostates, including a friend of hers whose parents she alleged had "placed a fatwa on him" after he came out to them.

Nonetheless, issues around gender fluidity were of far greater concern in the milieu than those around sexuality. Few users could understand or support transgender rights, revealing the strength of transphobia within the milieu. Lawrence's (40s, male, West Midlands) comment exemplifies this: "This is where I think the world's going totally mad yeah? [. . .] We all have a choice of choosing which gender we want to be today. [. . .] And in some ways, [. . .] being homosexual, being lesbian, OK, we all accept that today, yeah? But this thing about, [sighs] this thing about parents being able to say that their son who was born is actually a girl, they're gonna call it this name, it's like, what is it doing?"

The question Lawrence poses at the end of this quote reflects his confusion about the reasons behind challenges to gender norms and gender polarity. Like the conflations expressed by these users, his comment intimates a lack of basic understanding lying at the core of this disdain, perhaps underpinned by the notion that these movements were too bizarre to warrant efforts to comprehend them. While the flagrance of transphobia in the milieu was in itself disturbing, key to understanding political engagement in the pro-Brexit Facebook milieu is the way this manifested—as a bewilderment at and apprehension about liberal social change, and demonization of those deemed responsible for "forcing" through such change against society's will.

In the pro-Brexit Facebook milieu, acceptance of minority sexual and gender identities was sometimes depicted as a slippery slope, with the Left so consumed by their desire not to offend that they failed to recognize harmful forms of sexual deviance. That is, a clear link was frequently drawn in interviews and Facebook Posts between these identities and pedophilia. In an interview, Helen recounted some content she had recently seen on social media where "a drag queen child has been photographed with a naked male drag queen." She asked "Where is the outrage from the Left on that?" before linking this to a lack of outrage over "Muslim grooming gangs." It is no coincidence that children feature heavily in such narratives; children have often been at the heart of "loony left" moral panics (Petley 2018b, 60). Given their position as the most vulnerable and innocent segment of society, claims to be acting in defense of children have a special level of appeal and are particularly morally loaded. Helen's comment also makes explicit the "signification spiral" (Hall et al. 1978) that connects the Left's assumed agenda on social change with their alleged role in the harms of multiculturalism, and escalates this threat to the degeneration of the moral basis of society.

This points to something already alluded to in Carl's comment at the start of this section: issues around gender politics were found alongside and intertwined with narratives about the Left's race-relations politics. In the milieu, these were all considered part of one problem or agenda by the Left. Deborah said that she felt "very strongly" that deliberate representations of different categories of ethnic minority groups in television soaps were "like the lunatics are taking over the asylum" and were part of how "most of us are manipulated in some way." In her words, "It's as if somebody is working in the wings, trying desperately to make all people equal." This alleged "working" by the media and educational institutions was a key topic in the milieu that linked panics over social change to a deliberate left-wing agenda, and this will be explored next.

MEDIA BRAINWASHING

According to the narratives shared by users in the pro-Brexit Facebook milieu, the Left's deviant, anti-White, and Marxist agendas were achieved partly through propaganda. This was summarized by Mark's response to the question in an interview of why he thought certain individuals would want to "betray" (his term) Britain over Brexit. After struggling at first to articulate himself, he concluded:

> Over the last 40 years, all we've heard on news medias and things like that is political correctness, [. . .] and a lot of these people are so far ingrained with this political correctness that they can't think anything different. [. . .] They actually think that the political correctness and like, "let's have open borders" and "let's [. . .] give away British sovereignty to Europe" and things like that, [. . .] they actually do believe that that's what the majority think.

The pro-Brexit Facebook users were cognizant of the idea, prominent in the Cultural Marxism conspiracy theory, that "political correctness" was one of the Left's primary tools. This alleged strategy went hand-in-hand with positive messaging around immigration and the EU.

The left-wing brainwashing was seen as all-pervasive, but with major roots in the education system, particularly higher education. This purportedly explained why youth, especially middle-class youth, were the most prone to left-wing ideology and pro-EU sentiment. University lecturers and academics were portrayed in the milieu as part of (or paid off by) the liberal elite. Today's universities were said to be allegedly dumbing down students rather than promoting intelligence, and were teaching young people to "kick off" (Eileen), that is, throw tantrums and silence dissenting ideas. As Fred described, "University lecturers are without a doubt indoctrinating the students into EU, into [supporting 2016 Trump election rival Hillary] Clinton. [. . .] And a lot of young people who've gone to the universities [. . .] really believe in their heart and soul [. . .] that the EU is better."

However, it was the "mainstream media"—a term employed to create a juxtaposition with social or alternative media, but mostly used in the milieu to refer to television programming—that were seen as playing the largest role in the left-wing brainwashing machine. The targeting of "mainstream media" was popular in the transnational right-wing populist sphere at the time, where alternative information purveyors sought to deliberately discredit these media in order to garner credibility for their own messages and mobilize indignation (Figenschou and Ihlebæk 2019; Rone 2022). Kirk (60s, male, London) was emphatic that "the media have done more damage to this country and all countries, I think, because they think they know best and [. . .] they try and brainwash you." This brainwashing was able to succeed because "still the majority follow mainstream media" (Olivia), which was "feeding them left-wing anti-democratic stuff all the time" (Beatrice, 60s, female, North Wales). Televised debate shows such as "BBC Question Time" were used to exemplify an alleged left-wing, pro-EU bias and a failure by the public broadcaster to represent the views of pro-Brexit constituents in its guests and studio audiences. Fred articulated this narrative with reference to the BBC's programming and attributed it to a deliberate brainwashing agenda: "BBC especially, they are so anti-Brexit. I mean it was ridiculous. [. . .] At the time of [the] Brexit [referendum], even ordinary plays and comedies were putting over [. . .] an anti-Brexit message. [. . .] They've used program after program to try to brainwash the public into fearing Brexit."

In this way, the BBC was a particular target within the nebulous category of "mainstream media." As Britain's public broadcaster, the BBC's duty to provide impartial news and education is enshrined in the royal charter which forms its constitutional basis (Department for Culture, Media and Sport 2016). However, accusations of political bias have been aimed at the outlet from both sides of the political spectrum, dating back at least as far as the Thatcher years (Ayton and Tumber 2001). The public broadcaster status of the BBC was used by the pro-Brexit Facebook users to claim a hand-in-glove relationship between mainstream media content and the governing classes. This was illustrated by Mark's comment: "The BBC's an absolute disgrace. [. . .] It's actually highlighted it, how politicians are so unrepresentative and how, and how the media . . . I can't stand it!" Or, as Carl plainly put it, "The media are complicit with the government."

This narrative was linked back to Eurosceptic ideas of EU corruption through the notion that the BBC received funding from the EU and therefore must have a pro-EU bias. But other television channels such as Sky and Channel 4 were also portrayed as promoting panic over Brexit. This agenda was deemed "Project Fear" in pro-Brexit spaces. The pro-Brexit Facebook users ridiculed the sorts of claims that they said seemed to be emerging on a daily basis, such as "medicine's gunna grind to a halt" (Fred) and "we're not gunna have anybody to work in the NHS. Who's gunna cook our curries? There's gunna be no flowers for Mother's Day" (Helen). These were depicted as absurd speculations by unqualified and disingenuous "experts," or even deliberate lies. Kirk lamented the way that such predictions were rarely challenged on television programs, saying "You never ever get the other side of it."

Several participants Shared a video of pro-Leave Conservative MP Jacob Rees-Mogg reprimanding a Channel 4 journalist during an interview for using the term "crash out" to refer to a situation in which no exit deal with the EU was reached before the deadline—in this scenario, it was surmised that trade with the block would default to World Trade Organization rules. Rees-Mogg accused the journalist of bias for using the negatively nuanced term, and Mark reproduced the video's narrative in his interview: "Channel 4, I'm fed up of them cutting people off. [. . .] I'm fed up of the actual presenters or the people doing the questioning saying 'when we crash out.' [. . .] We don't know what's gunna [happen]."

According to the narratives of the pro-Brexit Facebook users, the problem with the "mainstream media" was not limited to Brexit but was a decades-long issue; the "mainstream media" was part of one all-encompassing left-wing bias and pervasive culture of political correctness, and this agenda was inextricably linked with Brexit. As Helen described, "I coulda written the headlines the other night. They'll be Brexit bashing, Boris bashing, Trump said a naughty word, and uh, 'there's too many White people in parliament.'"

In the pro-Brexit Facebook milieu, explanations for media bias ranged from the media going overboard in their efforts not to offend minority groups ("they've got to have a representation of LGBT and all the rest of it, you know" said Beatrice) to a deliberate agenda to indoctrinate people into multiculturalism and globalism. According to Eileen, "the mainstream media's trying to keep you calm and make you think multiculturalism is working. [. . .] They're trying to condition you for the future." In this way, the media was seen as just another part of a global system which was against "the people"; it worked to hide the truth regarding White victimization by not covering issues such as alleged "genocide" of "White farmers in Africa" (Lawrence), because exposing these was incompatible with the broader left-wing agenda.

This supposedly included the particularly favorable treatment of Islam and Muslims. As Eileen put it "If you attack Islam head on, in any way shape or form, you will lose, because they are protected. The whole society is [based] around 'must not upset [Muslims].'" The ill-famed "cover-up" of "grooming gangs" (see chapter 1) was referenced by many of the pro-Brexit Facebook users to illustrate this. Multiple users also made reference to an incident "barely" covered by the news media where one Muslim man allegedly beheaded another in a betting shop in the Midlands. I observed a Post intended to invoke frustration about this circulating in the milieu at the time. Olivia used this as evidence of a broader problem, saying, "It had one paragraph in the newspaper. And I just thought 'that is disgusting!' It's happening here all the time, and the general public don't know."

Media treatment of U.S. President Donald Trump and "Tommy Robinson" (see introduction in this book) were also repeatedly used to exemplify bias in the media as a whole. These individuals were portrayed by the pro-Brexit Facebook users as heroes and victims who were constantly attacked unfairly and portrayed dishonestly because they nobly refused to toe the line of political correctness in their pursuit of justice. As Neil (70s, male, South Wales) attested regarding Trump, "he's doing an amazing job which is not being published. [. . .] Whether you like Trump or not is irrelevant. The whole of the mainstream media in America is a get-Trump syndrome." Regarding "Tommy Robinson," Kirk spoke of the media's culpability in turning him into a pariah by disingenuously cutting interview content to make him "look like a [. . .] right-wing sort of monster."

Some of the interviews for this study took place not long after "Tommy Robinson" had released his online exposé video, *Panodrama*. This documentary-style film aimed to uncover an alleged plot by the BBC's flagship documentary series *Panorama* to maliciously defame "Robinson" by attempting to coerce a source into defaming him and uncritically accepting evidence that the source had deliberately fabricated. Alongside these allegations of the victimization of "Robinson," the film includes footage of *Panorama* producer John Sweeney making racist, classist, and homophobic remarks, and claims of bullying by the anti-racist advocacy group Hope Not Hate, thus promoting the idea that it is the Left, not the Right, who are intolerant. This simultaneously renders the Left hypocrites and the Right virtuous, and is reminiscent of the femonationalist and homonationalist logics discussed in chapter 4 that accuse those defending Islam of being complicit with homophobia and the subjugation of women from which it is assumed to be inseparable.

Olivia had traveled to attend the film's "premiere" outside the BBC offices in Salford, Greater Manchester, and said that although the content was shocking, she was not surprised by the accusations, as they confirmed her existing suspicions about the BBC's agenda. She pointed to the damning footage of Sweeney and said, "All of the lies that went on . . . And the thing that really irritated me the most was the way the BBC deliberately make fake news." Importantly, the film served to confirm the notion of left-wing media bias not only through its content but also the alleged lack of coverage of the film itself by the broader media. As Mark lamented, "There's been no mention of this John Sweeney [in the traditional media] and, it should be a big scandal what he's tried to do." According to the narrative in the pro-Brexit Facebook milieu, this was all part of a left-wing agenda in which "they don't want the people educated" (Neil).

The narrative that any favoring of Remain or left-wing agendas in the media was deliberate "brainwashing" was reinforced by the referendum result, which allegedly revealed that these media were made up of a left-wing elite minority removed from majority opinion. This narrative was, however, enabled by the ground laid by decades of anti-political correctness narratives by the Right.

POLITICAL CORRECTNESS AND THE ASSAULT ON FREE SPEECH

As noted above, "political correctness" is an integral concept within the far-right conspiracy theory of Cultural Marxism. It is alleged to be a key tool for delegitimizing criticism of left-wing agendas by labeling them as evil (Jamin 2014). However, the term is popular far beyond this theory and has been part of broader anti-left discourse since long before Cultural Marxism became more commonly known. Indeed, accusations of "political correctness" are themselves used as a device for delegitimizing left-wing pushes to recognize the social power of language and its role in marginalization and discrimination. Among the Right, there has been a "decades-long, carefully choreographed and well-financed campaign against political correctness" (Scatamburlo-D'Annibale 2019, 69).

The effects of this long-term campaign were evident in the narratives circulating in the pro-Brexit Facebook milieu. Interrelated with the above ideas around left-wing brainwashing agendas was a narrative that the people themselves were being prevented from speaking, from voicing individual opinions, criticisms, or other dissenting points of view. The users drew on normative discourses of freedom, in which individuals' entitlement to hold and voice their opinions represented not only a stalwart of modern democracy but a fundamental human right. In these narratives, pushes for politically correct or sensitive language, as well as practices of no-platforming that sought to counter the normalization of problematic and discriminatory discourses, were interpreted as the behavior of a generation of "snowflakes" who were intent on "getting offended" at everything and would not listen to the opinions of others. As these practices and sensitivities were fast becoming a societal norm, not only "freedom of speech" but healthy political debate was alleged to be stifled by the Left, threatening democracy. In Fred's words, "One time, you know, you could criticize anybody and they'd accept it because it's your opinion. Doesn't have to be right but, you know, you respect the fact that somebody has an opinion. But that has been taken away from us. We're not allowed to have an opinion now."

In this narrative, the number of things that "we" were no longer permitted to say was constantly growing to the point of absurdity. As Isaac (50s, male, Northwest England) remarked, "They seem to be cutting it down more and more, by limiting what we can talk about in open debate." The new social requirements to take care to use non-discriminatory terms were alleged to go against the principles of common sense because "where do you draw the line?" (Neil). The changed status of deeply racially prejudiced words describing Black and Asian people was also used as an example of how the forbidding of offensive terms could become, in these users' eyes, unreasonably restrictive. Kirk illustrated this perceived temporal decline: "When I was a kid, I had a dog, and that's what his name was, honestly, I mean that was the color. It's 'n***** brown.' [. . .] You can't say it now. [. . .] But then, [. . .] I could put on a rap music now from Black people and they don't stop saying the 'N,' like, that word, and [. . .] no one says anything. Soon as *you* say it, you're gunna get arrested for racial whatever. [. . .] I think it's too much they're stopping us saying" (Kirk's emphasis). This anecdote points to the intersection between White victimhood and Right victimhood in the milieu's ideology—not only did the media and those in power allegedly favor left-wing positions and silence right-wing ones, but in this narrative those who bore the brunt of the agenda of "political correctness" were invariably White.

The narrative claimed it was no longer possible to speak critically about immigration, Islam, or individuals of Black or minority ethnic origin without being accused of racism and bigotry. Importantly, the same was said to be true of openly supporting Britain's departure from the EU—both forms of self-censorship were understood as part of the same left-wing agenda. This was tantamount to "gag[ging] people" (Deborah). According to the pro-Brexit Facebook users, this was despite both sets of concerns being reasonable and widespread. Fred lamented that "people who are basically in the center of politics, perhaps marginally to the right, they're all being described as being far-right, extremists, which isn't true." This was deemed not only unfair but undemocratic and detrimental to the health of society.

Restrictions on criticism were portrayed as particularly stringent and socially harmful with regard to Islam. The narrative implied that native Brits were owed the right to debate the desirability of the increased visibility of Islam in public life. Furthermore, the inability to criticize religious practices was depicted as aiding and abetting organized child sexual exploitation and the oppression of women. Regarding the left-wing media reaction to Johnson's public criticisms of veiling, Eileen said: "A woman who is actually suffering health-wise, completely covered in black to go out, nobody will convince me that that's acceptable, [. . .] and I should be allowed to say that without being thought of as being racist. [. . .] I think it's common sense. [. . .] And if that is deemed racist then there's something wrong with society. We should be able to discuss these issues openly." Eileen's comment is a nod to the legacy of a long-running anti-multiculturalist discourse which has accused left-wing social agendas of supporting "reprehensible" Islamic cultural practices around gender and denying social problems allegedly related to immigration (Vertovec and Wessendorf 2010, 9–10). As Kundnani (2012, 156) notes, these multiculturalist principles of political correctness came to be understood as "destroying liberal ideas of the open society." These narratives fitted well with the milieu's concerns over left-wing social control and the appeals to democratic values that were so crucial to the pro-Brexit Facebook metanarrative (see chapter 3).

Participants also claimed that "patriotism"—particularly expression of English nationalism as compared with Scottish, Welsh, or Northern Irish—was being censored. This is a narrative that has been rehearsed in populist tabloid media and anti-multiculturalist vernacular for decades (Kundnani 2000, 14; 2001, 56; Rhodes 2010) and its presence here is in line with links between Brexit and English nationalism (Henderson et al. 2017; Virdee and McGeever 2018). For example, observational data from Mark's Facebook Timeline revealed that he Shared a Post expressing outrage over an army veteran who had allegedly been asked by the local council to take down St George's and Union Jack flags from his front lawn. When asked about this Post, Mark said, "Councils have been like that in this country for bloody 30, 40 years now, [. . .] and everybody knows it's stupidity." This Post was challenged by a Facebook Friend of Mark's, who accused him of falling for misinformation. But in Mark's eyes, "whether that's fake news or not, right, that's not the point. It's just, it does happen, right? And he knows it happens." In other words, this Post did not introduce this "loony left" urban myth to Mark—it was a narrative with which he was already familiar and which resonated with frustrations he already held. This was illustrative of a sense among the pro-Brexit Facebook users that "nationalism has become a dirty word" (Deborah). Such a development, much like left-wing pushes to normalize gender fluidity and promote transgender rights, was seen as inverting common sense, as evidently wrong. As Deborah exclaimed, "What's wrong with national pride? It's like suddenly everything's been turned on its head!"

SOCIAL MEDIA AND CENSORSHIP

Facebook was a forum where these users could finally express the sentiments that they felt were being silenced offline. However, even this sphere was now seen as being polluted by left-wing bias and censorship: "any bit of freedom of speech on Facebook is being removed. No freedom of speech on Facebook whatsoever. And on Twitter they too have very much a left-wing leaning" (Olivia). The users spoke of temporary, permanent, or "shadow" bans (a form of content moderation whereby Posts are hidden from audiences but the Posting user is not alerted, see Savolainen 2022) that they and others in their milieu had experienced after having Posted something that went against Facebook's alleged left-wing agenda. For instance, Lawrence attested that one of the temporary bans he received was for "stating the wrong thing regarding Islam. [. . .] I referred to um, the Mayor of London in Britain as being a 'goat shagger.'[1] [chuckles] [. . .] Nowadays you can say anything and somebody's going to get 'offended.' [. . .] It's control of anybody who has a point of view, [. . .] clamping down of anybody with a right-wing point of view." Lawrence's quote demonstrates the way in which the strategic deployment of discourses of "freedom" of speech and thought promote a relativism that serves to legitimize plainly racist statements like the one he made on Facebook, painting them as innocent "political views" or "jokes."

The bias in Facebook's censorship was either attributed to the left-wing leaning of the platform or those with power in its organization (sometimes referencing former UK Liberal Democrat Party leader Nick Clegg's appointment to Facebook's Vice President, Global Affairs and Communications, as evidence of this) or social media was said to be being manipulated by others for their own "left-wing" agenda. Beatrice, for example, described Facebook as "now actually coming in on this act" and being "used as a tool to undermine democracy." In her first interview, Eileen told of her experience of alleged "shadow banning" in which a Post of hers about German policy toward "migrants" was not technically removed by Facebook but was invisible to many of her Followers. In her eyes, this was the result of German Chancellor Angela Merkel having "allegedly done some sort of agreement with Mark Zuckerberg that 'no negative news about the migrant crisis'" and was part of the deliberate "attempt to stifle free speech."

Terms like "shut down," "silence," "gag," or "suppress" were used in interviews and Facebook Posts to paint a sinister picture of surveillance and censorship there. This was accompanied by direct comparisons to George Orwell's *1984*, connecting the alleged assault on free speech to a dystopian narrative of authoritarian control. "Tommy Robinson's" imprisonment for publishing information about a "grooming gangs" trial, and his permanent suspension from mainstream social media platforms before and during the project fieldwork was alleged to exemplify the silencing of everyday people; in the narrative, this was designed to keep the truth from getting out as well as to maintain control by punishing dissent. Audrey lamented, "['Tommy Robinson' is] still entitled to his speech. This is meant to be a free country, but it's becoming a bit like lock-down. If you say something they don't like, [. . .] you pay the price."

These narratives about the right to offend or to absolute freedom of expression were not necessarily coherent. When asked how censorship should be handled on social media, many of the users struggled to articulate where the line should be drawn or began to qualify their statements. Helen's assessment was, "I don't think they should stop anything. Unless it incites violence." Deborah went a step further, adding a variety of conditions: "I think any criticism of any kind should be allowed, if it's well constructed, well thought-out, and not just particularly intended to insult." Overall, the way in which users' ideas about civility were reconciled with the favored narrative of free speech and revoked rights was by concluding that there should be some restrictions, but not to the extent we have now, summarized by Kirk's comment that "they're stopping us 90 percent, but it should only be 50 percent."

These comments reflect a common shortcoming in the logic of anti-political correctness: the threshold between fair and unfair incursions of "freedoms" remains unclarified. The incoherency of course reflects the difficulty that drawing such a line poses for parties on all sides of the debate. However, such nuance was not compatible with narratives in the milieu about the virtue of freedom for freedom's sake, nor with narratives of societal decline and the deviance of the Left. As with all of the narratives that featured in the milieu, those about the assault on free speech were adopted and employed selectively, in ways that facilitated the justification of support for Brexit and the other right-wing populist issues engaged with on Facebook.

COMMUNIST ASPIRATIONS OF THE EU

While the pro-Brexit Facebook milieu concerned itself with many anti-left narratives that were not directly related to the EU, we have already seen how these were linked to Brexit in the minds of the users through their overlap with anti-Remainer narratives and the idea that the suppression of pro-Brexit views was part of a left-wing agenda. The link between anti-leftism and Euroscepticism did not stop there, however. In fact, the EU itself was perceived as not only a left-wing organization, but a "communist" one.

As the narrative went, the objective of the EU was a sort of Robin Hood approach; to take from the rich and give to the poor in order to even out the economic standing of member countries. This meant that Britain was unfairly penalized. In Fred's words, the EU had "milked us for everything that they can." Comments by Helen capture well the shared sense of outrage over this: "Oh, it's horrendous. [. . .] I mean we are the biggest net contributor after Germany. We're the ones that have got a crumbling NHS, a shortage of school places, massive potholes! Look at Poland. New hospitals, new roads. Don't get me started. We're a cash cow." Here, based on information Helen had learned online, Britain was being punished for its success, despite this success no longer being reflected in experiences of public services. There was also a common assumption that without exploiting comparatively rich countries like the UK, the EU would not be able to survive financially. As Eileen put it, "They're looking for excuses to keep our money pouring in. [. . .] They don't care about Britain."

The benevolence of the Robin Hood approach described here would appear to contradict narratives of the EU as a greedy or corrupt organization that were also prominent in the milieu. However, both were compatible with a representation of the EU as communist, which was understood as inextricably tied to authoritarian dysfunction. Having been born before 1980, most of the individuals who participated in this study had lived through a significant portion of the Cold War period. In their minds, communism and totalitarianism went hand in hand, and the EU had come to represent both. It was portrayed in Facebook Posts observed in the milieu and in users' interview narratives as a wicked bully, with a hunger for authoritarian control. Any redistributive socialist aspirations of the Union were able to be portrayed as communist, thanks to renewed media representations in the post-referendum period of socialists like Jeremy Corbyn as radical communists, "Leninists" or "Trots" (Cammaerts, DeCillia, and Magalhães 2020). This association laid the ground for the attribution of the oppression associated with Cold War communist regimes to European socialism, to EU governance, and to the broader contemporary left-wing movement.

Neil Shared a video to his Timeline from the Brexit Party's YouTube channel, in which one of the party's Members of European Parliament (MEPs) gave a scathing speech in the EU Parliament about the EU's "fantasy economics" and a "tax racket" among other MEPs. In the video, the representative goes on to say,

> Who knows what the future holds—socialist, communist, fascist governments, if Mr Corbyn was elected in the UK, or some of the crazy socialists in France get elected. [. . .] Until recently, most of the EU was run by Soviet communists. Who, quite frankly, is to say that they may not change back to the system they had before? [. . .] The European Union loves taxation to feed its overpaid bureaucrats and their gold-plated pensions, not to mention the corruption.

The EU's totalitarianism was purportedly attempting to rob the UK of its democratic sovereignty, including alleged plans to *force* the UK to join the Euro currency zone, create a centralized EU taxation system, and implement conscription into a planned EU army. The latter was a key fear of Beatrice, who said, "My grandchildren will be part of the EU army. [. . .] They've already signed away that. [. . .] [They] will be conscripted into the EU army. And nobody, nobody will be able to do anything about it."

This was all part of the way that the European project itself was seen as constituting a long-term plan to create a communist federation or "super-state." The planned superstate would do away with nation-states in Europe altogether, meaning, "no democracy, everybody being controlled like they're just ants, all currencies being the same, et cetera, et cetera" (Lawrence). This is captured in a quote recited by Eileen, which she attributed to European integrationist Jean Monnet: "the peoples of Europe should be guided toward a super-state without actually realizing why. This [. . .] can be disguised as having economic benefit." Concern over sovereignty has long been linked to Euroscepticism in Britain (Gifford 2010; Stephens 2005), with nationalist ideas of British exceptionalism shown to be particularly salient (Gifford 2006; Spiering 2004) and sovereignty being a key topic in right-wing pro-Brexit media coverage around the time of the referendum (Rone 2021). However, the narratives in the pro-Brexit Facebook milieu focused particularly on the idea that this federal agenda would be realized in a sinister, conspiratorial way, and with "communist" aspirations.

Eileen compared these aspirations to the sci-fi film and novel franchise *The Hunger Games* in both of her interviews and in some of the original content she Posted on Facebook, using the analogy to demonstrate the malevolent, communist nature of the EU. In an interview, she explained, "[In *The Hunger Games*] there was a parasitic elite, living a great life, [. . .] and then each section [. . .] was devoted to industry or farming or growing or cattle, but the people in these areas were poor, they had nothing. That's the only way the EU will go. If it survives. Because it's communist. And communism doesn't work."

The extremely bleak future painted by Eileen's analogy dramatizes the narrative of the EU's federalist agenda, casting it as a conflict between good and evil. According to the narratives circulating in the pro-Brexit Facebook milieu, the motivations of the EU were not simply at odds with what was best for the UK, but were fundamentally sinister. Importantly, the EU's purported ambitions were not separate from those of the Left in Britain. In a long text-based Facebook Post she had authored herself, Eileen wrote:

PEOPLE ARE NOW AFRAID, WHO DO THEY TURN TO?

> To governments that are not listening because they are too wrapped up with their own migrant long term agenda, I don't think so.
>
> Most people are not 'Far' anything they are centrists stalked by Marxists [. . .]
>
> Yes some of you still don't see the connection with this indifference to national needs, and the onslaught of a communist style regime.
>
> WE are permanently being bullied into feeling ashamed to question the intent and outcome of recent manipulated events. [. . .]
>
> Merkel is one of the most unpopular leaders but still rules the EU behind the scenes. [. . .]
>
> The Euro has nearly achieved its goal of bringing European wages down to Eastern European levels. [. . .]
>
> The EU is a counterfeit utopia designed to keep the wealth with the rich. [. . .]
>
> Welcome to the Hunger Games.

Here, Eileen connects the alleged communist aspirations of the EU to corruption, poverty of the masses, and migration. Her claim that "most people" are "centrists stalked by Marxists [. . .] being bullied into feeling ashamed" is emblematic of the depiction of the EU as in cahoots with the political correctness agenda of the Left, which victimized anyone who did not agree.

As compared with other left-wing actors in society, the threat of communism from the EU was conceptualized as more of a tangible one. It was focused not on subversion via brainwashing the masses, but on the use of military power to implement economic communism among members states and subjugating the people of Europe, in narratives and imagery that invoked the specter of the First and Second World Wars, and the brutality of the Nazi regime in particular. The concreteness of this aspect of the leftist threat empowered the dramaturgy and sense of urgency in the broader pro-Brexit Facebook metanarrative expounded in chapter 3.

The contrast between this communist depiction of the EU and the reality of its neoliberal foundations (Duman 2014; Hermann 2007; Souliotis and Alexandri 2017) is telling of the power of the communist bogeyman within the milieu. It is also telling of the influence of narratives propagated by the Alt-Right in the transnational right-wing populist sphere at the time. During the post-referendum negotiation period, this movement had begun to target the EU, even accusing the union of being Cultural Marxist (de Bruin 2022). As the same movement that had been popularizing the Kalergi Plan form of the Great Replacement conspiracy theory (see chapter 3) online, delegitimizing the EU through accusations of "communism" is highly compatible with the Alt-Right's ideological agenda.

CONCLUSION: "THE LUNATICS HAVE TAKEN OVER THE ASYLUM"

In the pro-Brexit Facebook milieu, a variety of ideologically-driven narratives were being collectively constructed, continually reconstructed, subtly elaborated, and selectively employed by users to account for their support for Brexit and engagement with it online. Giving primacy to the accounts of the users and their own motivations has enabled this section to reveal the ideologies that resonated most with these individuals. It has uncovered the fact that it was not only racist appeals that drove engagement in the pro-Brexit Facebook milieu—anti-leftist appeals also played a major role. Indeed, attention to users' narratives illuminates the connections between these two types of ideology, as well as their links with other online milieus and mobilizations around the world.

The anti-leftism underpinning this milieu was the product of the ground laid by the moral panic of 1980s Britain, which made folk devils of the "loony left." During the post-referendum negotiation period, these devices resurfaced to target Jeremy Corbyn and the Labour Party that he and his support base were driving leftward. These representations were then capitalized upon by transnational far-right and right-wing populist movements seeking to disseminate their conspiracy theories to new audiences. The absorption of ideas like those underpinning the theory of Cultural Marxism played a significant role in propelling the pro-Brexit Facebook milieu into the transnational right-wing populist sphere online.

Like many of the anxieties around race examined in chapter 4, this anti-leftism often incorporated concerns that were removed from the milieu's ostensible focus on EU membership. A closer look, however, reveals the role that support for Brexit played in the development of the malevolent representations of the Left examined here. The focus on race and racism that UKIP injected into the Brexit debate in the lead-up to the referendum meant that some of the loudest pro-Remain voices, particularly on social media, were from the anti-racist Left. The remainder came from those focused on the economic side of the debate, represented by Britain's financial center, London. What was more, a clear parallel could be drawn between accusations of bigotry directed at Leavers in the lead-up to and aftermath of the referendum, and the increasingly sensitive nature of discussions around race and immigration. Thus, Remain's considerable overlap with the metropolitan Left, and the group's shock, disappointment at, and opposition to the Leave result, paved the way for "snowflake" style imagery to be used that borrowed from existing anti-left discourse. The stage was set for far-right, anti-left ideas circulating on social media to permeate the pro-Brexit Facebook milieu.

Afterall, it was the Left who, it appeared, were promoting immigration and multiculturalism, key agendas to which Brexit promised to put an end. But the threat from the Left did not stop there. Their difficult to comprehend deconstructions of gender binaries and heteronormativity seemed intent on controverting the values by which the pro-Brexit Facebook users lived. The sinister specter of "political correctness," posited as a tool of the Left's oppressive social control, appealed effectively to these users in part because of the threat it allegedly posed to liberal democracy through the "stifling" of free speech and therefore open debate. When movements like the Alt-Right claimed that the EU itself was intending to implement not only Cultural Marxism but economic communism, this threat was made all the more tangible. The signification spiral here led to the doom prophesized in the pro-Brexit Facebook metanarrative.

As detractors of progressive left-wing agendas, allegedly "silenced," "gagged," or wrongly accused of malevolence by the Left, the pro-Brexit Facebook users claimed to be the victims of oppression. In this way, they were able to assert not only a White victimhood, but what I have termed Right victimhood. The importance of this second form of phantom victimhood and its online dissemination in this period should not be understated, precipitating as it has Britain's post-pandemic "war on woke" (Davies and MacRae 2023) and the broadening global influence of the far-right's theory of Cultural Marxism. The analysis here reveals the importance of a suspicious anti-leftism that has not been documented in studies of offline pro-Brexit sentiment or everyday racism. It demonstrates the embeddedness of the pro-Brexit Facebook milieu within the transnational online right ecosystem, and illustrates the way that radical and conspiratorial ideas travel beyond the boundaries of the groups or movements where they originate to permeate right-wing populist milieus that coagulated around ostensibly "mainstream" concerns.

NOTE

1. Serving his first term as Mayor of London at the time of the fieldwork, Sadiq Khan is a Labour Party member of British-Pakistani heritage who is a practicing Muslim and was the target of considerable ire in the milieu.

SECTION III

Knowledge

Chapter 6

Brexit, Facebook, and Epistemic Battlegrounds

In 2016, "post-truth" was crowned Oxford Dictionaries Word of the Year. There it was defined as the privileging of emotion over reason or personal beliefs over "objective" facts (Flood 2016). Bearing in mind that year's political events, and those events' victors, it is clear to whom this term was referring. The EU referendum itself was depicted "as a battle between 'heads' and 'hearts,' reason and emotion" (Moss, Robinson, and Watts 2020, 837), in which it was Leave supporters who were characterized as hot-headed, irrational, and driven by emotions like nostalgia, nationalism, or xenophobia. This has not only been the case in popular discourse but also in academic analyses, with scholars like Campanella & Dassù (2019, 103) describing the decision to vote Leave as "def[ying] any rational cost–benefit analysis" and "fundamentally irrational [in] nature."

Such discourse is tied up with a growing global awareness of the problem of dis- and misinformation (Hall, Chadwick, and Vaccari 2023). At the same time as Russian disinformation was implicated in Trump's election to the U.S. presidency (Intelligence Community Assessment 2017), the UK saw accusations that many of the Leave campaign's messages—such as claims about EU bans on bent bananas and the financial benefits of leaving the EU—had been false or misleading. As Carl et al. (2019, 90) note of the referendum, "there has been considerable debate about whether voters (particularly Leave voters) were well informed prior to making their decision."

The pro-Brexit Facebook users were clearly aware of these discourses, and this shaped the way they engaged with pro-Leave and other right-wing content online. This final section of the book is dedicated to examining the milieu's relationship with knowledge—broadly construed to encompass ideas of truth, facts, and information—and the role this played in online political engagement there. As we saw in chapter 5, these users' political engagement was partly driven by a strong sense of Right victimhood that was closely related to their pro-Brexit stances. The analysis reveals that this had an important impact on how they related to knowledge. These users sought to assert their epistemic capital (Maton 2003) in order to reclaim a stake in political knowledge production and subvert what they saw as a pro-left regime of truth (Foucault 1976). This effort both drew on and empowered a broader transnational movement within online right-wing populism toward weaponizing "facts" as part of a contemporary struggle for cultural hegemony.

RATIONALITY, EMOTION, AND POLITICAL ENGAGEMENT

The abovementioned post-truth is one of the most influential concepts used to characterize support for Brexit and other racist and right-wing populist causes (Boler and Davis 2018; Marshall and Drieschova 2018; Rose 2017; D. Sayer 2017). The concept presents a binary opposition between "emotion" and "reason" (Durnová 2019), and it is argued that the growing role of social media in news and information consumption is contributing to this (Marshall and Drieschova 2018). Scholars commenting on the role of social media and the internet in the rise of right-wing populist and nativist politics have even claimed that "we now live in a post-truth world, where emotions and beliefs trump evidence-based arguments" (Cosentino 2020), or "modern rationality has been dangerously discarded and replaced by a strange form of powerful irrationality" (Overell and Nicholls 2019, vii). The idea that emotion and reason are distinct and competing may resonate with common conceptions of how these two forces operate. But to what extent does this reflect the reality of political engagement?

In fact, emotionality and rationality should be understood as interacting, rather than mutually exclusive (Ahmed 2014; Durnová 2019). It was Raymond Williams (1977, 132) who aptly observed that it is "not feeling against thought, but thought as felt and feeling as thought." Insights from affective intelligence theory have demonstrated how emotions like anxiety, anger, and hope are key determinants of which information we choose to inform our decision-making (Marcus 2003). Kevin McDonald (2018, 166) notes in his seminal volume on online radicalization, "In order to be able to believe certain things, we have to be able to feel certain things," and in this way our experience of the world is always both "sensuous-emotional" and "intellectual." That is, emotions should be understood not as in direct contention with reason or rationality, but as constituting "a form of human reasoning" (Mizen 2015, 168). They are an integral part of how we make judgments about matters that affect ourselves and those we care about, including decisions about politics (A. Sayer 2011; Wahl-Jorgensen 2019).

Post-truth's popularity as a concept is rooted in the Le Bon-esque idea of "the unreason of the masses" and the incapacity of ordinary people to stand back and engage with "the facts" (Walkerdine 2020, 146). The attribution of recent democratic political outcomes to the vice of illegitimate emotionality is based on a prevailing notion that political communication is "chiefly a conduit for factual information" (Musolff 2017, 642) and "liberal democracy [is] governed via modes of regulation in which reasoning or being reasonable win the day" (Walkerdine 2020, 146). This, however, does not reflect reality. Rather, as Moss and colleagues (2020) point out, it is based on an emotional regime (Reddy 2001) that governs what is seen as legitimate forms of political engagement. Emotion is understood as a dangerous source of irrational voting behavior that has no place in formal politics. Popular understandings construct emotion and reason as competing in a zero-sum game, despite the two being inextricably linked (Moss, Robinson, and Watts 2020, 851). However, these understandings are also imbued with new epistemic norms that have emerged from a growing public awareness of the problem of misinformation, whereby nominally "objective" and hyper-critical stances toward the media are valorized (Hall, Chadwick, and Vaccari 2023).

Of course, support for Brexit is inarguably underpinned by particular emotions. The passionate users in this study are a prime example, and the preceding chapters of this book are full of testimonies of frustration, anger, disappointment, hope, fear, and even hate. Multiple empirical studies have demonstrated the role that emotions played in voting decisions at the EU referendum, including evidence of a correlation between "negative emotional reactions" to the EU and voting to Leave (H. D. Clarke, Goodwin, and Whiteley 2017), a correlation between "negative emotions" and Euroscepticism (Verbalyte and Scheve 2018), and a stronger correlation between anger toward the EU and wanting to Leave, compared with anxiety (Vasilopoulou and Wagner 2017). On social media, Rosa and Ruiz (2020) demonstrated how in the final weeks before the referendum, tweets by key political actors that appealed to emotions or debased opposing views generated the most engagement. Hobolt and colleagues (2020) also identify an "affective polarization" between Leavers and Remainers that was engendered by the referendum debate and has drawn new and lasting boundaries of political identification that are emotionally loaded.

However, this is not evidence that the preponderance of emotionality in politics is new to a recent "post-truth" age. Politics are unlikely to have somehow become more emotional since 2016, emotions being a historically well-evidenced political motivator (Ahmed 2014). Anger, for example, is described by Wahl-Jorgensen (2019, 169) as "the essential political emotion" because it "energizes groups of individuals toward a collective response to shared grievances." Rather, it is more likely that "there has been a shift in awareness of emotion as a determining factor" (Boler and Davis 2018, 75). Such a shift could be seen as an attempt to make sense of recent gains made by racism, nativism, cultural conservatism, and economic isolationism—which appear to liberal or globally minded commentators as irrational reversals of progressive developments that are seen by these commentators as universally "good." In this sense, the rise of the term "post-truth" in itself illustrates the rift between two competing visions for society. Issues like Brexit and Trumpism have become proxies for this rift in public life.

A second key facet of the post-truth concept as it is understood by social scientists is the indeterminability of truth. This is often presented as inextricable from—or is even conflated with—the above-described supposed new prominence of emotionality in politics. In the post-truth age, according to theorists, claims to objective truth have been "devalued" (d'Ancona 2017; in Marshall and Drieschova 2018, 91) and "the distinction between truth and falsehood has become irrelevant" (Kalpokas 2019, 9). This is of course underpinned by concern over the rise of right-wing populist politicians, such as Donald Trump and Boris Johnson, whose demonstrably poor record for truthfulness did not seem to dampen their electoral success (Judge 2022; Kellner 2018; McGranahan 2017; Oborne 2021). But as Laybats and Tredinnick (2016, 204) point out, "this is not the first time in which the value of truth has been put under question." The philosopher whose work is often drawn upon by recent post-truth theorists, Jean Baudrillard, actually heralded the "destruction" of meaning more than forty years ago (Baudrillard 1981). Furthermore, the problem of "fake news" is an age-old one, demonstrated for example in the "loony left" myths propagated by Britain's right-wing press in the 1980s (see chapter 5).

The conditions for this relativization of truth are seen as inhering in social media's ability to spread dis- and misinformation (e.g., Marshall and Drieschova 2018), in mediatization more broadly (e.g., Kalpokas 2019), in postmodernism's rejection of absolute truth (e.g., Cosentino 2020; cf. Fischer 2019), or in a purported growing distrust in institutions of authority and expert knowledge (e.g., Marshall and Drieschova 2018). In particular, the latter has often been used as evidence that Brexit defied rationality. A broader trend of declining trust in institutions and media allowed the referendum result to be characterized as a "revolt against 'expertise'" (J. Clarke and Newman 2017, 110). This is infamously exemplified by Leave campaigner Michael Gove's assertion in a Sky News interview in the lead-up to the referendum that "we have had enough of experts' (Ryan 2020). Although the quote is commonly truncated as such, Gove's comment in full was "the people of this country have had enough of experts from organizations with acronyms saying they know what is best *and getting it consistently wrong*" (emphasis added) and was a reference in particular to the failings of economists to predict or prevent the 2008 global financial crisis (Lowe 2016). What this full and contextualized quote demonstrates is not necessarily a propensity to privilege emotions over rationality or facts, but rather a populist rejection of the kind of expertise on offer from a perceived elite political establishment, based on a sense that this expertise was not only flawed but also condescending, and did not reflect the lived realities of "the people." Moreover, these feelings did not suddenly emerge in 2016. As Clarke and Newman (2017) argue, a challenge to the "'depoliticizing' consequences of technocratic governance" brought about by Tony Blair's Labour government (1997–2007) and its "third way" was "appropriated and mobilized to support a new populist project, here being articulated through a binary between expertise and the wisdom of the people" (ibid., 111).

Situating the epistemic foundations of support for Brexit within the context of populist appeals enables a more nuanced understanding that transcends the post-truth binary between emotion and reason. Populism like that mobilized in the Leave campaign, has long had a fraught relationship with expertise. A history of anti-intellectualism and the valorizing of common sense are well-known tenets of populism and compatible with its emphasis on anti-elitism (Wodak 2015, 22). The term "epistemological populism" has even been coined to refer to manifestations of populism that focus on disparaging elite knowledge (Saurette and Gunster 2011). This sort of populism is well captured in the assertion by pro-Brexit Labour MP Gisela Stuart during the referendum campaign that "There is only one expert that matters and that's you, the voter" (in J. Clarke and Newman 2017, 111).

However, this is complicated by Ylä-Anttila's (2018, 358) analysis, which asserts that such reverence of common sense is characteristic only of traditional "rural" forms of populism. Meanwhile, he contends, contemporary right-wing populism may be more likely to champion not emotion or common sense but "facts," expertise, and evidence, in the form of "counter-knowledge." This is defined as "alternative knowledge which challenges establishment knowledge, replacing knowledge authorities with new ones, thus providing an opportunity for political mobilisation" (ibid., 359). Ylä-Anttila applies the concept to Finnish anti-immigrant groups online and observes that the activists there advocate not common sense, but "a particular kind of *objectivist* counter-expertise" (ibid., 357, emphasis added). "[P]rofessing strictly positivist views, and strongly opposing ambivalent or relativist truth orientations" these groups "often employ 'scientific' language and engage in popularisation of scientific knowledge and rhetoric" (ibid., 358). In fact, these groups characterized their *opponents* as driven by emotions rather than "facts"—"[f]or them, it is the 'multiculturalist elite' who are 'post-truth'" (ibid., 357–358).

In other words, Ylä-Anttila's findings directly challenge claims by post-truth theorists that online right-wing populism prioritizes emotions over facts and renders the distinction between fact and fiction irrelevant. In fact, scholars are beginning to recognize a trend within online right-wing spaces toward rhetoric that reveres facticity and objectivity. In these spaces, "leftist" epistemic authority is challenged, with "post-positivist" social science blamed for "'distorted,' 'subjective' and 'biased' views on truth" (Ylä-Anttila 2018, 369). This is epitomized in the way popular Alt-Right intellectual Jordan Peterson publicly "battles" leftists in viral online videos, constructing himself as calm and reasonable and his opponents as ideological and emotionally vulnerable "snowflakes" (Nicholls 2019). In Nicholls' (2019, 63) analysis, Peterson's "dispassionate performance sets the voice of reason up in a binary relationship against the emotional, passionate postmodern other." Similarly, Facebook-based "anti-vax" movements, which in Covid-19 times have been affiliated with and capitalized upon by the online far-right, evidence their position by citing scientific studies and challenging the mainstream media's own objectivity (Berriche 2021).

Hong and Hermann (2020) have demonstrated a contemporary trend for popular "microinfluencers" in the right-wing online milieu to weaponize "fact signaling" to build effective solidarity. This is defined as "the performative invocation of the idea of Fact and Reason, distinct from the concrete presentation of evidence or reasoning" (ibid., 1). In other words, online performances by right-wing actors appeal to the notion of objectively undeniable "facts" like "a man is a man and a woman is a woman" in order to dismiss progressive and left-wing cultural claims, and create a sense of legitimacy for, and affective community around, the "traditional values" they promote. This trend is also embodied in the burgeoning industry of right-wing alternative news and information sites that now exist. As noted in chapter 5, these sites challenge the authority of the mainstream media through criticism of its content and motives, and use populist appeals to emphasize their own knowledge, experience, and positions of victimhood (Figenschou and Ihlebæk 2019). Online alternative news and information outlets, popular among distrusting and disenchanted right-wing citizens (Thorbjørnsrud and Figenschou 2022) cater to, and in turn propagate, this notion that the (allegedly left-leaning) mainstream media are withholding information in order to control people's opinions (Holt 2019). Paternotte and Verloo (2021, 556) characterize these alternative information trends as a deliberate attempt by right-wing actors to dismantle existing institutions of knowledge production. They identify the theory of Cultural Marxism (discussed in chapters 3 and 5) as a "diagnosis and prognosis frame" used by these actors. The effectiveness of such devices on individual social media users engaging in these right-wing spheres has yet to be examined.

In the case of Brexit supporters, there was arguably a particular sensitization to the importance of self-presentation as "factual" and rational because of the high profile of representations of this group as emotionally-charged and irrational. Indeed, Remainer respondents to a Mass Observation Archive directive around Brexit "often portrayed Leave voters as uneducated, either unwilling or unable to understand and engage with expert arguments, and therefore more susceptible to lies" (Moss, Robinson, and Watts 2020, 847). These recriminations were being played out at the forefront of national media, Brexit being a dominant news issue throughout the negotiation period. Accusations of racism served to heighten sensitivities, as "racism and legitimacy are conventionally treated as mutually exclusive terms in a zero-sum game" (Mintchev 2021, 126). Mintchev argues that these connotations mean such accusations are experienced as performative, adversarial acts of delegitimation and discrediting that prompt "equally performative responses" in defense of one's legitimacy (ibid.). These sensitivities have been exacerbated by "a culture of political frustration and mutual recrimination between Leave and Remain supporters" (Mintchev 2021, 125; see also Mintchev and Moore 2019; Tyler, Degnen, and Blamire 2022). The framing of Brexit as not only racist but economically reckless added to the moralization of these discourses and raised the stakes for deflecting such accusations. Moreover, Brexit was a particularly contested "truth" space in this period because the United Kingdom had yet to leave the EU. Public discourse about Brexit thus centered on Leave and Remain camps' conflicting "predictions" of what the consequences of leaving would look like, from an exodus of manufacturing, global finance businesses, and unprecedented economic instability, to £350 million per week of additional funds for building and staffing Britain's hospitals (see Zappettini 2019).

Within this contested space, knowledge was treated by pro-Brexit Facebook users as a valuable resource and weapon. As I will demonstrate in this chapter, these users sought to lay claim to political truth in the name of their conservative and nationalist values, to challenge the perceived regime of truth (Foucault 1976) in politics. However, as "Brexiteers," their legitimacy to do so—their epistemic capital (Maton 2003)—had been revoked. According to the contemporary emotional regime of politics, this emotional and irrational group did not have a legitimate claim to epistemic authority. In the following sections, I will demonstrate how these individuals sought to reclaim this epistemic capital by asserting their reverence of objective "facts" and constructing their opponents—Remainers and "lefties"—as emotional, irrational, and fact-less. In this as yet overlooked relationship with knowledge lies a mechanism crucial to understanding motivations for engaging in the pro-Brexit Facebook milieu.

KNOWLEDGE REVERENCE IN THE
PRO-BREXIT FACEBOOK MILIEU

I will begin by demonstrating the value that was placed on finding and Sharing knowledge, and knowledge for knowledge's sake, in the pro-Brexit Facebook milieu. Interviews and immersive, qualitative observations in this study indicated that users were intensely preoccupied with knowledge. As discussed in chapter 2, for them the "point" of using social media was to find and share information. In interviews, these individuals spent significant time and energy talking about the facts and "truths" they had discovered through their online engagement. Some users, such as Jessica (40s, female, London), Neil (70s, male, South Wales), Eileen (60s, female, Northwest England), and Olivia (50s, female, Southeast England), were so passionate about these discoveries that they divulged this information at length unprompted—one question from me about their use of Facebook could prompt a fifteen minute monologue about the EU or Islam. These users' eagerness to share such detailed accounts illustrated not only their desire to justify their political stances, but also their passion for uncovering "truths" and sharing these with others. In Kirk's (60s, male, London) words, "It's just education. Any education's good."

Facebook posts in the milieu were also awash with "facts" and figures. Olivia said that the reason she chose to Share videos rather than images on Facebook was strategic: in her view, "you can't tell a story from a picture [...] and you can't see the facts." One of Helen's (50s, female, West Midlands) Facebook Posts was a screenshot of a tweet by Conservative MP David Davis. Davis had resigned as Secretary of State for Exiting the European Union in July 2018 in protest over then Prime Minister Theresa May's "soft" Brexit plans. This combined with his critical stance toward the BBC (deemed an enemy of Brexit, see chapter 5) meant he was broadly considered an ally in the pro-Brexit Facebook milieu. In the tweet, Davis raised the issue of the BBC's planned scrapping of free TV licenses for over-seventy-fives, deliberately using "hard" facts and figures to evidence his argument that this policy was unfair and hypocritical. He gave a figure for the "average weekly income" of over-seventy-fives, claimed one-fifth of this group was living "below the poverty line," and compared this with a figure claimed to be the annual income the outlet paid some of its performers.

Eileen's primarily self-authored Posts were also commonly designed to convey these sort of "facts." In one post, she claimed that "1 in 5 people arrested in Britain are foreign nationals" and that a "crime tourism" suspect was "arrested every 3 minutes." In her interviews, Eileen criticized Katie Hopkins, "Tommy Robinson," Raheem Kassam, and similar online right-wing microinfluencers for prioritizing "growing" their brands and generating income over informing the public. She contrasted this behavior with her own attitude toward Sharing on Facebook: "[People]'re following you cos they want to know if you've got any information for them. [. . .] I'm not interested in me getting my way. I'm interested in other people making a choice from an informed platform. That's the difference."

The preparation for the pro-Brexit demonstration that Beatrice (60s, female, North Wales) was undertaking at the time of our second interview (see chapter 1) was also demonstrative: she was creating flyers filled with facts and figures gathered from Facebook content. This included the percentage of pro-Brexit guests on the BBC's Andrew Marr and Sunday politics shows compared with anti-Brexit guests, and supposedly damning details about the "UN Migration Pact" (see chapter 4). She hoped to distribute these flyers to passers-by at the demonstration in order to spread the word. As discussed in chapter 1, Beatrice had made it her "mission" to warn people about the supposed threats facing Britain and the British people.

Illustrated here is the sense that the more these users and their allies could collectively learn, the better they felt they could equip themselves and others against nefarious forces. It was for this reason that Eileen attested she was happy to admit when she had been mistaken and to clarify the truth for her followers. Similarly, Jessica said that within the milieu, when a previously Shared piece of information was found to have been false, users were keen to call this out, because "we've gotta keep on track here—only the truth has gotta come out." Neil said he always encouraged friends online to "expand your brain. Expand your knowledge." When asked in an interview whether ignorance might be preferable to discovering distressing truths about things like purported globalist plans to exterminate 90 percent of the Earth's population, he answered categorically in the negative: "These people are evil. [. . .] If you say 'well I don't want to know,' then don't be surprised if bad things happen. People need to know." This comment was illustrative of the characterization of truth and facts as weapons against the kind of oppression constructed in the metanarrative outlined in chapter 3.

In this way, an important part of challenging the dominant regime of truth and constructing their own epistemic capital was to assert that the "real" truth was being hidden by those in power. Within the covert plot of the metanarrative, the mainstream media and other institutions of authority were "continuing to lie to us" (Fred, 60s, male, Northeast England) or "omit information" (Neil). This meant that knowledge needed to be sought and uncovered by individuals who had to "find out for themselves" (Eileen). As discussed in chapter 2, with the advent of social media, Brexiteers could finally uncover these "truths," and social media was where these discoveries took place. As Beatrice said, social media was "the only way, fair way that you could actually [. . .] learn about stuff, find out what was really going on in the world."

Of course, given growing censorship of far-right and conspiracy-related content on Facebook and other social media platforms at the time, the pro-Brexit Facebook users were also aware that the knowledge they sought was becoming increasingly difficult to find. As Jessica put it, "What they're trying to do now is try to curb that information from being shared." Eileen also alluded to this difficulty when she said, "I'm just telling the truth, and not many people are."

CHALLENGING THE REGIME OF TRUTH

The pro-Brexit Facebook milieu's preoccupation with knowledge, seen for example in the Facebook Posts referred to above, demonstrates the central role of "hard" facts and figures in their efforts to evidence their political positions on Facebook. In this way, knowledge was not only a valuable resource to share with allies, but also a weapon in an epistemological struggle with their political opponents. The pro-Brexit Facebook users sought to challenge the perceived pro-Remain, left-wing regime of truth in politics, which they did not feel represented their interests or their understandings of the world.

In a comment already touched upon in chapter 1, Mark (50s, male, Yorkshire), for example, described his dismay at what he felt was Islamist-sympathizing coverage by the BBC: "I thought, 'this is not what I hear on the streets. This is not what I hear in the pubs. This is no way a reflection of any society I know.'" Mark's comment illustrates the sense of unjust exclusion from knowledge production that was a strong theme in the users' narratives. For Beatrice, this exclusion was embroiled in the deception by those in power, which added to Leavers' humiliation: "It's the lying and the, and by inference, [. . .] they are insulting my intelligence [. . .] I know you said *that* last week, now you're standing there and saying *this* this week. And [. . .] you're telling me that I'm uneducated and all the rest of it, [. . .] and [Remainers are] trying to fight for a second referendum because 'we didn't know what we were doing.' [. . .] I'm sorry, but I knew what I was doing!" (Beatrice's emphasis).

Comments like Beatrice's illustrate the awareness amongst the pro-Brexit Facebook users of their characterization as misinformed or ignorant. Part of their approach to rejecting this characterization was challenging the claims made by the Remain and left-wing camps, and this was played out in interactions on Facebook. As discussed in chapter 2, conflict with these groups was a central element of the users' online political engagement. This was illustrated in the language Carl (50s, male, Northwest England) used when he attested that the reason he liked to keep an eye on "the crap [the mainstream media] come out with" was "because I want to educate meself on what they're saying, so I can *defend* meself when they're saying it" (emphasis added). Debates about the benefits or consequences of leaving the European Union were particularly heated, and mutual understanding was often seen as futile. The argument that Lawrence (40s, male, West Midlands) had with his stepsister via Facebook which resulted in their estrangement (see chapter 2) was an example of this: "It was about the referendum. [. . .] 'We must remain, to help the NHS,' but it was like, but if we leave, we're saving 39 billion a year, and we can help put our NHS back where we need it and we govern our own NHS rather than the EU controlling everything. But she didn't see it that way."

Lawrence conflates here the 39 billion pound "divorce bill," a financial settlement negotiated by then-Prime Minister Theresa May that was highly publicized during the negotiation period, with the UK's annual contribution to the EU (estimated at net nine billion pounds) (Reality Check 2019). These figures were points of hot contention at the time, with Remainers disputing the validity of estimates or accusing them of being misleading (Kettell and Kerr 2021). To Lawrence and many in the pro-Brexit Facebook milieu, however, these inarguably vast sums represented hard proof of the benefits of leaving the EU and were employed frequently.

Eileen's Facebook activity was particularly focused on antagonistic encounters with the Remainer and left-wing opposition. During the fieldwork, she self-authored multiple Facebook Posts meant as cynical responses to Private Messages she had allegedly received from critics. The below example of an extract from one of these Posts alludes to the demeaning stereotypes that users felt were attributed to them by those on the opposite side of politics and particularly by young people. The Post also challenges the perceived claims to expertise of these opponents:

> Thanks for the message [. . .] and pointing out I'm a thick northerner, if you can't even accept me, someone from your own country who has a regional accent how come you welcome migrants? You say you have a degree! [. . .] We left school at 16 and became adults at 16 and three quarters [. . .] A gap year was usually had one week in July in Blackpool in a sea front hotel [. . .] Anyway I can't stay I'm just giving birth to my 14 illegitimate child, at the number 32 bus stop and I haven't got the right change I'm all fingers and thumbs and the heads out! [. . .] [sic] (Eileen's Facebook Timeline, original text Post)

Whether or not she actually sent these messages to the individuals in question is unclear, but to Eileen her victory was in publicly shaming her attackers. Eileen's sarcastic rejection of a representation of working-class Northerners as having large numbers of (potentially illegitimate) children alludes to the regionally classed nature of understandings of Remainer prejudices and of her own sense of being devalued within this. In response, Eileen employs alternative gendered and classed forms of respectability (Skeggs 1997) via a depiction of Northern women as responsible, hardworking and pragmatic.

George (70s, male, Northeast England) described a similar sense of being dismissed and patronized in an argument with a younger Remainer Facebook user:

> He was really getting abusive, you know, too much. Cos I just wouldn't agree with what he was saying. [. . .] It was all about Brexit, and it went on for a long time. And he has a view which is exactly opposite to mine, and because I'm older, he doesn't think older people should have the same sort of voting rights as younger people. [. . .] He was trying to use his accountancy knowledge to say how he was better informed than anybody else and when this friend of mine said "well, I'm in the same sort of job as you," he very quickly changed his tack.

These sort of heated disputes with Remainers over which side was "right" were a common experience in the milieu. In this anecdote, George rejects the interlocuter's claim to hold greater knowledge than Leavers, and portrays his unwarranted arrogance as having been caught red-handed. He also refers to the well-publicized age dimension to the Brexit vote, which prompted sensational claims by sections of the Left that older people should not be allowed to vote based on their being the least affected by electoral outcomes *and* because their views were imagined as too bigoted (Nast 2016; Schrieberg 2016). Such arguments illustrate how pro-Brexit Facebook users' feelings of marginalization from political knowledge production were also related to a more tangible threat of exclusion from democratic suffrage itself. In the face of these high stakes, the pro-Brexit Facebook users actively asserted their own epistemic capital, a strategy which I will turn to now.

ASSERTING AND RECLAIMING EPISTEMIC CAPITAL

As I will demonstrate in this section, the pro-Brexit Facebook users' reverence of knowledge and practices of engaging in arguments over the facts can also be understood as part of their attempts to assert their epistemic capital, something they felt had been revoked by delegitimizing characterizations of Brexiteers. One of the things that Fred Shared to Facebook during the fieldwork was a Post originally from a Public Page containing a link to a *Telegraph* news article entitled "Trading on World Trade Organisation terms offers the best Brexit deal" (Bootle 2018). It was accompanied by the following text (not a Comment added by Fred, but part of the original Post):

> The remainers really need to educate themselves.
>
> 90% of world economic growth is outside the EU
>
> 82% of the world GDP is outside the EU
>
> 60% of UK exports not to EU.
>
> Over 100 countries doing well outside the EU.
>
> Proving the 17.4 million voting to leave were cognizant of being outside the EU, without a deal, is our best option. [sic]

The above text focuses heavily on quantitative evidence, which is used to position a "no-deal" Brexit as irrefutably preferable. However, what becomes clear in the last line of the text is that this evidence is also intended to demonstrate the epistemological position of Brexit supporters. It seeks to refute an alluded-to characterization of this group as not having known what they voted for.

In the face of this characterization, the pro-Brexit Facebook users sought to claim epistemic capital. They performed their knowledge wealth in interviews and Facebook Posts, and constructed themselves as rational, objective beings who actively researched and verified information and thus were more informed than most. Carl and Jessica, for example, often asked me in interviews "Did you know *that*?" and Carl also said he prided himself on knowing "more [about Islam] than a lot of Muslims."

Users like Eileen and Olivia, who dedicated themselves to researching Brexit and Islam respectively (Olivia frequently referring to Islam as her "topic") were particularly proud of their knowledge. Each positioning themself as an authority on their subject matter, they described in interviews how even those with similar political views tended to be naïve, easily convinced by appealing manifestos or political promises. As noted in chapter 5, Eileen was able to recite almost word for word a quote attributed to a 1952 letter from Jean Monet that she claimed demonstrated the gradual and covert orchestration of a European superstate. She said, "An element of my Followers will trust what I say, because I save them having to do their research. I've done it all first. And because of a proven track record in not letting people down, they can afford to put their trust in me. [. . .] I'm on[line] every day doing this."

Deborah (50s, female, Northwest England) demonstrated a similar view when she spoke of altercations with her son-in-law. Alluding to a frustration at being talked down to by the opposition, she told me, "I spend a lot of time going into these issues, and I get quite annoyed when people that have only skimmed the surface try to inform me and tell me I'm wrong."

Part of these individuals' assertion of their epistemic capital was their claim to always "do their research." As touched upon in chapter 2, the users were adamant that they did not blindly believe everything they read, but rather investigated and verified claims online, particularly before Sharing content. Contrasting themselves with others online (particularly Remainers and those on the Left) the pro-Brexit Facebook users assured me they "try not to comment on something I know nothing about" but rather "usually investigate further" (George). Mark insisted, "I'll always research things. I don't just blindly put things on." This was ordinarily a case of utilizing search engines like Google as a starting point to "seek to validate [information] by going on to other places and following other leads" described by Neil as doing "due diligence." Other methods of verifying information included enquiring with a reputable "source" (Eileen) or relative (Audrey, 50s, female, Northwest England), or in Isaac's (50s, male, Northwest England) case Posting the content to his Wall and waiting for "friends that are that big a spotters" to discredit it. The users generally professed an awareness that there was "an awful lot of fake news out there" (Neil) and were adamant that "I don't believe them all" (Kirk).

As noted in chapter 2, these claims to "do their research" may seem to contradict the individuals' own descriptions of their passive information-seeking practices on Facebook. However, they did not necessarily claim to seek information from a range of sources in the first instance, but rather to verify the information that they encountered on the Facebook platform. It should also be noted that narratives around practices did not always reflect reality. In some cases there were direct and obvious contradictions, within the same interview, between statements like "I always check before I Post things on" and admissions that a Post "was one of those things I didn't have a chance to research [because] there was so many other things going on" (Neil). Ontological narratives (see Somers 1994, 618) about research-driven objectivity were also overshadowed by some instances of quite easily falsifiable "fake news" that I observed being Shared. This is not necessarily surprising as online misinformation involves variegated and sophisticated deceptions that may render any individual vulnerable (Chadwick and Stanyer 2022). What is important here is these users' assertion of their identity as savvy information seekers.

These claims to "do their own research" also reflect a popular refrain within the broader, transnational online right. Similar attitudes were expressed, for example, by respondents in Pilkington's (2020, 128) ethnographic study of far-right street movements when speaking about their online activities. The refrain is also reminiscent of attitudes in conspiracy milieus (Buzzell and Rini 2022; Marwick and Partin 2022). However, this "act of epistemic superheroism" (Buzzell and Rini 2022) is to some extent a product of the contemporary condition of society in which we all not only contend with an overwhelming volume of information, but do so in an "adversarial information environment" where the normative concept of epistemic virtue is "implausibly individualistic" (ibid., 1). Indeed, determining fact from fiction was portrayed as an active and individual process by the pro-Brexit Facebook users; as Isaac said, "I just like gathering information in and then I make me own mind up." These neoliberal norms of information seeking are reflected in the emergent epistemic norms mentioned above (Hall, Chadwick, and Vaccari 2023) and their relationship to the emotional regime surrounding political engagement.

The pro-Brexit Facebook users appeared to be aware of these norms. Finding things out for oneself and coming to one's own conclusions in an informed and rational manner was not just a self-characterized attitude, but was encouraged and expected of others. As Carl assured me, "Anything to do with the 'religion-of-not-peace' [. . .] I always say, 'research it yourself first.'" Similarly, Neil stressed that when he Posted content he always reminded people "Don't just take my word for it." Both Neil and Jessica also attributed their interest in QAnon (see chapter 1) to the way its curator (known as "Q") "tells you to go and investigate for yourself" (Jessica). Eileen, although priding herself on providing her Followers with information, attested that part of her mission was "encouraging people above all else to research stuff before they just Share the tripe that comes up on Facebook."

These normative expectations signal the value the users in this milieu claimed to place on rationality and objectivity, and in itself contributes to their assertion of epistemic capital. According to their ontological narratives, for the users to believe something, there needed to be proof. Mark explained that his inclination to defend figures like Jacob Rees Mogg, "Tommy Robinson," and Nigel Farage from accusations of unsavory character was based on not being able to find sufficient evidence to support such claims online:

> Where's the evidence for all this? [. . .] I won't just turn round and say somebody is this and somebody is that because they don't believe the same thing as me. [. . .] If people are gunna start labelling somebody I want to know why they're labelling em [. . .] and, as far as I can see and as far as my recent looking on Facebook and things like that and looking on Google, the man [Farage] has never directly came out and said anything he shouldn't.

While the motives behind such accusations by the left were also the object of criticism, Mark explicitly accounted for his own assessment on the basis of what was considered rational, factual research. Mark used the same logic in his defense of "Tommy Robinson," saying that while "the man's name's tarnished, [. . .] I'm also not gunna go and say he's an evil man unless I find evidence that he is evil. I can't find it." By his second interview, Mark had "done quite a bit of looking him up" and conceded "the jury's still out."

However, he defended "Robinson" at length, pointing to how the activist had apologized for things he had said in the past, and sympathizing with him for being shouted down and called names by the media. This incident highlights the importance Mark claimed to place on "evidence" and doing one's own research. It also reveals how, even if he was not sure whether he liked or agreed with "Robinson," what Mark purported to disagree with most were the Left's personal, allegedly baseless attacks on him. This representation of the Left as morally repugnant, explored in chapter 5, was reinforced by the epistemic norms asserted by users, as I will explore in the next section.

CHALLENGING OPPONENTS' EPISTEMIC CAPITAL

A key way in which the pro-Brexit Facebook users constructed themselves as holders of epistemic capital was by creating a binary with Remainers and "lefties," who were portrayed as lacking this form of credibility. That is, to reject their own characterization as irrational dupes, the users threw these accusations back at their opponents, representing them as irrational "snowflakes" who had been duped by "Project Fear," did not want to face the facts, or were too emotional and easily offended. For instance, Fred told of how his sister had switched from a pro-Remain to a pro-Leave position based on new information she had learned after the referendum: "My sister was absolutely adamant that she wanted to stay in the EU. Absolutely no question about it—she would not be turned. Now she has, because she's seen the facts that have come out. She's realized the lies that she was told."

Fred's description intimates his perceptions of the Remain camp: Remainers were "misinformed, or they've accepted what the media have told them instead of checking their facts out." Thus, contrary to mainstream media portrayals, in this account it was Leavers who held "the facts." In Fred's analysis, "I try to be reasonable and put forward a structured argument, [. . .] but they, perhaps just they don't have an argument to put back [so] they turn to abuse."

As noted above, much of the contestation over Brexit during the fieldwork period revolved around predicting the consequences of leaving the EU. Accusations of irresponsibility and irrationality leveled at Leavers by Remainers were often justified using economic arguments of hardship that would be inflicted on hard-working families and free-movement rights lost for children (Zappettini 2019). These predictions were dubbed "Project Fear" in the milieu to construct them as a form of emotionally-manipulative propaganda. The Remain camp, it was argued, was lying or grasping at straws, because there was no way to determine what would happen in the unprecedented post-Brexit future. In other words, users challenged Remainers' power to produce this particular knowledge, based on the assertion that no one actually had claim to it. As George said about the exchange rate, "The fact is it's been fluctuating for years. [...] You can't just blame Brexit. [...] It could be anything." Similarly, Mark claimed, "The Remain people are just all over the place. They'll talk about car crashes and falling over cliffs and things like that. [...] Nobody can tell what the future's gonna hold."

Remainers and those on the left were also portrayed as actively ignoring the facts, privileging instead emotions in their politics. About her conflicts over what she claimed were violent teachings of Islam, Jessica said, "So, there's a lot of people that still don't want to face the facts. [...] I'm just telling you the facts of what [the Quran] says." Here there is no room for subjectivity when it comes to the truth: facts are facts and Remainers and "lefties" need only accept them. Olivia echoed this when she relayed an encounter she had with an acquaintance, Ted,[1] who she described as "incredibly opinionated" and "not prepared to discuss or debate anything." At a gathering of friends, the topic of Brexit came up, and Ted was passionately disagreeing with another individual's pro-Leave position, "f-ing and blinding screaming and shouting at [the other man]." Olivia intervened and told him,

> "You have to look at the evidence." I said, "I'm not interested in opinions. I'm only ever interested in the evidence. [...] The evidence is there." [...] But he's one of these people that seems to be so brainwashed [...] that he wasn't prepared, Natalie, to listen or even read the actual facts. [...] I said "well you give me one good reason." [...] He wasn't *able* to give a reason [...] and I said, "and however I voted is irrelevant. [...] It's factual whether you like it or not, Ted, this is the biggest vote in history." [...] Then, of course, he came out with the usual diatribe, didn't he? "Oh, people don't know what they were voting for." What, 17 and a half million of them?! [laughs]

In this anecdote, Olivia simultaneously constructs herself as evidence-based, factual and unbiased, while depicting Ted as emotional, fact-less, and ridiculous, able only to repeat meaningless slogans. This was summarized well by Helen when she said, "Brexiteers are far more informed and [...] less emotional. It's almost as if the people that want to remain are having some kind of tantrum."

Contrary to claims in the post-truth literature, the pro-Brexit Facebook users derided emotionality and called for *more* facticity. For instance, Deborah criticized journalists for having become "far too opinionated. [...] To me a journalist should be there to observe and report, but they're not anymore." Some users made reference to anti-racist challenges to traditionally accepted historical narratives and, typical of racist and right-wing populist discourses, presented these as ignoring or attempting to change the facts of history itself (e.g., Walker, Topping, and Morris 2020). Such controversy had particularly come to the fore since the "Unite the Right" rally held in Charlottesville, Virginia, against the removal of a statue of a Confederate general in August 2017 (Winter 2017). Such issues were used to construct those on the left as irrational, ridiculous, ignorant, and even hateful. As Neil said, "You can't pretend it never happened."

These narratives use a post-racial frame to deny racist and colonial histories (Joseph-Salisbury 2019). However, to the individuals in the milieu, it was anti-racism that was "destroying [. . .] history statues and history" and ignorant of the "facts": "[if] you read back into it, it's only gone on for, they've only had that statue for 200 years or something, 100 years, you know" (Isaac). These strategies are used broadly by the online right; in Joseph-Salisbury's (2019) analysis of the online backlash to a piece he wrote that challenged the glorification of Winston Churchill, he demonstrates the way in which he as the author was portrayed by online commenters as racist, pathologically confused, unintelligent, and motivated by emotions such as jealousy and intolerance.

While accusations in the pro-Brexit Facebook milieu generally centered on such epistemic arguments, Mark's narrative below hints at how this was simultaneously a matter of defending national pride and identity:

> "Oh, colonialists," as if it's some really bad thing and everything about the British was, has been awful and shocking and terrible. [. . .] Well actually I'm quite proud that it was us [that] had an empire [. . .] cos if it hadn't have been the British Empire it woulda been the French empire or the Spanish empire. [. . .] If there'd never been any empires in the whole wide world, brilliant, that's even better, but there's always gunna be empires, or there's always been empires. We just happened to have the biggest empire in the world. [. . .] What was right then might not be right now. But don't say that that's a disgrace and belittle it [. . .] because it's not a disgrace. It's not.

Mark clearly did not want to have the version of history he cherished discarded. Like many users, his perceived exclusion (or the exclusion of what he saw as the ignored majority group to which he belonged) from decisions about historical and other forms of knowledge was a source of dismay. Mark's narrative also reflects the romanticization of the empire by the Leave campaign and the imputed specter of its revival post-Brexit (Virdee and McGeever 2018). His privileging of identity demonstrates the way in which these individuals' claims of being entirely rational and factual were not always consistent with the values that they emphasized, a point I will return to later. More importantly, however, it illustrates the way in which claims to knowledge were tied up with pride and the experience of status loss, which went to the heart of the milieu's quest to reclaim epistemic capital.

RECONCILING "HARD FACTS" WITH "COMMON SENSE"

In Ylä-Anttila's (2018) study of Posts in Finnish online anti-immigration forums (see above)—much like the claims to revere and to be the bearers of knowledge within the pro-Brexit Facebook milieu—there was a strong emphasis on "knowledge" based frames. Meanwhile, frames dealing with experiential knowledge or "common sense" that are prominent in more traditional forms of epistemological populism were not present. Ylä-Anttila characterizes this shift in epistemic emphasis as a feature of contemporary right-wing populism. Given the prominence of objectivist claims in the pro-Brexit Facebook milieu, we might assume the same absence of appeals to "common sense" or what is sometimes referred to in the study of epistemological populism as "folk wisdom," but was this actually the case?

In fact, despite professing to be objective and revere evidence, the pro-Brexit Facebook users indicated that they also valued "common sense" in making determinations about truth, sometimes even using "common sense" to justify their positions and argue against the legitimacy of their opponents. As Neil told me, "To know which path to take, which one to believe, who to follow, [. . .] that's something that comes with time, with experience, and from common sense." Kirk also exemplified this when speaking in an interview about a Post he had written rejecting the way the media was attributing job losses at Nissan to Brexit; given the direction of the automobile industry more broadly, he explained, "My common sense tells me it's not right."

Unfortunately, in users' perceptions of left-wing-driven politics today, common sense was a resource in short supply. Much like knowledge and rationality, this was constructed as something that users and their allies had, while "lefties" and Remainers did not. Isaac, for instance, expressed his exasperation with protracted Brexit negotiations which he believed should have been simple: "They wanna trade with us, we wanna trade with them. Businesses wanna trade. It's only the politicians that are pissing about basically. [. . .] What's the hassle?" In fact, in users' views there were a range of issues that could be solved with common sense—a form of knowledge held by "ordinary" people, not by experts. For instance, immigration: "I mean, if you're gunna let too many people in your country and you don't vet them, [. . .] what are they gunna do?" (Carl); social media censorship: "Well obviously there are certain terms that are derogatory. And I think most people know what those are" (Deborah); and global poverty, "What would work is send some people over to Africa, put some coffee processing plants up, [. . .] give them some actual work [. . .] [instead] Angela Merkel invites a load of people, the bitch, and what does she know?" (Eileen).

Users also frequently drew on analogies that spoke to a sort of folk wisdom in order to account for their positions. As Kirk explained regarding calls for a second referendum on Brexit, "It's like the Ryder Cup. [. . .] If America beat us by half a point and took the Ryder Cup off us, and we all went, 'oh no, so close [. . .] we wanna do that again,' you can't at the Ryder Cup. [. . .] They won, and that's it—[even] by the smallest margin, it's a win. But I think [it's] because [Remainers] ain't got any common sense."

Alongside such analogies, users also frequently extrapolated from anecdotal evidence, including from content they encountered on social media and from their own experiences. For instance, Kirk referred to an incident in which a young girl "got stabbed somewhere" in the UK and said "The guy was from, not Moldovia [sic] or, or some country out there. [. . .] If he wasn't in the country she'd still be alive. Simple plain fact. So immigration ain't great." Accounting for her opposition to foreign aid, Jessica compared her own experience with controversial comments made by then-U.S. President Donald Trump the previous year to assert that "[the money's] not really going to the people otherwise Africa would be very rich by now." Similarly, Helen attested that contrary to the narrative that it was "mainly older people that voted out," she knew "loads of youngsters that voted Brexit! They will never tell you, because of what my daughter went through at school. *Fact*" (Helen's emphasis).

Notable here is the populist way in which this logic is employed to challenge elite claims to knowledge. This is also illustrated by users' claims to represent majority opinion based on their interactions within their own milieus. As Helen told me, "There are so many people that feel as I do. [. . .] They *know* it's happening. They're not wrong—it's what they *see*. You can't argue with what you see" (Helen's emphasis). Here Helen does not only claim to understand and represent the majority, but also emphasizes the epistemic logic of felt and situated knowledge. In this way, "common sense" did not merely represent a gut feeling or the inevitable subjectivity of human values. It symbolized the rejection of elite knowledge. As Eileen Shared on her Facebook Timeline, "Common sense is a gift often unrecognisable to those who think they've had an education during their indoctrination" (original text Post authored by Eileen).

Of course, placing high levels of trust in individual anecdotes, experiences, or gut feelings would appear to be at odds with users' self-narratives about being rational and objective in their information-seeking. However, as discussed at the start of this chapter, the two need not be understood as mutually exclusive. In this case, they coexist, serving distinct yet complementary functions. On the one hand, claims to objectivity and facticity were employed by the pro-Brexit Facebook users to reject their characterization as misinformed or ignorant, while on the other, claims to folk knowledge served the populist function of positioning the users' views as majoritarian, inarguable and morally correct. This reflects findings by Moss et al. (2020, 842) of "contradictory yet overlapping understandings of emotion" in narratives around Brexit, whereby emotionality was a negative accusation at the same time as "gut feelings" were valorized as authentic or legitimate sources of knowledge. In the pro-Brexit Facebook milieu, folk wisdom and positivist epistemologies were employed side-by-side; "common sense" was not viewed as deviating from rationality, but was used to reframe what was rational around what resonated with users.

EPISTEMOLOGICAL LEADERS

A microcosm which reflects this complexity can be found in the reverence of particular epistemological leaders in the milieu. Although the pro-Brexit Facebook users stressed the necessity of their "own judgment" (Deborah) for discerning truth from falsity, these individuals, who included politicians and microinfluencers, served as venerated experts offering trustworthy information and agreeable viewpoints. Narratives around trustworthy figures, while in many ways consistent with the above-discussed self-constructions as evidenced-based and rational, also reflected the importance the users placed on common sense or "straight-talking."

On the one hand, these personalities were Followed because they provided "lots and lots of information" (Neil). As Olivia explained about one individual, "The reason I like him is because he does Post up factual information. So, like I say, he will use things such as Pew Research to show statistical figures in certain topics. [. . .] When they can show proof, those are the people that I Follow: [. . .] anyone that is labelled as a true scholar, and who really knows their topic." Neil also described those whom he trusted online as "accredited doctors, medical professors, research people, [. . .] people that you learn to trust because things they've said and done in the past have come true."

On the other hand, as Kirk said about one microinfluencer, "I'll sit and listen to her, cos she talks straight common sense." Donald Trump, whose electoral appeal is characterized by a discourse of "authenticity" rather than one of "truth" (Montgomery 2017) was also viewed broadly positively in the milieu. Populist leaders capitalize on down-to-earth identities in order to "signify closeness to 'the people,' as opposed to the perceived remoteness of mainstream political elites" (Ekström, Patrona, and Thornborrow 2018, 4). According to Eileen, "[Trump] is politically, um, undiplomatic, but he's the best thing to happen to politics in a long time because he tells it like it is." Some users acknowledged Trump's flaws. Carl even went so far as to say "I mean, probably Donald Trump is corrupt, but the point is he's at least trying to give us something back, give the people back . . . Not like Hillary Clinton. [. . .] She's just a puppet." This seeming contradiction arguably reflects the relationship between authenticity and fallibility. In a populist epistemology that emphasizes the importance of "average" people, common sense, and "real" experience, individuals who are not perfect are more real and thus more credible.

Indeed, when it came to common sense and rationality, one need not beget the other, and no politician exemplified this better in pro-Brexit Facebook users' minds than Conservative MP Jacob Rees-Mogg. By far the most widely respected British politician in the pro-Brexit Facebook milieu throughout the course of the fieldwork, Rees-Mogg "talks common sense, *and* he knows his facts" (Fred, emphasis added). That Rees-Mogg was extremely well-informed and direct was repeated by all the users who spoke about him. He was not the only politician publicly and unwaveringly defending Brexit at the time, and in fact, was a backbencher and had been generally unknown to these individuals until recent months. However, his particularly calm and composed demeanor and evidence-based responses to Remain arguments during media appearances appealed to users' desire to be taken seriously and not have their pro-Brexit position dismissed as irrational or non-factual.

Beatrice emphasized the way in which Jacob Rees-Mogg when challenged, rather than becoming angry, "very politely and succinctly [would] just say 'no, that's not true.'" As Fred's description exemplified, "He can deal with any argument that's put to him. I've never seen him lost for words yet. And he comes up with the facts and he's bang on." This was contrasted with portrayals of Shadow Home Secretary Diane Abbott, whose misspeaking on budget spending in the run-up to the 2017 General Election became a familiar meme in the milieu and led to her being ridiculed and called sarcastic names like "Diane Abacus" (Carl). The racialized and gendered nature of the appraisals embodied in this comparison cannot be ignored of course, but the criteria by which these value judgments are *claimed* to be made are evidence of the deliberate emphasis on facticity in the milieu.

The following assessment of Rees-Mogg by Kirk also alluded to dissatisfaction with the perceived corrupt nature of politics: "he don't beat around the bush. [. . .] It's a more direct and truthful side of a politician." Despite being extremely wealthy and an unapologetic member of the upper class, Rees-Mogg stood out among other politicians who, it was claimed, "are in it just for the money and the perks" (Fred). Like Trump, who was similarly described as "direct" in a way that was preferred by "the common person" (Kirk), Rees-Mogg gave users a "straight talking," and presumably incorruptibly wealthy, representative for their views, "a voice for us" (Kirk). Interestingly, users stressed that they did not always agree with Rees-Mogg's stances on issues like abortion or his negative assessment of "Tommy

Robinson," but these disagreements could be overlooked (or put down to a Trump-like authentic flawedness) given the credible and undefeatable manner in which he defended their claims to knowledge in the public arena.

In this sense, while narratives in the milieu about who and what to trust and how to discern fact from fiction online sometimes contradicted claims to rationality and objectivity, these narratives did mirror the desire discussed in the previous section to reclaim control of knowledge from "left-wing" forms of knowledge production that seemed entirely removed from their lived experiences and sensibilities. Populist epistemes are not a zero-sum game, and seemingly contradictory forms of epistemic logic can be used in overlapping and complementary ways. This also constitutes further evidence that rationality and emotionality, facts and feelings, are not distinct or competing but ever symbiotic. This complex relationship will continue to be explored in the following section.

RECONCILING RATIONALITY WITH EMOTION

As noted in the opening sections of this chapter, we have already seen throughout this book how engagement in the pro-Brexit Facebook milieu, like all forms of political engagement, was clearly saturated with emotions. High levels of obvious passion and emotionality were evident throughout the interviews and Facebook observations, and there were clear ways in which these emotions mattered in users' sense-making online. For instance, they frequently used emotions like disgust, disdain, and resentment not only to sustain racism and marginalize immigrants and Muslims (Ahmed 2014, 86–94), but to deny the epistemic capital of their political opponents, using terms like "grotesque" (Lawrence) and "smirking, know it all, irritating, annoying, low life scumbag. [. . .] Face only a mother could love" (Mark, self-authored comment accompanying a Facebook Post on his Timeline). In other words, while these individuals placed a high value on knowledge and "facts," their engagement with these was not unemotional or unaffected.

Take, for example, a comment by Helen: "You've got people like Diane Abbott going 'oh this place is too white.' [. . .] Hate that woman, and I don't say that about many people. And one of their colleagues, [. . .] Emily Thornberry. Hate that woman. I don't hate, I just despise what comes out of her mouth, do you know what I mean? I don't hate anybody." During this portion of the interview, Helen was becoming increasingly worked up about her contempt for left-wing politics. Perhaps all too aware of the accusations of emotionality aimed at Brexiteers and those on the right, she quickly back-peddled and assured me that she was not someone who "hates" others, only the things they say.

The users also spoke frequently of the fears and anxieties underpinning their political engagement. For instance, Fred located his issue with Islam not in any form of hatred or disgust, but in his "worry" about extremism and violence, before transposing responsibility for that anxiety onto the Muslim population more broadly:

> I've got Muslim friends, you know. I don't have a problem with Muslims as such. It's the extremists, the radical side, they're the ones I'm concerned about. But I'm also worried that the moderate Muslims who are just getting on with life aren't condemning it. I'm worried that mosques are covering up what's happening, as has been exposed recently, [. . .] that there was an extremist speaker there [at the Didsbury mosque in Manchester] days before the Ariani [sic: Ariana Grande] thing.[2] [. . .] The actual talk that he gave was recorded, and it is very violent and is very anti-British and is encouraging people to go and do exactly what he did.

Fred's problematization of Islam and Muslims, like that of many of the users, was thus expressed in terms of fear. Like Helen, however, he made clear attempts to assure me that his negative emotions were not irrational or baseless, by providing evidence of the allegedly insidious nature of British Muslims.

It is notable that the Facebook Posts observed in this study, even while often focusing on facts and figures, seemed almost invariably designed to both convey *and invoke* strong emotions in their audience. For example, one meme-style Post Shared by Kirk featured a list of four anti-Brexit statements followed by a pro-Brexit response, set against a Union Jack background. These included "'No one really knew what Brexit meant' . . . Yes they did. A leaflet costing £9m was delivered to every house in the country which 'clearly laid out' what leaving the EU would mean." At the bottom was written "You need to talk to people outside the M25 and stop peddling your Westminster LIES!" Emphatic markers like exclamation marks and all-caps are used to convey anger and frustration, while the use of "hard" facts like the cost of nine million pounds simultaneously conveys a sense of facticity and seeks to inflame outrage in the reader. The final statement separates those living inside the M25 ring road motorway (that is, Londoners) from the majority of people who are assumed to be more authentic and accuses the government of deceit. The Union Jack background signals that the arguments of Brexiteers are those of "real" Brits, and is meant to invoke a sense of patriotic pride—or anti-patriotic shame—in the reader.

Affective devices that promote community building, such as humor and empathy, were also prevalent in the milieu. Eileen's scathing responses to critics (see above) were representative of the generally sarcastic tone she used when producing content and of the intertwining of humor with claims to epistemic capital. In the case of empathy, this was used not only to reinforce a sense of transnational White victimhood shared with, for example, White Africans claimed to be persecuted, but also to position the Right and Brexiteers as morally superior vis-à-vis the Left and Remain. Appeals to protect society's vulnerable—in the form of elderly, veterans, and children—were used in many Posts Shared by the users, to create a sense of feeling good about doing the right thing and to delineate this milieu from political opponents who allegedly did not care.

In all of the above ways, a conflict existed between the pro-Brexit Facebook users' condemnation and dismissal of emotions and emotionality, and their genuinely emotional engagement with the subject matter and the medium. Like the Brexit voters in Moss and colleagues' (2020, 839) study, these individuals were eager to deny their emotionality because they had "feelings about feelings" in political life. This was arguably in part due to an "emotional regime" (Reddy 2001) which "both valorises individual feelings and maintains the belief that they are separate from, and inferior to, reason" (Moss, Robinson, and Watts 2020, 852). This hierarchical and adversarial understanding of emotion and reason was reflected in public narratives about the referendum which assumed that those who voted to Leave did so out of emotion, while those who voted to Remain were driven by rationality (ibid., 840) and clearly contributed to pro-Brexit Facebook users' feelings of being "marginalized" or sense of Right victimhood. Feelings and knowledge in this milieu were not discrete or mutually exclusive elements. Rather, narratives around factfulness were informed by feelings of marginalization or disempowerment within the perceived dominant regime of truth.

CONCLUSION: "WE'RE SICK OF BEING TOLD THEY KNOW BETTER THAN WE DO"

The online political engagement of pro-Brexit Facebook users was underpinned by a palpable sense of political disempowerment. These individuals felt that, as Brexit supporters, they were dismissed by media and politicians as not having known what they were voting for in the referendum, as racist for objecting to immigration and problematizing Islam, and as having "abandoned rationality in favour of passion" (Moss, Robinson, and Watts 2020, 838; e.g., Hewitt 2016), with all of the recriminations that this (rightly) entails in contemporary society (Mintchev 2021; Tyler, Degnen, and Blamire 2022). In a perceived contemporary hierarchy of legitimacy, they felt looked down upon by Remainers and those on the left who seemed to enjoy an undeserved higher status in public life and the right to determine the regime of truth around politics. According to the worldview of these individuals, their own right to this—or their epistemic capital—had been revoked, and with it their status as worthy citizens.

In response, the pro-Brexit Facebook users sought to assert their epistemic capital and reclaim their stake in the production of political knowledge. They used Facebook to construct themselves as fact-rich and rational and assert their reverence of knowledge. They threw accusations of irrationality and ignorance back at Remainers, challenging the perceived anti-Brexit and pro-left regime of truth and in turn reinforcing their own appreciation of facts and evidence. In this way, knowledge was viewed in this milieu as an invaluable weapon in a struggle for cultural hegemony. Reclaiming a stake in knowledge production meant reclaiming the right to participate in decisions about the direction of British society and claim a stake in its future. Thus, narratives of valuing information and of researching for oneself—through the practices discussed in section I, and in the context of the disempowerment described in section II—can be seen as appealing to these individuals' desire to exercise their agency.

This effort was part of a broader, transnational right-wing populist objective to discredit left-wing politics by shifting the focus of political debate to the arena of epistemic legitimacy. From Jordan Peterson to Ben Shapiro, new right YouTube pundits across English-speaking countries and beyond are preoccupied with epistemic claims and fact signaling (Hong and Hermann 2020; Nicholls 2019). The conflict over truth in which the pro-Brexit Facebook users were engaged mirrored that played out in the theory of Cultural Marxism promoted by the Alt-Right (Mirrlees 2018). The rise of QAnon has prompted a renewed focus on construction of alternative facts and the importance of epistemic capital in far-right conspiracy milieus (Marwick and Partin 2022; Morelock and Narita 2022; Robertson and Amarasingam 2022). In climate change denial movements too—said to have learned their tactics from the tobacco industry's campaign to discredit medical science (Supran and Oreskes 2021)—it is not scientific data that are rejected so much as "the sociopolitical dynamics that have generated it" (Fischer 2019). Post-Brexit, right-wing populists like Nigel Farage have begun to focus their ire on "net-zero" emissions reduction policies (Atkins 2022), indicating that climate science will continue to be an important arena for contestation of epistemic authority going forward. While it is cultural values that are at stake in this battle, the battle itself is being fought through discursive maneuvers to claim epistemic legitimacy.

This is not coincidental. It is a product of our contemporary emotional regime around politics, which stipulates the value of objectivity and rationality vis-à-vis emotion in political life. If "[o]ne of the core assumptions in the public discourse of the referendum was that Leave was the emotional choice and Remain the rational one" (Moss, Robinson, and Watts 2020, 840), then it is no surprise that the pro-Brexit Facebook users felt that their knowledge claims were ridiculed and marginalized. The same normative conditions have given rise to the misplaced popularity of the concept of post-truth. The findings here underscore the inadequacy of post-truth to explain right-wing populist engagement online. They challenge the post-truth notion that Brexit and its related right-wing populist movements online are part of a new era in which emotions are valued over rationality or facts. Moreover, the findings refute post-truth's representation of emotions and rationality as distinct and competing. The emphasis placed on knowledge, facts, and rationality by the pro-Brexit Facebook users did not beget the actual emotionality of their engagement. Like all political engagement, it was highly affective, with emotions like anger, pride, and amusement playing significant roles. Indeed, the users' desire to stake a claim in knowledge production itself reveals the importance of feelings of marginalization, frustration, and fundamentally, pride to these individuals.

Given that emotion is integral to the way in which individuals on both sides of the political spectrum engage in politics, theories of post-truth, which focus on the emotionality of right-wing politics, are also normatively loaded, creating hierarchies between emotions that are morally right and "rational" and those that are wrong and "irrational." This only serves to add to the kinds of discontent which fueled online right-wing populist engagement. In the worldview of the pro-Brexit Facebook milieu, it was not new emotional and irrational challenges to left-wing truths that were the problem. Rather, this view of their engagements was itself the problem, because it was one which rendered them and their claims (rightly or wrongly) devalued, demonized, and ignored. As Helen put it, "We're sick of being told we're wrong. We're sick of being told we're stupid. We're sick of being told they know better than we do." Analysis of the pro-Brexit Facebook milieu's relationship to knowledge demonstrates the way that the contemporary struggles over truth being played out online and in broader media are not mere "truth-games" (Cosentino 2020, 21) within a new flat hierarchy between ontologies (ibid., 19). To the actors involved they are in fact serious challenges to power, and thus have important political consequences.

NOTES

1. A pseudonym.
2. This is in reference to the Islamist terrorist attack that occurred at Ariana Grande's concert in Manchester in 2017. The suicide bomber responsible was a regular at the Didsbury mosque in South Manchester, which during the project fieldwork

made headlines due to covertly filmed footage of the imam there making positive remarks about armed jihad in a sermon before the bomber planned the attack (Thomas and Titheradge 2018). The Facebook observations in this project revealed that this was a popular topic in the pro-Brexit Facebook milieu at the time.

Conclusion
Taking Back Control?

This book has examined engagement with Brexit and right-wing populist politics on Facebook, the motivations behind it, the meaning with which it was imputed, and its sociological consequences. Based on an original piece of in-depth, qualitative research, the book has sought to connect online and offline experiences and to situate this social media-based engagement within the lives of those involved. The political transformations of these individuals, their interpretations of the world around them, and their claims to victimhood, legitimacy, and epistemic capital, took place within the particular context of Britain's Brexit politics and the identities and resentments that this engendered. But the engagement of these individuals also represents a case study of transnational right-wing populism on social media. The findings have important implications for how we understand the role of social media platforms like Facebook in engagement with right-wing populist politics globally, and in the propagation of the exclusionary, illiberal, and racist ideas with which this politics is inextricably bound up. In this chapter, I synthesize the analysis of the previous chapters to provide the overall findings of the study and elucidate these implications.

As we have seen in this book, although Brexit was not the only concern of the pro-Brexit Facebook users, it was a significant crystallizing force. The issue of Brexit, with the help of the technological opportunity provided by Facebook, acted as a catalyst for engagement with right-wing populism online. It served as the core that brought this milieu together, which judging by the number of Likes and Followers on certain pro-Brexit Pages during the fieldwork, could have numbered in the hundreds of thousands. Brexit offered a tangible, agentic goal for these individuals to work toward. It acted as a vehicle for explaining, expressing, empowering and legitimizing a range of discontents, bringing together issues of national belonging and entitlement, and entwining them with matters of sovereignty and control. Thanks to the way in which Brexit was being debated in the arenas of mainstream politics and the media, and continued to be long after the referendum, individuals were provided with economic and legal discourses to use as justification for isolationism and exclusion, and a seemingly more legitimate language with which to express their discontents about multiculturalism and liberal social change. As a cause, Brexit was also imbued with the dramaturgy of an imperative to act, painted as a crucial historic moment in which the members of the milieu were participating and on which the fate of Britain, and even the Western world, depended.

And yet, Brexit was merely a starting point, a launch pad for the development and articulation of an array of concerns that at many times bore no obvious relation to the issue of Britain's membership in the EU. According to the metanarrative around which the concerns in the milieu cohered, the EU was just one actor in a broad, sinister agenda to facilitate undesirable social change and multiculturalism. As Beatrice said, "It's just, everything! Everything is geared against us." Leaving the EU was seen as merely one, albeit very important, step toward mitigating unwanted liberal social change and reclaiming control over the direction of British society. This control, it was posited, had been unjustly taken away from the users and the White British majority they claimed to represent. The appeal of the moralized, Manichean (good versus evil) structure of this metanarrative, points to a desire to make sense of a world seen to have "gone mad." The pro-Brexit Facebook users understood themselves as participating in a crucial juncture which would establish the fate of indisputably virtuous values like democracy and freedom.

Brexit also acted as a vehicle for right-wing populism. This apparatus may have been established by the rhetoric of the Leave campaign (Clarke & Newman, 2017), but was extended and amplified in the post-referendum exit deal negotiation period. In the context of the uncertainty surrounding Britain's departure from the EU, the notion that the democratic mandate for Brexit was being derailed meant conditions were ripe for populist appeals to democracy and the "will of the people." Right-wing populism provided the pro-Brexit Facebook milieu with a vernacular with which to understand and articulate their discontents. It attributed blame to institutions like the EU and "out-of-touch" politicians like Theresa May. Populism imbued the category of Brexiteer with an identity of the wrongfully disempowered victim, made possible by the dismissive representations of Leave voters by Remainers and some liberal media. It reassured the users that as members of the "majority"—seen as enshrined in the referendum result, regardless of the fact that voters had variegated reasons for choosing Leave—their illiberal views were valid, virtuous, and more valuable than those of their opponents.

In order to highlight the importance to this milieu of such discursive appeals to majoritarian disempowerment, throughout this book I have spoken of "right-wing populist" engagement. However, the analysis has demonstrated that engagement in the pro-Brexit Facebook milieu was built on more than these populist appeals. The way the milieu brought together seemingly disparate villains and threats is evidence of the fact that these appeals cannot be understood outside of the political, ideological, and social contexts through which they came into being and came to have meaning to these individuals. As noted in the introduction to this book, the analytical lens of populism is prone to obscuring the importance of racism in engagement with this form of politics. To understand how and why individuals engage in right-wing populist politics online we must situate this within the broader context of their social and political world, and acknowledge the racialized inequalities that structure that world. This study has highlighted the key role played by racism, including differentialist racism, cultural racism, nativism, and Islamophobia. Racist attitudes and racialized categories of belonging were not only something that ran through the narratives used to legitimate these users' political stances. They were also a key underlying factor that both predated and motivated these individuals' online political engagement. They bred the logic of White victimhood which acted as a driver of the counter-narratives and agentic engagement practices in the pro-Brexit Facebook milieu. Though emboldened by the issue of Brexit and transnational right-wing populism, the racisms represented in the narratives of the pro-Brexit Facebook milieu were informed by the enduring and historically embedded status of racism in social life. The particular prominence of Islamophobia in the milieu reflects the focus of racist attitudes in Britain today on Islam and Muslims. The narratives around this also point to the importance of the historical moment in which this engagement was embedded, one marred by the legacy of the "war on terror," the rise of the Islamic State, and the "migrant crisis." The reactionary political rhetoric and inflammatory media coverage of these events undoubtedly played a major role in the conditions of online right-wing populist engagement we see today.

Meanwhile, anti-leftism and anti-communism also featured prominently in the milieu's narratives and motivations—from characterizations of the EU's alleged federal agenda, to accusations of media bias, to depictions of the Left and Remainers as depraved and idiotic. These negative depictions and moral panics were in part a product of long-standing efforts by right-wing actors and the right-leaning press to cultivate hegemonic conservative values (Smith, 1994). The particular significance of "communism," its conflation with socialism and association with totalitarianism and corruption, points to the importance among the participant group, all born before 1980, of lived experiences of the Cold War and Thatcher eras. This was reignited by an active media campaign during the post-referendum period against popular Labour Party leader Jeremy Corbyn and the socialist movement he represented (Cammaerts et al., 2020; Piazza & Lashmar, 2017). At the same time, new social cleavages had arisen around Leave and Remain identities, and Remainers came to be synonymous with a "snowflake"-dominated Left. These conditions laid the ground for the contemporary left-wing movement and the milieu's Brexit adversaries to be associated with the oppression of Cold War communist regimes and thus to be designated not only ideologically opposed to the milieu, but a threat to freedom and democracy. These attitudes prevailed despite the generalized sense of indignation and societal decline engendered by more than a decade of Conservative Party-led austerity policy, sentiments that also formed the backdrop for the users' politicization. Animosity toward the left in this milieu was focused on their cultural policies, meaning that the promise of parties like Labour to put an end to such socio-economic conditions appeared to hold no weight. Instead, anti-left sensibilities found an outlet in far-right conspiracy theories like Cultural Marxism, engendering not only animosity but fear and a call to action.

The important role played by these external social contexts demonstrates how online political engagement cannot be understood by focusing on platform affordances alone. To sever online behaviors from offline lives is to limit social scientific enquiry to a superficial and fragmented account of the embedded, everyday experience of social media use. In this study, attending to historical and contemporary social context revealed the ways in which engaging in pro-Brexit and right-wing populist politics on Facebook became meaningful to these individuals. Facebook offered them something that offline engagement could not. For one thing, it provided opportunities to connect with likeminded individuals and similar causes across the world. This taught them that they were not "alone" in their concerns, lending validity to their anxieties over ethnic, cultural, and religious diversity and liberal social change, and ultimately their desire to exclude and discriminate against others. It gave them unbridled quantities of globally-situated material with which to evidence their claims to White victimhood and Right victimhood. It also connected them with those who held views that conflicted with their own, interactions with whom reinforced these phantom victimizations and galvanized their identities.

Facebook enabled and encouraged the members of this milieu to engage with pro-Brexit and right-wing politics in a way that made them feel valuable and in control. Most importantly, within the context of populist appeals to their own disempowerment, Facebook provided these individuals with a sense of agency, the ability to take action, and generate alternative ways of making value (Skeggs & Loveday, 2012). As Deborah said, "we just, we want out. We want to be able to have our own sovereignty back, and Facebook gives us an outlet for that." Facebook allowed the users to share in counter-narratives that positioned their practices on Facebook as part of something greater than their individual networks, that is, as participation in the historic moment at which the fate of Britain (and beyond) would be decided. In this sense, Facebook offered the opportunity to become not only victims but heroes. It allowed the users to find and Share knowledge that was understood as otherwise hidden from them. Within the struggle in which this milieu was embroiled, knowledge was power. It was a valuable defense against the covert workings of nefarious forces and a weapon in discursive battles with Remainers and lefties over the perceived regime of truth (Foucault, 1976). Knowledge was claimed and performed by those in the pro-Brexit Facebook milieu in order to assert their epistemic capital (Maton, 2003). In so doing, they sought to recover their legitimacy as citizens that they understood to have been revoked by certain characterizations of Brexiteers, and thus reclaim their stake in decisions about the direction of British society. In short, Facebook provided an opportunity to "take back control."

However, the sense of validation and agency that these users garnered from their online political engagement belied the reality of the power that Facebook exerted over this. In addition to the logics of the platform that shaped these individuals' online engagement practices, Facebook's algorithms also controlled the content that they encountered, and thus the ideas that they inevitably engaged with. Born of the system of surveillance capitalism (Zuboff, 2019) and the demands of the attention economy, these algorithms are designed not only to show users more of the content they have thus far been actively engaging with, but also to keep users engaged by presenting them with increasingly provocative content. In fact, as noted in chapter 2, leaked internal documents, known as the "Facebook Papers" have revealed that Meta is aware of the divisive and harmful outcomes of Facebook's core design, and that despite this the company chooses user engagement over safety (Lima, 2021). The relative lack of awareness among the pro-Brexit Facebook users of the power of algorithmic targeting stood in contrast to their extremely critical stances toward news media and their characterizations of Facebook as a left-biased platform. They viewed their information discovery as despite control over information dissemination, rather than because of it, thanks to their construction of themselves in opposition to a perceived "left-wing" bias in the media and those in power. In this way, these users' allegedly critical information consumption attitudes fueled rather than weakened the power held by Facebook over their engagement.

The consequences of this power can be seen in the way in which Facebook connected the pro-Brexit Facebook users to a range of transnational ideologies. For many of these individuals, what started as support for and curiosities around Britain's departure from the EU ultimately led to engagement with much more extreme ideas. These included ideas drawn from far-right and Alt-Right conspiracy theories like the Great Replacement and Cultural Marxism and the kind of "fact signaling" (Hong & Hermann, 2020) that is becoming a trend in far-right and Alt-Right online content. While the milieu did not center around any one particular conspiracy, ideas from these theories permeated the narratives that circulated within the milieu, seen in claims of impending Islamization and the normalization of deviance by the left. The presence of these extreme ideas in the narratives circulated among the pro-Brexit Facebook milieu was part of what separated it from what has been documented about support for Brexit more broadly. This points to the role of Facebook in facilitating global connection and promoting and extending harmful ideologies.

That many of the users in this study were not typical conspiracy theorists should in fact be treated as an alarming finding, as it is a symptom of the increasing reach and potential for normalization of these far-right, racist ideas. It is not only the pre-existence of racist ideas that made the pro-Brexit Facebook milieu fertile ground for far-right ways of making sense of the world. Far-right conspiracy theories provide an alternative episteme for those who, like the users, claim to be epistemically marginalized. The distorted Gramscian logic offered by the Cultural Marxism conspiracy theory particularly resonated with the struggle for cultural hegemony in which the users saw themselves as embroiled. In this way, the Right's recent emphasis on combatting "woke-ism" is a canny recruitment strategy that should be carefully monitored going forward.

The importance in the pro-Brexit Facebook milieu of ideas drawn from these far-right and Alt-Right theories indicates the possibility that extreme right actors deliberately capitalized upon the unique combination of the technological and ideological opportunities of the Brexit-Facebook conjuncture to disseminate their ideology to a new audience. On Facebook, it is not only automated algorithms that extend the reach of problematic content, but the ability of nefarious actors to manipulate these algorithms, including through paid advertising and coordinated bot and humanoid campaigns. The Cambridge Analytica affair featured at the start of this book is certainly not the most sinister known example of this. It is well-documented that "troll farms" based in Russia and other states have been seeking to disrupt Western societies via social media (Al-Rawi, 2021; Golovchenko et al., 2020). In fact, at the time of writing, it has come to light that a team of hackers have been selling social media-based disinformation services to political actors, and claim to have already manipulated more than thirty elections globally (Kirchgaessner et al., 2023).

As a case study, the pro-Brexit Facebook milieu demonstrates the power of right-wing populist vernacular to galvanize pre-existing discontents and, harnessing the opportunities provided by social media, mobilize individuals who might not otherwise have become politically engaged. Examining how this process took place, from the perspective of the users involved, can offer valuable insights to help us understand how the far and populist right has similarly been extending its reach via, for example, popular support for Trump in the United States, or discontent at Covid-19 related restrictions and vaccine enforcement the world over. Each of these have resulted in real world harms, whether the injury, trauma, and loss of life at the January 6 Capitol Hill insurrection by pro-Trump groups who, like the pro-Brexit Facebook milieu, were (wrongly) convinced that democracy was under attack (Armaly et al., 2022); or the innumerable Covid-19 infections and deaths that undoubtedly resulted from the propagation of suspicion and appeals to "freedom" by far-right and right-wing populist actors during the pandemic (Brubaker, 2021; Eberl et al., 2021). The social harms of these however, like those caused by engagement with Brexit, are ongoing. They reverberate in loss of trust in institutions of democracy, science, and governance. They live on in social divisions and animosity toward campaigns for social progress, minority rights protection, and a more inclusive society. They manifest in the emboldening of far-right and right-wing populist political actors, the mainstreaming of far-right ideas, and experiences of everyday racism, transphobia, homophobia, and misogyny.

The case of the pro-Brexit Facebook milieu also serves as a cautionary tale that may inform the identification and amelioration of future right-wing populist mobilizations. The UK has left the EU, Trump has left office, and concerns about immigration and multiculturalism may have since been overshadowed by the Covid-19 pandemic and Russia's war against Ukraine. However, the shape-shifting force of right-wing populism finds new arenas in which to thrive. Indeed, there are many avenues for the global right to build on and learn from their relative success in the pro-Brexit Facebook milieu in order to continue to extend the reach of their ideas via similar right-wing populist causes around the world. This may be particularly true given the significant relaxing of moderation policies at Twitter (now known as "X"), and the reinstating of Trump's account on Twitter (now known as "X"), Facebook, and Instagram, two years after he was banned from these platforms for inciting violence. The dissemination potential of mainstream platforms is exponentially greater than that of alternative "free speech" social media, such as Gab or Truth Social. Recently created reactionary right-wing media outlets like GB News and Talk TV, available on television and online, have also significantly expanded the potential reach of right-wing populist ideas.

Right-wing, pro-Brexit actors have recently been using similar populist appeals to democracy and the rights of "the people" in their mobilization against "net zero" policies in Britain (Atkins, 2022; Huber, 2022). This builds on decades of right-wing efforts to provoke doubt in climate science in the face of the threat that such science poses to the sustainability of the capitalist systems in which the right is invested (Fischer, 2019). The lens of populist appeals offers a more nuanced account of the epistemic battlegrounds plaguing politics today than the concept of "post-truth" is able. When those in power are understood as not representing the interests of "real" people, challenges to the regime of truth seen as constructed by those in power may follow. However, as demonstrated by the pro-Brexit Facebook milieu, the concept of epistemological populism is not sufficient to fully understand the way in which "truth," "facts," and knowledge are weaponized in these milieus. In Ylä-Anttila's words (2018, p. 361), "Instead of truth value alone, the social origins, meanings, and implications of knowledge claims are crucial." The findings of the current study also encourage scholars to move beyond the lens of "conspiracy" that has recently been advanced by the rise of QAnon when seeking to understand online alternative epistemic appeals (Marwick & Partin, 2022), and incorporate insights from the concept of "epistemic capital" (Maton, 2003; Robertson & Amarasingam, 2022). In the right's struggle for cultural hegemony, these epistemic appeals should be understood as discursive maneuvers used to claim legitimacy and disparage left-wing opponents.

The analysis here also demonstrates how these epistemic struggles are not mere "truth-games" (Cosentino, 2020, p. 21) but rather constitute serious challenges to power. Sensationalist concepts like post-truth do more than flatten these socially-embedded phenomena into a binary between emotion and reason. They also advance particular value judgments born of the emotional regime in politics today (Reddy, 2001; see Moss et al., 2020). Emotions are integral to and inseparable from political engagement, on both sides of the political spectrum. It has even been argued that they are useful or desirable for progressive politics (Nussbaum, 2013). The results of the current study highlight the consequences of attributing right-wing political phenomena to individualized problems of emotionality or lack of engagement with "facts," and using these characterizations to dismiss those who engage with this phenomena as irrational or misinformed. Awareness of these characterizations went to the heart of engagement in the pro-Brexit Facebook milieu. As Tyler et al. (2022) aptly note, the reduction of racism to a characteristic of "types of people" who are either racist or not obscures the collectively constructed nature of racism in which the whole of society is implicated. This should not be taken to mean that harmful ideologies should not be strongly condemned and discouraged within social discourse, but to draw attention to the potential for *how* we do so to contribute to the creation of populist pariahs and the challenge that this presents.

It is difficult to disentangle the "senses" of political disempowerment expressed by the pro-Brexit Facebook users from the manipulative populist appeals that gave them discursive life. This is particularly the case given the irreconcilability of such claims to Right victimhood with the reality of the ongoing mainstreaming of the far-right in politics (Mondon & Winter, 2020).

However, throughout this book I have attempted to recognize these "experiences" insomuch as they were real to the individuals in question, by privileging their interpretations in my analysis. To do so is not to legitimate the views or discontents of these individuals, which were often socially harmful in their exclusionary, discriminatory, and illiberal nature. Although the voices of those groups who were targeted by the milieu do not feature here, it has been my mission throughout this volume not to diminish the harm caused to these groups by the ideologies in question. I hope, however, that I have demonstrated the indispensable nature of close-up, interpretive attempts to understand the causes and meanings of this social phenomenon, and the role that these understandings may play in ameliorating this harm.

The insights presented here about the motivations, meanings, and consequences of engagement in the pro-Brexit Facebook milieu have not been previously documented. The novel contribution these findings provide for the study of online right-wing populist engagement were made possible by the elicitation of users' own interpretations. They could not have been garnered via a research approach that relies on scraping online data. Quantitative analysis of social media content, or the artefacts of users' engagement with it, cannot on their own answer the question of which ideas, ideologies, and discursive appeals resonate most with the individuals in question, and why. It cannot tell us how engagement with this online content comes about, or what participating in online milieus means in the context of individuals' everyday lives and their social and political worlds. It cannot, I contend, elucidate the role of social media platforms in political life. It is not the case, as some have alleged, that individuals engaging with "distasteful" (Esseveld & Eyerman, 1992) ideologies on social media cannot be recruited to consentingly and openly speak to researchers about their worldviews (cf. Fuchs, 2018a). I hope that this volume has demonstrated the advantages of interpretive, sociological research into political social media use and inspires researchers to look beyond the novelty of the computational opportunities of "big data."

Appendix
Participant Characteristics

Table A.1

Name	Gender	Age	Location	Occupation
Audrey	F	50s	Northwest England	Care worker
Beatrice	F	60s	North Wales	Retired (special needs teacher)
Carl	M	50s	Northwest England	Self-employed (van driver)
Deborah	F	50s	Northwest England	Retired (various)
Eileen	F	60s	Northwest England	Self-employed (property entrepreneur)
Fred	M	60s	Northeast England	Retired (administrative)
George	M	70s	Northeast England	Retired (civil servant)
Helen	F	50s	West Midlands	Not working—full-time caring responsibilities
Isaac	M	50s	Northwest England	Care worker (ex-military)
Jessica	F	40s	London	Unemployed (previously self-employed: removals)
Kirk	M	60s	London	Self-employed (renovations)
Lawrence	M	40s	West Midlands	Steelworker
Mark	M	50s	Yorkshire	Secondary teacher
Neil	M	70s	South Wales	Retired (head teacher)
Olivia	F	50s	Southeast England	Self-employed (property entrepreneur)

Note: All names are pseudonyms.

References

Abbas, M.-S. (2019). Conflating the Muslim refugee and the terror suspect: Responses to the Syrian refugee "crisis" in Brexit Britain. *Ethnic and Racial Studies*, *42*(14), 2450–2469. https://doi.org/10.1080/01419870.2019.1588339

Abranches, M., Theuerkauf, U. G., Scott, C., & White, C. S. (2021). Cultural violence in the aftermath of the Brexit Referendum: Manifestations of post-racial xeno-racism. *Ethnic and Racial Studies*, *44*(15), 2876–2894. https://doi.org/10.1080/01419870.2020.1841257

Adler, M. (2018). *Cruel, Inhuman or Degrading Treatment? Benefit Sanctions in the UK*. Palgrave Pivot.

Ahmed, S. (2014). *The Cultural Politics of Emotion* (2nd ed.). Edinburgh University Press.

Alexander, C. (2017). Raceing Islamophobia. In F. Elahi & O. Khan (Eds.), *Islamophobia: Still a Challenge for Us All*. Runnymede Trust.

Alexander, D. (2011, March 21). Why MPs must say yes on Libya. *The Guardian*. http://www.theguardian.com/commentisfree/2011/mar/21/mps-must-say-yes-on-libya

Allchorn, W. (2018, July 18). Tommy Robinson and the UK's post-EDL far right: How extremists are mobilising in response to online restrictions and developing a new "victimisation" narrative. *VOX– Pol*. https://www.voxpol.eu/tommy-robinson-and-the-uks-post-edl-far-right-how-extremists-are-mobilising-in-response-to-online-restrictions-and-developing-a-new-victimisation-narrative/

Allen, C. (2011). Opposing Islamification or promoting Islamophobia? Understanding the English Defence League. *Patterns of Prejudice*, *45*(4), 279–294. https://doi.org/10.1080/0031322X.2011.585014

Allen, C. (2020). From Go Back Home to Letterboxes: Islamophobia and Muslim Women. In C. Allen (Ed.), *Reconfiguring Islamophobia: A Radical Rethinking of a Contested Concept* (pp. 51–62). Springer International Publishing. https://doi.org/10.1007/978-3-030-33047-7_5

Allen, N. (2018). "Brexit means Brexit": Theresa May and post-referendum British politics. *British Politics*, *13*(1), 105–120. https://doi.org/10.1057/s41293-017-0067-3

Al-Rawi, A. (2021). How did Russian and Iranian trolls' disinformation toward Canadian issues diverge and converge? *Digital War*, *2*(1), 21–34. https://doi.org/10.1057/s42984-020-00029-4

Altheide, D. L., & Snow, R. P. (1979). *Media Logic*. Sage.

Anspach, N. M. (2017). The new personal influence: How our Facebook friends influence the news we read. *Political Communication*, *34*(4), 590–606. https://doi.org/10.1080/10584609.2017.1316329

Antonucci, L., Horvath, L., Kutiyski, Y., & Krouwel, A. (2017). The malaise of the squeezed middle: Challenging the narrative of the "left behind" Brexiter. *Competition & Change*, *21*(3), 211–229. https://doi.org/10.1177/1024529417704135

Applebaum, B. (2010). *Being White, Being Good: White Complicity, White Moral Responsibility, and Social Justice*. Lexington Books.

Argentino, M.-A. (2021, January 7). QAnon and the storm of the U.S. Capitol: The offline effect of online conspiracy theories. *The Conversation*. http://theconversation.com/qanon-and-the-storm-of-the-u-s-capitol-the-offline-effect-of-online-conspiracy-theories-152815

Armaly, M. T., Buckley, D. T., & Enders, A. M. (2022). Christian nationalism and political violence: Victimhood, racial identity, conspiracy, and support for the Capitol attacks. *Political Behavior*, *44*(2), 937–960. https://doi.org/10.1007/s11109-021-09758-y

Ashcroft, Lord. (2016). How the United Kingdom voted on Thursday . . . And why—Lord Ashcroft Polls. *Lord Ashcroft Polls*. https://lordashcroftpolls.com/2016/06/how-the-united-kingdom-voted-and-why/

Atkins, E. (2022). 'Bigger than Brexit': Exploring right-wing populism and net-zero policies in the United Kingdom. *Energy Research & Social Science*, *90*, 102681. https://doi.org/10.1016/j.erss.2022.102681

Ayton, P., & Tumber, H. (2001). The rise and fall of perceived bias at the BBC. *Intermedia*, *29*(4). http://www.staff.city.ac.uk/p.ayton/Intermedia2001.PDF

Bail, C. A., Argyle, L. P., Brown, T. W., Bumpus, J. P., Chen, H., Hunzaker, M. B. F., Lee, J., Mann, M., Merhout, F., & Volfovsky, A. (2018). Exposure to opposing views on social media can increase political polarization. *Proceedings of the National Academy of Sciences*, *115*(37), 9216–9221. https://doi.org/10.1073/pnas.1804840115

Balibar, E. (1991). Is There a Neo-Racism? In E. B. Wallerstein & Immanuel (Eds.), *Race, Nation, Class: Ambiguous Identities*. Verso.

Balthazar, A. C. (2017). Made in Britain: Brexit, teacups, and the materiality of the nation. *American Ethnologist*, *44*(2), 220–224. https://doi.org/10.1111/amet.12471

Banaji, S., Bhat, R., Agarwal, A., Passanha, N., & Sadhana Pravin, M. (2019). *WhatsApp vigilantes: An exploration of citizen reception and circulation of WhatsApp misinformation linked to mob violence in India* [Monograph]. Department of Media and Communications, London School of Economics and Political Science. https://eprints.lse.ac.uk/104316/1/Banaji_whatsapp_vigilantes_exploration_of_citizen_reception_published.pdf

Barberá, P., Jost, J. T., Nagler, J., Tucker, J. A., & Bonneau, R. (2015). Tweeting from left to right: Is online political communication more than an echo chamber? *Psychological Science*, *26*(10), 1531–1542. https://doi.org/10.1177/0956797615594620

Barker, M. (1981). *The New Racism: Conservatives and the Ideology of the Tribe*. Junction Books.

Bartlett, J., Reffin, J., Rumball, N., & Williamson, S. (2014). *Anti-Social Media*. Demos. https://demos.co.uk/wp-content/uploads/files/DEMOS_Anti-social_Media.pdf

Bastos, M. T., & Mercea, D. (2019). The Brexit botnet and user-generated hyperpartisan news. *Social Science Computer Review*, *37*(1), 38–54. https://doi.org/10.1177/0894439317734157

Baudrillard, J. (1981). *Simulacres et Simulation*. Galilée.

BBC News. (2016a, June 24). Brexit: Nicola Sturgeon says second Scottish independence vote "highly likely." *BBC News*. https://www.bbc.com/news/uk-scotland-scotland-politics-36621030

BBC News. (2016b, July 9). Brexit: Petition for second EU referendum rejected. *BBC News*. https://www.bbc.com/news/uk-politics-36754376

BBC News. (2018, February 17). UKIP members vote to sack embattled leader Henry Bolton. *BBC News*. https://www.bbc.co.uk/news/uk-politics-43098646

BBC News. (2019a, March 23). Brexit march: Million joined Brexit protest, organisers say. *BBC News*. https://www.bbc.com/news/uk-politics-47678763

BBC News. (2019b, October 30). Facebook agrees to pay Cambridge Analytica fine to UK. *BBC News*. https://www.bbc.com/news/technology-50234141

BBC News. (2020a, April 18). Home secretary vows to stop illegal Channel crossings. *BBC News*. https://www.bbc.com/news/uk-england-kent-52338124

BBC News. (2020b, October 7). Cambridge Analytica "not involved" in Brexit referendum, says watchdog. *BBC News*. https://www.bbc.com/news/uk-politics-54457407

BBC News. (2022, November 23). Home secretary: I will tell you who is at fault. *BBC News*. https://www.bbc.co.uk/news/av/uk-politics-63730140

Begum, N. (2023). "The European family? Wouldn't that be the white people?": Brexit and British ethnic minority attitudes towards Europe. *Ethnic and Racial Studies*, 1–23. https://doi.org/10.1080/01419870.2023.2205499

Beider, H. (2015). *White Working-Class Voice: Multiculturalism, Community-Building and Change*. Policy Press.

Beneito-Montagut, R., Rosales, A., & Fernández-Ardèvol, M. (2022). Emerging digital inequalities: A comparative study of older Aadults' smartphone use. *Social Media + Society*, *8*(4), 20563051221138756. https://doi.org/10.1177/20563051221138756

Bennett, W. L., & Livingston, S. (2018). The disinformation order: Disruptive communication and the decline of democratic institutions. *European Journal of Communication*, *33*(2), 122–139. https://doi.org/10.1177/0267323118760317

Berger, B. (2009). Political theory, political Sscience and the end of civic engagement. *Perspectives on Politics*, *7*(2), 335–350. https://doi.org/10.1017/S153759270909080X

Berger, J. (2018). *The alt-right Twitter census: Defining and describing the audience for alt-right content on Twitter*. Vox-Pol Network of Excellence.

Berriche, M. (2021). En quête de sources. Preuves et mises à l'épreuve des internautes dans la controverse vaccinale sur Facebook. *Politiques de communication*, *16*(1), 115–154. https://doi.org/10.3917/pdc.016.0115

Berry, J. M., & Sobieraj, S. (2013). *The Outrage Industry: Political Opinion Media and the New Incivility*. Oxford University Press.

Berry, M., Garcia-Blanco, I., & Moore, K. (2015). *Press Coverage of the Refugee and Migrant Crisis in the EU: A Content Analysis of Five European Countries*. UNHCR. https://www.unhcr.org/protection/operations/56bb369c9/press-coverage-refugee-migrant-crisis-eu-content-analysis-five-european.html

Bhambra, G. K. (2017). Brexit, Trump, and "methodological whiteness": On the misrecognition of race and class. *British Journal of Sociology*, *68*(S1), S214–S232. https://doi.org/10.1111/1468-4446.12317

Bhatt, C. (2012). The new xenologies of Europe: Civil tensions and mythic pasts. *Journal of Civil Society* *8*(3), 307–326. https://doi.org/10.1080/17448689.2012.732456

Bhattacharyya, G. (2008). *Dangerous Brown Men*. Zed Books. https://www.bloomsbury.com/uk/dangerous-brown-men-9781842778791/

Binns, A., Bateman, M., & Mair, J. (2018). The *remoaner queen under attack*: The trolling of Gina Miller. In. Mair, T. Clark, N. Fowler, & R. Snoddy, (Eds.), *Anti-Social Media* (pp. 10–16). Abramis. http://www.abramis.co.uk/books/bookdetails.php?id=184549729

Blee, K. (2002). *Inside Organized Racism: Women in the Hate Movement*. University of California Press.

Bogerts, L., & Fielitz, M. (2019). 'Do you want meme war?' Understanding the visual memes of the German far right. In M. Fielitz & N. Thurston (Eds.), *Post-digital cultures of the far right: Online actions and offline consequences in Europe and the US* (pp. 137–153). Transcript Publishing.

Boler, M., & Davis, E. (2018). The affective politics of the "post-truth" era: Feeling rules and networked subjectivity. *Emotion, Space and Society*, *27*, 75–85. https://doi.org/10.1016/j.emospa.2018.03.002

Bonacchi, C., Altaweel, M., & Krzyzanska, M. (2018). The heritage of Brexit: Roles of the past in the construction of political identities through social media. *Journal of Social Archaeology*, *18*(2), 174–192. https://doi.org/10.1177/1469605318759713

Bonilla-Silva, E. (2006). *Racism without Racists: Color-Blind Racism and the Persistence of Racial Inequality in the United States*. Rowman & Littlefield Publishers.

Bootle, R. (2018, September 9). Trading on World Trade Organisation terms offers the best Brexit deal. *The Telegraph*. https://www.telegraph.co.uk/business/2018/09/09/trading-world-trade-organisation-terms-offers-best-brexit-deal/

Bosotti, A. (2018, June 24). Gina Miller rallies Remoaners to pressure Government into 2nd vote. *Express.Co.Uk*. https://www.express.co.uk/news/uk/978577/Brexit-news-gina-miller-brexit-people-s-vote-march-second-referendum-latest-video

Bossetta, M., Segesten, A. D., & Trenz, H.-J. (2018). Political participation on Facebook during Brexit: Does user engagement on media pages stimulate engagement with campaigns? *Journal of Language and Politics*, *17*(2), 173–194. https://doi.org/10.1075/jlp.17009.dut

Bossetta, M., Segesten, A. D., Zimmerman, C., & Bonacci, D. (2018). Shouting at the Wall: Does Negativity Drive Ideological Cross-posting in Brexit Facebook Comments? *Proceedings of the 9th International Conference on Social Media and Society*, 246–250. https://doi.org/10.1145/3217804.3217922

Bouko, C., & Garcia, D. (2020). Patterns of emotional tweets: The case of Brexit after the referendum results. In G. Bouvier & J. E. Rosenbaum (Eds.), *Twitter, the Public Sphere, and the Chaos of Online Deliberation* (pp. 175–203). Springer International Publishing. https://doi.org/10.1007/978-3-030-41421-4_8

Brändle, V. K., Galpin, C., & Trenz, H.-J. (2022). Brexit as "politics of division": Social media campaigning after the referendum. *Social Movement Studies*, *21*(1–2), 234–253. https://doi.org/10.1080/14742837.2021.1928484

Bright, J. (2017). *Explaining the Emergence of Echo Chambers on Social Media: The Role of Ideology and Extremism* (SSRN Scholarly Paper ID 2839728). Social Science Research Network. https://doi.org/10.2139/ssrn.2839728

Bright, L. F., Kleiser, S. B., & Grau, S. L. (2015). Too much Facebook? An exploratory examination of social media fatigue. *Computers in Human Behavior*, *44*, 148–155. https://doi.org/10.1016/j.chb.2014.11.048

British Social Attitudes 39. (2022). *Culture Wars: Keeping the Brexit divide alive?* Natcen Social Research. https://www.bsa.natcen.ac.uk/media/39478/bsa39_culture-wars.pdf

Brown, A. (2018). What is so special about online (as compared to offline) hate speech? In *Ethnicities*, *18* (3), 297–326. https://doi.org/10.1177/1468796817709846

Brown, K., Mondon, A., & Winter, A. (2021). The far right, the mainstream and mainstreaming: Towards a heuristic framework. *Journal of Political Ideologies*, 1–18. https://doi.org/10.1080/13569317.2021.1949829

Browning, C. S. (2019). Brexit populism and fantasies of fulfilment. *Cambridge Review of International Affairs*, *32*(3), 222–244. https://doi.org/10.1080/09557571.2019.1567461

Brubaker, R. (2017a). Between nationalism and civilizationism: The European populist moment in comparative perspective. *Ethnic and Racial Studies*, *40*(8), 1191–1226. https://doi.org/10.1080/01419870.2017.1294700

Brubaker, R. (2017b). Why populism? *Theory and Society*, *46*(5), 357–385. https://doi.org/10.1007/s11186-017-9301-7

Brubaker, R. (2021). Paradoxes of populism during the pandemic. *Thesis Eleven*, *164*(1), 73–87. https://doi.org/10.1177/0725513620970804

Bucher, T. (2017). The algorithmic imaginary: Exploring the ordinary affects of Facebook algorithms. *Information, Communication & Society*, *20*(1), 30–44. https://doi.org/10.1080/1369118X.2016.1154086

Burke, S. (2018). The discursive "othering" of Jews and Muslims in the Britain First solidarity patrol. *Journal of Community & Applied Social Psychology*, *28*(5), 365–377. https://doi.org/10.1002/casp.2373

Busbridge, R., Moffitt, B., & Thorburn, J. (2020). Cultural Marxism: Far-right conspiracy theory in Australia's culture wars. *Social Identities*, *26*(6), 722–738. https://doi.org/10.1080/13504630.2020.1787822

Buzzell, A., & Rini, R. (2022). Doing your own research and other impossible acts of epistemic superheroism. *Philosophical Psychology*, *0*(0), 1–25. https://doi.org/10.1080/09515089.2022.2138019

Cadwalladr, C., & Graham-Harrison, E. (2018, March 17). Revealed: 50 million Facebook profiles harvested for Cambridge Analytica in major data breach. *The Guardian*. https://www.theguardian.com/news/2018/mar/17/cambridge-analytica-facebook-influence-us-election

Calhoun, C. (2017). Populism, nationalism and Brexit. In W. Outhwaite (Ed.), *Brexit* (pp. 57–76). Anthem Press; JSTOR. https://www.jstor.org/stable/j.ctt1kft8cd.8

Cammaerts, B., DeCillia, B., & Magalhães, J. C. (2020). Journalistic transgressions in the representation of Jeremy Corbyn: From watchdog to attackdog. *Journalism*, *21*(2), 191–208. https://doi.org/10.1177/1464884917734055

Campanella, E., & Dassù, M. (2019). Brexit and Nostalgia. *Survival*, *61*(3), 103–111. https://doi.org/10.1080/00396338.2019.1614781

Carl, N., Richards, L., & Heath, A. (2019). Leave and Remain voters' knowledge of the EU after the referendum of 2016. *Electoral Studies*, *57*, 90–98. https://doi.org/10.1016/j.electstud.2018.11.003

Chadwick, A., & Stanyer, J. (2022). Deception as a bridging concept in the study of disinformation, misinformation, and misperceptions: Toward a holistic framework. *Communication Theory*, *32*(1), 1–24. https://doi.org/10.1093/ct/qtab019

Chadwick, A., Vaccari, C., & Hall, N.-A. (2023). What explains the spread of misinformation in online personal messaging networks? Exploring the role of conflict avoidance. *Digital Journalism*, 1–20. https://doi.org/10.1080/21670811.2023.2206038

Chaykowski, K. (2016, June 29). *Facebook News Feed Change Prioritizes Posts from Friends Users Care About*. Forbes. https://www.forbes.com/sites/kathleenchaykowski/2016/06/29/facebook-tweaks-news-feed-algorithm-to-prioritize-posts-from-friends-you-care-about/

Clarke, H. D., Goodwin, M., & Whiteley, P. (2017). *Brexit: Why Britain Voted to Leave the European Union*. Cambridge University Press. https://doi.org/10.1017/9781316584408

Clarke, H., Whiteley, P., Borges, W., Sanders, D., & Stewart, M. (2016). Modelling the dynamics of support for a right-wing populist party: The case of UKIP. *Journal of Elections, Public Opinion and Parties*, *26*(2), 135–154. https://doi.org/10.1080/17457289.2016.1146286

Clarke, J., & Newman, J. (2017). "People in this country have had enough of experts": Brexit and the paradoxes of populism. *Critical Policy Studies*, *11*(1), 101–116. https://doi.org/10.1080/19460171.2017.1282376

Cleland, J. (2020). Charismatic leadership in a far-right movement: An analysis of an English defence league message board following the resignation of Tommy Robinson. *Social Identities*, *26*(1), 48–60. https://doi.org/10.1080/13504630.2019.1671182

Clements, B. (2013). Public opinion and military intervention: Afghanistan, Iraq and Libya. *The Political Quarterly, 84*(1), 119–131. https://doi.org/10.1111/j.1467-923X.2013.02427.x

Cockbain, E., & Tufail, W. (2020). Failing victims, fuelling hate: Challenging the harms of the "Muslim grooming gangs" narrative. *Race & Class, 61*(3), 3–32. https://doi.org/10.1177/0306396819895727

Cohen, S. (1972). *Folk Devils and Moral Panics: The Creation of the Mods and Rockers*. MacGibbon and Kee.

Colleoni, E., Rozza, A., & Arvidsson, A. (2014). Echo chamber or public sphere? Predicting political orientation and measuring political homophily in Twitter using big data. *Journal of Communication, 64*(2), 317–332. https://doi.org/10.1111/jcom.12084

Cosentino, G. (2020). *Social Media and the Post-Truth World Order: The Global Dynamics of Misinformation*. Springer International Publishing. https://doi.org/10.1007/978-3-030-43005-4_3

Costa, E. (2018). Affordances-in-practice: An ethnographic critique of social media logic and context collapse. *New Media & Society, 20*(10), 3641–3656. https://doi.org/10.1177/1461444818756290

Coudenhove-Kalergi, R. N. (1925). *Praktischer Idealismus [practical idealism]*. Pan-Europa-Verlag.

Cox, M. (2017). The rise of populism and the crisis of globalisation: Brexit, Trump and beyond. *Irish Studies in International Affairs, 28*, 9–17. JSTOR. https://doi.org/10.3318/isia.2017.28.12

Curato, N. (2017). Flirting with authoritarian fantasies? Rodrigo Duterte and the new terms of Philippine populism. *Journal of Contemporary Asia, 47*(1), 142–153. https://doi.org/10.1080/00472336.2016.1239751

Curran, J. (2018). Rise of the "Loony Left." In J. Curran, I. Gaber, & J. Petley (Eds.), *Culture Wars: The Media and the British Left* (2nd ed.). Routledge.

Curtice, J. (2019, June 23). *Three Years On: Still Divided*. What UK Thinks: EU. https://whatukthinks.org/eu/three-years-on-still-divided/

Cutts, D., Goodwin, M., Heath, O., & Surridge, P. (2020). Brexit, the 2019 general election and the realignment of British politics. *The Political Quarterly, 91*(1), 7–23. https://doi.org/10.1111/1467-923X.12815

d'Ancona, M. (2017). *Post-Truth: The New War on Truth and How to Fight Back*. Ebury Press.

Dahlgreen, W. (2016, February 23). *EU referendum neck and neck as campaign kicks off*. YouGov. https://yougov.co.uk/topics/politics/articles-reports/2016/02/23/eu-referendum-leave-leads-one

Dajani, D., Gillespie, M., & Crilley, R. (2019). Differentiated visibilities: RT Arabic's narration of Russia's role in the Syrian war. *Media, War & Conflict*, 1750635219889075. https://doi.org/10.1177/1750635219889075

Dan, V., Paris, B., Donovan, J., Hameleers, M., Roozenbeek, J., van der Linden, S., & von Sikorski, C. (2021). Visual mis- and disinformation, social media, and democracy. *Journalism & Mass Communication Quarterly, 98*(3), 641–664. https://doi.org/10.1177/10776990211035395

Davidson, T., & Berezin, M. (2018). Britain First and the UK Independence Party: Social media and movement-party dynamics. *Mobilization: An International Quarterly*, *23*(4), 485–510. https://doi.org/10.17813/1086-671X-23-4-485

Davies, H. C., & MacRae, S. E. (2023). An anatomy of the British war on woke. *Race & Class*, 03063968231164905. https://doi.org/10.1177/03063968231164905

Davies, K. (2022). Sticking together in "Divided Britain": Talking Brexit in everyday family relationships. *Sociology*, *56*(1), 97–113. https://doi.org/10.1177/00380385211011569

Davis, J. L., & Chouinard, J. B. (2016). Theorizing affordances: From request to refuse. *Bulletin of Science, Technology & Society*, *36*(4), 241–248. https://doi.org/10.1177/0270467617714944

Davis, J. L., & Jurgenson, N. (2014). Context collapse: Theorizing context collusions and collisions. *Information, Communication & Society*, *17*(4), 476–485. https://doi.org/10.1080/1369118X.2014.888458

Davis, M. (2019). Transnationalising the anti-public sphere: Australian anti-publics and reactionary online media. In M. Peucker & D. Smith (Eds.), *The Far-Right in Contemporary Australia* (pp. 127–149). Springer. https://doi.org/10.1007/978-981-13-8351-9_6

de Bruin, R. (2017). Alt-right claims that would put the Soviets to shame: The alleged conspiracies of conservative reformers like count Coudenhove-Kalergi and the Bilderberg Group. *EuroVisie*, *13*(2), 28–31.

de Bruin, R. (2022). European union as a road to serfdom: The Alt-Right's inversion of narratives on European integration. *Journal of Contemporary European Studies*, *30*(1), 52–66. https://doi.org/10.1080/14782804.2021.1960489

De Genova, N. (2018a). Rebordering "the people": Notes on theorizing populism. *South Atlantic Quarterly*, *117*(2), 357–374. https://doi.org/10.1215/00382876-4374878

De Genova, N. (2018b). The "migrant crisis" as racial crisis: Do Black Lives Matter in Europe? *Ethnic and Racial Studies*, *41*(10), 1765–1782. https://doi.org/10.1080/01419870.2017.1361543

de Oliver, M. (2011). Nativism and the obsolescence of grand narrative: Comprehending the quandary of anti-immigration groups in the Neoliberal era. *Journal of Ethnic and Migration Studies*, *37*(7), 977–997. https://doi.org/10.1080/1369183X.2011.559029

Deacon, D., & Wring, D. (2016). The UK Independence Party, populism and the British news media: Competition, collaboration or containment? *European Journal of Communication*, *31*(2), 169–184. https://doi.org/10.1177/0267323115612215

Dearden, L. (2018, August 13). "Letterbox" insults against Muslim women spike in wake of Johnson comments. *The Independent*. https://www.independent.co.uk/news/uk/home-news/boris-johnson-burqa-muslim-women-veil-attacks-islamophobia-letterboxes-rise-a8488651.html

Dearden, L. (2019, December 28). Almost 19,000 children sexually groomed in England in year, official figures suggest. *The Independent*. https://www.independent.co.uk/news/uk/home-news/grooming-child-sex-abuse-exploitation-rotherham-rochdale-police-a9215261.html

DeCook, Julia R. 2018. Memes and Symbolic Violence: #proudboys and the Use of Memes for Propaganda and the Construction of Collective Identity. *Learning, Media and Technology 43*(4): 485–504. https://doi.org/10.1080/17439884.2018.1544149

Del Vicario, M., Zollo, F., Caldarelli, G., Scala, A., & Quattrociocchi, W. (2017). Mapping social dynamics on Facebook: The Brexit debate. *Social Networks*, *50*, 6–16. https://doi.org/10.1016/j.socnet.2017.02.002

Demianyk, G. (2020, October 29). Nigel Farage Gives Gushing Speech at Donald Trump Rally in Arizona. *HuffPost UK*. https://www.huffingtonpost.co.uk/entry/nigel-farage-donald-trump-rall_uk_5f99fb4bc5b6a4a2dc81f2c9

Department for Culture, Media and Sport. (2016). Broadcasting: Copy of Royal Charter for the continuance of the British Broadcasting Corporation. http://downloads.bbc.co.uk/bbctrust/assets/files/pdf/about/how_we_govern/2016/charter.pdf

DeVito, M. A. (2017). From editors to algorithms. *Digital Journalism*, *5*(6), 753–773. https://doi.org/10.1080/21670811.2016.1178592

Dixon, S. (2022, October 21). UK Facebook users 2022. Statista. https://www.statista.com/statistics/1012080/uk-monthly-numbers-facebook-users/

Dixon, S. (2023, February 13). Facebook MAU worldwide 2022. Statista. https://www.statista.com/statistics/264810/number-of-monthly-active-facebook-users-worldwide/

Dobreva, D., Grinnell, D., & Innes, M. (2019). Prophets and Loss: How "Soft Facts" on Social Media Influenced the Brexit Campaign and Social Reactions to the Murder of Jo Cox MP. *Policy & Internet*, *12*(2), 144–164.

Doerr, N. (2017). Bridging language barriers, bonding against immigrants: A visual case study of transnational network publics created by far-right activists in Europe. *Discourse & Society*, *28*(1), 3–23. https://doi.org/10.1177/0957926516676689

Dubois, E., & Blank, G. (2018). The echo chamber is overstated: The moderating effect of political interest and diverse media. *Information, Communication & Society*, *21*(5), 729–745. https://doi.org/10.1080/1369118X.2018.1428656

Due, C. (2011). "Aussie humour" or racism? Hey hey it's Saturday and the denial of racism in online responses to news media articles. *Platform: Journal of Media and Communication*, *3*(1), 36–53.

Duguay, S. (2018). Social media's breaking news: The logic of automation in Facebook trending topics and Twitter moments. *Media International Australia*, *166*(1), 20–33. https://doi.org/10.1177/1329878X17737407

Duman, Ö. S. (2014). The rise and consolidation of neoliberalism in the European Union: A comparative analysis of social and employment policies in Greece and Turkey. *European Journal of Industrial Relations*, *20*(4), 367–382. https://doi.org/10.1177/0959680113520274

Durnová, A. (2019). Unpacking emotional contexts of post-truth. *Critical Policy Studies*, *13*(4), 447–450. https://doi.org/10.1080/19460171.2019.1670222

Duvall, S.-S. (2020). Too famous to Pprotest: Far-right online community bonding over collective desecration of Colin Kaepernick, fame, and celebrity activism. *Journal of Communication Inquiry*, *44*(3), 256–278. https://doi.org/10.1177/0196859920911650

Eberl, J.-M., Huber, R. A., & Greussing, E. (2021). From populism to the "plandemic": Why populists believe in COVID-19 conspiracies. *Journal of Elections, Public Opinion and Parties*, *31*(sup1), 272–284. https://doi.org/10.1080/17457289.2021.1924730

Edgerly, S., Thorson, K., & Wells, C. (2018). Young citizens, social media, and the dynamics of political learning in the U.S. presidential primary election. *American Behavioral Scientist*, *62*(8), 1042–1060. https://doi.org/10.1177/0002764218764236

Ekström, M., Patrona, M., & Thornborrow, J. (2018). Right-wing populism and the dynamics of style: A discourse-analytic perspective on mediated political performances. *Palgrave Communications*, *4*(1), Article 1. https://doi.org/10.1057/s41599-018-0132-6

Ekström, M., & Shehata, A. (2018). Social media, porous boundaries, and the development of online political engagement among young citizens. *New Media & Society*, *20*(2), 740–759. https://doi.org/10.1177/1461444816670325

Engesser, S., Ernst, N., Esser, F., & Büchel, F. (2017). Populism and social media: How politicians spread a fragmented ideology. *Information, Communication & Society*, *20*(8), 1109–1126. https://doi.org/10.1080/1369118X.2016.1207697

Eslami, M., Rickman, A., Vaccaro, K., Aleyasen, A., Vuong, A., Karahalios, K., Hamilton, K., & Sandvig, C. (2015). "I always assumed that I wasn't really that close to [her]": Reasoning about invisible algorithms in news feeds. *Proceedings of the 33rd Annual ACM Conference on Human Factors in Computing Systems*, 153–162. https://doi.org/10.1145/2702123.2702556

Esseveld, J., & Eyerman, R. (1992). Which side are you on? Reflections on methdological issues in the study of 'distasteful' social movements. In M. Diani & R. Eyerman (Eds.), *Studying Collective Action*. Sage.

Evans, G. (1998). Euroscepticism and conservative electoral support: How an asset became a liability. *British Journal of Political Science*, *28*(4), 573–590. https://doi.org/10.1017/S0007123498000258

Evans, S. K., Pearce, K. E., Vitak, J., & Treem, J. W. (2017). Explicating affordances: A conceptual framework for understanding affordances in communication research. *Journal of Computer-Mediated Communication*, *22*(1), 35–52. https://doi.org/10.1111/jcc4.12180

Farris, S. R. (2017). *In the Name of Women's Rights: The Rise of Femonationalism*. Duke University Press.

Faulkner, D., & Watson, I. (2023, March 7). Sunak says he is up for the fight on illegal Channel crossings. *BBC News*. https://www.bbc.com/news/uk-64881908

Faulkner, S., Guy, H., & Vis, F. (2021). Right-wing populism, visual disinformation, and Brexit: From the UKIP "Breaking Point" poster to the aftermath of the London Westminster bridge attack. In H. Tumber & S. Waisbord (Eds.), *The Routledge Companion to Media Disinformation and Populism*. Routledge.

Fekete, L. (2009). *A Suitable Enemy: Racism, Migration and Islamophobia in Europe*. Pluto Press.

Fekete, L. (2012). The Muslim conspiracy theory and the Oslo massacre. *Race & Class*, *53*(3), 30–47. https://doi.org/10.1177/0306396811425984

Ferree, M. M., Gamson, W. A., Rucht, D., & Gerhards, J. (2002). *Shaping Abortion Discourse: Democracy and the Public Sphere in Germany and the United States*. Cambridge University Press.

Fielding, R. (2011, August 16). Gartner: Consumers suffering social media fatigue [Text]. MyCustomer. https://www.mycustomer.com/marketing/technology/gartner-consumers-suffering-social-media-fatigue

Figenschou, T. U., & Ihlebæk, K. A. (2019). Challenging journalistic authority. *Journalism Studies*, *20*(9), 1221–1237. https://doi.org/10.1080/1461670X.2018.1500868

Fischer, F. (2019). Knowledge politics and post-truth in climate denial: On the social construction of alternative facts. *Critical Policy Studies*, *13*(2), 133–152. https://doi.org/10.1080/19460171.2019.1602067

Fitzgerald, D., Hinterberger, A., Narayan, J., & Williams, R. (2020). Brexit as heredity redux: Imperialism, biomedicine and the NHS in Britain. *The Sociological Review*, *68*(6), 1161–1178. https://doi.org/10.1177/0038026120914177

Flemmen, M., & Savage, M. (2017). The politics of nationalism and white racism in the UK. *British Journal of Sociology*, *68*, S233–S264. https://doi.org/10.1111/1468-4446.12311

Fletcher, R., & Park, S. (2017). The impact of trust in the news media on online news consumption and participation. *Digital Journalism*, *5*(10), 1281–1299. https://doi.org/10.1080/21670811.2017.1279979

Flood, A. (2016, November 15). "Post-truth" named word of the year by Oxford Dictionaries. *The Guardian*. https://www.theguardian.com/books/2016/nov/15/post-truth-named-word-of-the-year-by-oxford-dictionaries

Ford, R. (2016, June 25). Older "left-behind" voters turned against a political class with values opposed to theirs. *The Observer*. https://www.theguardian.com/politics/2016/jun/25/left-behind-eu-referendum-vote-ukip-revolt-brexit

Ford, R., & Goodwin, M. (2014). *Revolt on the Right: Explaining Support for the Radical Right in Britain*. Routledge.

Foste, Z. (2020). Remaining vigilant: Reflexive considerations for white researchers studying whiteness. *Whiteness and Education*, *5*(2), 131–146. https://doi.org/10.1080/23793406.2020.1738264

Foucault, M. (1976). Truth and power. In *Power: The Essential Works of Foucault 1954–1984*. New Press.

Fox, B. (2018). Making the headlines: EU immigration to the UK and the wave of new racism after Brexit. In E. Balica & V. Marinescu (Eds.), *Migration and Crime: Realities and Media Representations* (pp. 87–107). Springer International Publishing. https://doi.org/10.1007/978-3-319-95813-2_5

Fox, J. E., Moroşanu, L., & Szilassy, E. (2012). The racialization of the new European migration to the UK. *Sociology*, *46* (4), 680–695. https://doi.org/10.1177/0038038511425558

Freedland, J. (2016, July 20). *Jonathan Freedland on a roar of rage from the Left Behind*. The New European. https://www.theneweuropean.co.uk/top-stories/jonathan-freedland-on-a-roar-of-rage-from-the-left-behind-1-4625460

Froio, C. (2018). Race, religion, or culture? Framing Islam between racism and neo-racism in the online network of the French far right. *Perspectives on Politics*, *16*(3), 696–709. https://doi.org/10.1017/S1537592718001573

Froio, C., & Ganesh, B. (2019). The transnationalisation of far right discourse on Twitter: Issues and actors that cross borders in Western European democracies. *European Societies*, *21*(4), 513–539. https://doi.org/10.1080/14616696.2018.1494295

Fuchs, C. (2017). From digital positivism and administrative big data analytics towards critical digital and social media research! *European Journal of Communication*, *32*(1), 37–49. https://doi.org/10.1177/0267323116682804

Fuchs, C. (2018a). "Dear Mr. Neo-Nazi, can you please give me your informed consent so that I can quote your Fascist Tweet?": Questions of social media research ethics in online ideology critique. In G. Meikle (Ed.), *The Routledge Companion to Media and Activism* (pp. 385–394). Routledge. https://westminsterresearch.westminster.ac.uk/item/q4z4v/-dear-mr-neo-nazi-can-you-please-give-me-your-informed-consent-so-that-i-can-quote-your-fascist-tweet-questions-of-social-media-research-ethics-in-online-ideology-critique

Fuchs, C. (2018b). *Nationalism 2.0: The Making of Brexit on Social Media*. Pluto Press. https://www.plutobooks.com/9781786802996/nationalism-2-0/

Fujioka, B. J., & DeCook, J. R. (2021). Digital cynical romanticism: Japan's 2channel and the precursors to online extremist cultures. *Internet Histories*, 1–17. https://doi.org/10.1080/24701475.2021.1919966

Gabriel, D. (2017). The othering and objectification of Diane Abbott MP in the 2017 UK General Election. In E. Thorsen, D. Jackson, & D. Lilleker (Eds.), *UK Election Analysis 2017: Media, Voters and the Campaign. Early Reflections from Leading Academics* (pp. 129–130). Centre for the Study of Journalism, Culture & Community, Bournemouth University, Centre for Media Research, Bournemouth University and Political Studies Association. http://www.electionanalysis.uk/

Garner, S. (2010). *Racisms*. Sage Publications.

Gaston, S. (2018). *Out of the Shadows: Conspiracy Thinking on Immigration* (p. 60). Henry Jackson Society. https://henryjacksonsociety.org/wp-content/uploads/2018/12/Out-of-the-Shadows-Conspiracy-thinking-on-immigration.pdf

Geertz, C. (1977). *The Interpretation of Cultures*. Basic Books.

Generation D. (2017). *Handbuch Für Medienguerillas: Teil I. Shitpos- ting 1×1*. https://www.hogesatzbau.de/wp-content/uploads/2018/01/HANDBUCH-F%c3%9cR-MEDIENGUERILLAS.pdf

George, S. (2000). Britain: Anatomy of a Eurosceptic state. *Journal of European Integration*, *22*(1), 15–33. https://doi.org/10.1080/07036330008429077

Gerbaudo, P. (2018). Social media and populism: An elective affinity? *Media, Culture & Society*, *40*(5), 745–753. https://doi.org/10.1177/0163443718772192

Gest, J., Reny, T., & Mayer, J. (2018). Roots of the Radical Right: Nostalgic Deprivation in the United States and Britain. *Comparative Political Studies*, *51*(13), 1694–1719. https://doi.org/10.1177/0010414017720705

Gifford, C. (2006). The rise of post-imperial populism: The case of right-wing Euroscepticism in Britain. *European Journal of Political Research*, *45*(5), 851–869. https://doi.org/10.1111/j.1475-6765.2006.00638.x

Gifford, C. (2010). The UK and the European Union: Dimensions of sovereignty and the problem of Eurosceptic Britishness. *Parliamentary Affairs*, *63*(2), 321–338. https://doi.org/10.1093/pa/gsp031

Gillespie, T. (2014). The relevance of algorithms. In P. Boczkowski & K. Foot (Eds.), *Media Technologies: Essays on Communication, Materiality, and Society* (pp. 167–193). MIT Press.

Gilroy, P. (1987). *There Ain't No Black in the Union Jack: The Cultural Politics of Race and Nation*. Routledge.

Golovchenko, Y., Buntain, C., Eady, G., Brown, M. A., & Tucker, J. A. (2020). Cross-platform state propaganda: Russian trolls on Twitter and YouTube during the 2016 U.S. presidential election. *International Journal of Press/Politics*, *25*(3), 357–389. https://doi.org/10.1177/1940161220912682

Goodwin, M. (2015). Ukip, the 2015 general election and Britain's EU referendum. *Political Insight*, *6*(3), 12–15. https://doi.org/10.1111/2041-9066.12107

Goodwin, M., & Heath, O. (2016). The 2016 referendum, Brexit and the Left Behind: An aggregate-level analysis of the result. *The Political Quarterly*, *87*(3), 323–332.

Goodwin, M., & Milazzo, C. (2015). *Britain, the European Union and the Referendum: What Drives Euroscepticism?* Chatham House.

Goodwin, M., & Milazzo, C. (2017). Taking back control? Investigating the role of immigration in the 2016 vote for Brexit. *British Journal of Politics and International Relations*, *19*(3), 450–464. https://doi.org/10.1177/1369148117710799

Gorodnichenko, Y., Pham, T., & Talavera, O. (2018). *Social Media, Sentiment and Public Opinions: Evidence from #Brexit and #USElection*. National Bureau of Economic Research Working Paper Series No. 24631.

Gran, A.-B., Booth, P., & Bucher, T. (2020). To be or not to be algorithm aware: A question of a new digital divide? *Information, Communication & Society*, 1–18. https://doi.org/10.1080/1369118X.2020.1736124

Green, J., & Prosser, C. (2016). Party system fragmentation and single-party government: The British general election of 2015. *West European Politics*, *39*(6), 1299–1310. https://doi.org/10.1080/01402382.2016.1173335

Greene, V. S. (2019). "Deplorable" satire: Alt-right memes, white genocide tweets, and redpilling normies. *Studies in American Humor*, *5*(1), 31–69. https://doi.org/10.5325/studamerhumor.5.1.0031

Grygiel, J. (2019, July 24). Facebook algorithm changes suppressed journalism and meddled with democracy. *The Conversation*. http://theconversation.com/facebook-algorithm-changes-suppressed-journalism-and-meddled-with-democracy-119446

Guhl, J. (2019, July 2). Too little, too late. *Friedrich Ebert Stiftung*. https://www.fes.de/en/displacement-migration-integration/article-page-flight-migration-integration/too-little-too-late/

Gupta, S., & Virdee, S. (2018). Introduction: European crises: contemporary nationalisms and the language of "race." *Ethnic and Racial Studies*, *41*(10), 1747–1764. https://doi.org/10.1080/01419870.2017.1361545

Hackett, R. A. (2016). Alternative media for global crisis. *Journal of Alternative & Community Media*, *1*(1), 14–16. https://doi.org/10.1386/joacm_00007_1

Hackl, A. (2022). Good immigrants, permitted outsiders: Conditional inclusion and citizenship in comparison. *Ethnic and Racial Studies*, *45*(6), 989–1010. https://doi.org/10.1080/01419870.2021.2011938

Haidt, J., Graham, J., & Joseph, C. (2009). Above and below left–right: Ideological narratives and moral foundations. *Psychological Inquiry*, *20*(2–3), 110–119. https://doi.org/10.1080/10478400903028573

Hakoköngäs, E., Halmesvaara, O., & Sakki, I. (2020). Persuasion through bitter humor: Multimodal discourse analysis of rhetoric in internet memes of two far-right groups in Finland. *Social Media + Society*, *6*(2), 2056305120921575. https://doi.org/10.1177/2056305120921575

Hall, N.-A. (2022a). RT UK's Facebook audiences' interpretation of Russia's strategic narrative of the Syrian conflict. *Digital War*. https://doi.org/10.1057/s42984-022-00058-1

Hall, N.-A. (2022b). RT's appeal to British audiences on Facebook: Outsider in an untrustworthy media. *Participations*, *19*(1).

Hall, N.-A. (2022c). Understanding Brexit on Facebook: Developing close-up,q methodologies for social media research. *Sociological Research Online*, *27*(3), 707–723. https://doi.org/10.1177/13607804211037356

Hall, N.-A., Chadwick, A., & Vaccari, C. (2023, May). Online Misinformation, Epistemic Cultural Capital and Social Distinction. ICA 2023, Toronto.

Hall, S., Roberts, B., Clarke, J., Jefferson, T., & Critcher, C. (1978). *Policing the Crisis*. Palgrave. https://www.goodreads.com/work/best_book/121583-policing-the-crisis-mugging-the-state-and-law-and-order-critical-soc

Halliday, J., & Barr, L. B. C. (2018, December 7). Revealed: The hidden global network behind Tommy Robinson. *The Guardian*. https://www.theguardian.com/uk-news/2018/dec/07/tommy-robinson-global-support-brexit-march

Hänska, M., & Bauchowitz, S. (2017). Tweeting for Brexit: How social media influenced the referendum. In J. Mair, T. Clark, N. Fowler, R. Snoddy, & R. Tait (Eds.), *Brexit, Trump and the Media* (pp. 31–35). Abramis Academic Publishing. http://www.abramis.co.uk/publish/home.php

Harris, Richard, and Martin Charlton. 2016. Voting out of the European Union: Exploring the Geography of Leave. *Environment and Planning A: Economy and Space* 48(11): 2116–28. https://doi.org/10.1177/0308518X16665844

Hartzell, S., L. (2018). Alt-White: Conceptualizing the "Alt-Right" as a rhetorical bridge between White nationalism and mainstream public discourse. *Journal of Contemporary Rhetoric*, *8*(1/2), 6–25.

Harvey, D. (2007). *A Brief History of Neoliberalism*. OUP Oxford.

Haynes, J. (2019). From Huntington to Trump: Twenty-five years of the "Clash of Civilizations." *The Review of Faith & International Affairs*, *17*(1), 11–23. https://doi.org/10.1080/15570274.2019.1570755

Henderson, A., Jeffery, C., Wincott, D., & Wyn Jones, R. (2017). How Brexit was made in England. *British Journal of Politics and International Relations*, *19*(4), 631–646. https://doi.org/10.1177/1369148117730542

Hermann, C. (2007). Neoliberalism in the European Union. *Studies in Political Economy*, *79*(1), 61–90. https://doi.org/10.1080/19187033.2007.11675092

Hern, A., & Rawlinson, K. (2018, March 14). Facebook bans Britain First and its leaders. *The Guardian*. https://www.theguardian.com/world/2018/mar/14/facebook-bans-britain-first-and-its-leaders

Hertner, I. (2016, June 13). "Seven, or seven and a half out of 10": Jeremy Corbyn's conspicuous absence from the referendum campaign [Online resource]. *LSE Brexit*. http://blogs.lse.ac.uk/brexit/

Hewitt, G. (2016, April 14). EU Referendum: Don't discount raw emotion. *BBC News*. https://www.bbc.com/news/uk-politics-eu-referendum-36029874

Hewitt, R. (2005). *White Backlash and the Politics of Multiculturalism*. Cambridge University Press.

Hickson, K. (2018). Enoch Powell's "Rivers of Blood" Speech: Fifty years on. *The Political Quarterly*, *89*(3), 352–357. https://doi.org/10.1111/1467-923X.12554

Hillis, K., Paasonen, S., & Petit, M. (2015). *Networked Affect*. MIT Press.

Hine, C. (2015). *Ethnography for the Internet: Embedded, Embodied and Everyday*. Bloomsbury Academic.

Hmielowski, J. D., Hutchens, M. J., & Cicchirillo, V. J. (2014). Living in an age of online incivility: Examining the conditional indirect effects of online discussion on political flaming. *Information, Communication & Society*, *17*(10), 1196–1211. https://doi.org/10.1080/1369118X.2014.899609

Hobolt, S. B. (2016). The Brexit vote: A divided nation, a divided continent. *Journal of European Public Policy*, *23*(9), 1259–1277. https://doi.org/10.1080/13501763.2016.1225785

Hobolt, S. B., Leeper, T. J., & Tilley, J. (2020). Divided by the vote: Affective polarization in the wake of Brexit. *British Journal of Political Science, online first*, 34.

Hogan, B. (2010). The presentation of self in the age of social media: Distinguishing performances and exhibitions Online. *Bulletin of Science, Technology & Society*, *30*(6), 377–386. https://doi.org/10.1177/0270467610385893

Holt, K. (2019). *Right-Wing Alternative Media*. Routledge. https://doi.org/10.4324/9780429454691

Holt, K., Figenschou, T. U., & Frischlich, L. (2019). Key dimensions of alternative news media. *Digital Journalism*, *7*(7), 860–869. https://doi.org/10.1080/21670811.2019.1625715

Holt, T. J., Freilich, J. D., & Chermak, S. M. (2022). Examining the online expression of ideology among far-right extremist forum users. *Terrorism and Political Violence*, *34*(2), 364–384. https://doi.org/10.1080/09546553.2019.1701446

Hong, S., & Hermann, S. N. (2020, October 5). "Fuck your feelings": The affective weaponisation of facts and reason. *AoIR Selected Papers of #AoIR2020*. The 21st

Annual Conference of the Association of Internet Researchers. https://doi.org/10.5210/spir.v2020i0.11236

Horaczek, S. (2012, February 2). People upload an average of 250 million photos per day to Facebook. *Popular Photography*. https://www.popphoto.com/news/2012/02/people-upload-average-250-million-photos-day-to-facebook/

Horsti, K. (2017). Digital Islamophobia: The Swedish woman as a figure of pure and dangerous whiteness. *New Media & Society*, *19*(19), 1440–1457. https://doi.org/10.1177/1461444816642169

Howard, P., & Kollanyi, B. (2016). Bots, #Strongerin, and #Brexit: Computational Propaganda During the UK-EU Referendum. https://dx.doi.org/10.2139/ssrn.2798311

Huber, L. P., Lopez, C. B., Malagon, M. C., Velez, V., & Solorzano, D. G. (2008). Getting beyond the "symptom," acknowledging the "disease": Theorizing racist nativism. *Contemporary Justice Review*, *11*(1), 39–51. https://doi.org/10.1080/10282580701850397

Huber, R. (2022). Populism and Climate Change. In *The Populism Interviews*. Routledge.

Hussein, S. (2015). Not eating the Muslim other: Halal certification, scaremongering, and the racialisation of Muslim identity. *International Journal for Crime, Justice and Social Democracy*. https://search.informit.org/doi/abs/10.3316/informit.252514045117578

Hwang, H., Kim, Y., & Huh, C. U. (2014). Seeing is believing: Effects of uncivil online debate on political polarization and expectations of deliberation. *Journal of Broadcasting & Electronic Media*, *58*(4), 621–633. https://doi.org/10.1080/08838151.2014.966365

Iakhnis, E., Rathbun, B., Reifler, J., & Scotto, T. J. (2018). Populist referendum: Was "Brexit" an expression of nativist and anti-elitist sentiment? *Research & Politics*, *5*(2), 1–7. https://doi.org/10.1177/2053168018773964

Intelligence Community Assessment. (2017). Assessing Russian activities and intentions in recent US elections. National Intelligence Council.

Ipsos MORI. (2022). *Is*sues Index: 2007 onwards. Ipsos MORI. https://www.ipsos.com/ipsos-mori/en-uk/issues-index-2007-onwards

Jackson, L. B. (2018). *Islamophobia in Britain: The Making of a Muslim Enemy*. Palgrave Macmillan. https://doi.org/10.1007/978-3-319-58350-1

Jackson, P., & Shekhovtsov, A. (Eds.). (2014). *The Post-War Anglo-American Far Right*. Palgrave Macmillan UK. https://doi.org/10.1057/9781137396211

Jacobs, K., Sandberg, L., & Spierings, N. (2020). Twitter and Facebook: Populists' double-barreled gun? *New Media & Society*, *22*(4), 611–633. https://doi.org/10.1177/1461444819893991

Jamin, J. (2014). Cultural Marxism and the Radical Right. In P. Jackson & A. Shekhovtsov (Eds.), *The Post-War Anglo-American Far Right: A Special Relationship of Hate* (pp. 84–103). Palgrave Macmillan UK. https://doi.org/10.1057/9781137396211_4

Jasser, G., McSwiney, J., Pertwee, E., & Zannettou, S. (2021). "Welcome to #GabFam": Far-right virtual community on Gab. *New Media & Society*, 14614448211024546. https://doi.org/10.1177/14614448211024546

Jay, A. (2014). *Independent Inquiry into Child Sexual Exploitation in Rotherham: 1997–2013*. Rotherham Metropolitan Borough Council. https://www.rotherham.gov.uk/downloads/file/279/independent-inquiry-into-child-sexual-exploitation-in-rotherham

Joseph-Salisbury, R. (2019). "Does anybody really care what a racist says?" Anti-racism in 'post-racial' times. *The Sociological Review*, *67*(1), 63–78. https://doi.org/10.1177/0038026118807672

Jovicic, S. (2020). Scrolling and the in-between spaces of boredom: Marginalized youths on the periphery of Vienna. *Ethos*, *48*(4), 498–516. https://doi.org/10.1111/etho.12294

Judge, D. (2022). "Would I Lie to You?": Boris Johnson and lying in the House of Commons. *The Political Quarterly*, *93*(1), 77–86. https://doi.org/10.1111/1467-923X.13105

Kalpokas, I. (2019). *A Political Theory of Post-truth*. Springer International Publishing. https://doi.org/10.1007/978-3-319-97713-3_1

Kalsnes, B., Larsson, A. O., & Enli, G. S. (2017). The social media logic of political interaction: Exploring citizens' and politicians' relationship on Facebook and Twitter. *First Monday 22*(2). https://doi.org/10.5210/fm.v22i2.6348

Karlsen, R., Steen-Johnsen, K., Wollebæk, D., & Enjolras, B. (2017). Echo chamber and trench warfare dynamics in online debates. *European Journal of Communication*, *32*(3), 257–273. https://doi.org/10.1177/0267323117695734

Kellner, D. (2018). Donald Trump and the politics of lying. In M. A. Peters, S. Rider, M. Hyvönen, & T. Besley (Eds.), *Post-Truth, Fake News: Viral Modernity & Higher Education* (pp. 89–100). Springer. https://doi.org/10.1007/978-981-10-8013-5_7

Kemp, S. (2021, February 9). Digital in Canada: All the Statistics You Need in 2021. DataReportal – Global Digital Insights. https://datareportal.com/reports/digital-2021-canada

Ker-Lindsay, J. (2018). Turkey's EU accession as a factor in the 2016 Brexit referendum. *Turkish Studies*, *19*(1), 1–22. https://doi.org/10.1080/14683849.2017.1366860

Kettell, S., & Kerr, P. (2021). The Brexit religion and the Holy Grail of the NHS. *Social Policy and Society*, *20*(2), 282–295. https://doi.org/10.1017/S1474746420000561

Kim, D. H., & Ellison, N. B. (2021). From observation on social media to offline political participation: The social media affordances approach. *New Media & Society*, 1461444821998346. https://doi.org/10.1177/1461444821998346

Kim, Y., & Kim, Y. (2019). Incivility on Facebook and political polarization: The mediating role of seeking further comments and negative emotion. *Computers in Human Behavior*, *99*, 219–227. https://doi.org/10.1016/j.chb.2019.05.022

Kinnvall, C. (2015). Borders and fear: Insecurity, gender and the Far Right in Europe. *Journal of Contemporary European Studies*, *23*(4), 514–529. https://doi.org/10.1080/14782804.2015.1056115

Kirchgaessner, S., Ganguly, M., Pegg, D., Cadwalladr, C., & Burke, J. (2023, February 15). Revealed: The hacking and disinformation team meddling in elections. *The Guardian*. https://www.theguardian.com/world/2023/feb/15/revealed-disinformation-team-jorge-claim-meddling-elections-tal-hanan

Klinger, U., & Svensson, J. (2015). The emergence of network media logic in political communication: A theoretical approach. *New Media & Society, 17*(8), 1241–1257. https://doi.org/10.1177/1461444814522952

Koch, I. (2017). What's in a vote? Brexit beyond culture wars. *American Ethnologist, 44*(2), 225–230. https://doi.org/10.1111/amet.12472

Koehler, D. (2014). The radical online: Individual radicalization processes and the role of the internet. *Journal for Deradicalization, 1*, Article 1.

Koram, K. (2020, June 4). Systemic racism and police brutality are British problems too. *The Guardian*. https://www.theguardian.com/commentisfree/2020/jun/04/systemic-racism-police-brutality-british-problems-black-lives-matter

Krämer, B. (2017). Populist online practices: The function of the internet in right-wing populism. *Information, Communication & Society, 20*(9), 1293–1309. https://doi.org/10.1080/1369118X.2017.1328520

Kundnani, A. (2000). "Stumbling on": Race, class and England. *Race & Class, 41*(4), 1–18. https://doi.org/10.1177/0306396800414005

Kundnani, A. (2001). In a foreign land: The new popular racism. *Race & Class, 43*(2), 41–60. https://doi.org/10.1177/0306396801432004

Kundnani, A. (2002). The Death of Multiculturalism. *Race & Class, 43*(4), 67–72. https://doi.org/10.1177/030639680204300406

Kundnani, A. (2007). Integrationism: The politics of anti-Muslim racism. *Race & Class, 48*(4), 24–44. https://doi.org/10.1177/0306396807077069

Kundnani, A. (2012). Multiculturalism and its discontents: Left, Right and liberal. *European Journal of Cultural Studies, 15*(2), 155–166. https://doi.org/10.1177/1367549411432027

Kundnani, A. (2014). *The Muslims Are Coming!: Islamophobia, Extremism, and the Domestic War on Terror*. Verso Books.

Laclau, E. (2005). *On Populist Reason*. Verso.

Langlois, G., & Elmer, G. (2013). The Research Politics of Social Media Platforms. *Culture Machine, 14*. https://culturemachine.net/wp-content/uploads/2019/05/505-1170-1-PB.pdf

Latzko-Toth, G., Bonneau, C., & Millette, M. (2016). Small data, thick data: Thickening strategies for trace-based social media research. In *The SAGE Handbook of Social Media Research Methods* (pp. 199–214). SAGE Publications Ltd. https://doi.org/10.4135/9781473983847

Laybats, C., & Tredinnick, L. (2016). Post truth, information, and emotion. *Business Information Review, 33*(4), 204–206. https://doi.org/10.1177/0266382116680741

Lee, B. (2019). Overview of the far-right. Centre for Research and Evidence on Security Threats (CREST). https://assets.publishing.service.gov.uk/government/uploads/system/uploads/attachment_data/file/834424/Ben_Lee_-_Overview_of_the_far_right.pdf

Leidig, E. (2021). From love jihad to grooming gangs: Tracing flows of the hypersexual Muslim male through far-right female ifluencers. *Religions*, *12*(12), Article 12. https://doi.org/10.3390/rel12121083

Lentin, A. (2014). Post-race, post politics: The paradoxical rise of culture after multiculturalism. *Ethnic and Racial Studies*, *37*(8), 1268–1285. https://doi.org/10.1080/01419870.2012.664278

Lentin, A. (2018). Beyond denial: "Not racism" as racist violence. *Continuum*, *32*(4), 400–414. https://doi.org/10.1080/10304312.2018.1480309

Lewis, P., & Hilder, P. (2018, March 23). Cambridge Analytica misled MPs over work for Leave.EU, says ex-director. *The Guardian*. https://www.theguardian.com/news/2018/mar/23/cambridge-analytica-misled-mps-over-work-for-leave-eu-says-ex-director-brittany-kaiser

Lewis, R. (2020). "This is what the news won't show you": YouTube creators and the reactionary politics of micro-celebrity. *Television & New Media*, *21*(2), 201–217. https://doi.org/10.1177/1527476419879919

Lilleker, D. G., & Bonacci, D. (2017). The structure of political e-expression: What the Brexit campaign can teach us about political talk on Facebook. *International Journal of Digital Television*, *8*(3), 335–350. https://doi.org/10.1386/jdtv.8.3.335_1

Lima, C. (2021). A whistleblower's power: Key takeaways from the Facebook Papers. *Washington Post*, October 26. https://www.washingtonpost.com/technology/2021/10/25/what-are-the-facebook-papers/

Lippard, C. D. (2011). Racist nativism in the 21st century. *Sociology Compass*, *5*(7), 591–606.

Little, O., & Richards, A. (2021, October 5). TikTok's algorithm leads users from transphobic videos to far-right rabbit holes. Media Matters for America. https://www.mediamatters.org/tiktok/tiktoks-algorithm-leads-users-transphobic-videos-far-right-rabbit-holes

Loader, B. D., Vromen, A., & Xenos, M. A. (2014). The networked young citizen: Social media, political participation and civic engagement. *Information, Communication & Society*, *17*(2), 143–150. https://doi.org/10.1080/1369118X.2013.871571

Logan, K., Bright, L. F., & Grau, S. L. (2018). "Unfriend me, please!": Social media fatigue and the theory of rational choice. *Journal of Marketing Theory and Practice*, *26*(4), 357–367. https://doi.org/10.1080/10696679.2018.1488219

Loke, J. (2012). Public expressions of private sentiments: Unveiling the pulse of racial tolerance through online news readers' comments. *Howard Journal of Communications*, *23*(3), 235–252. https://doi.org/10.1080/10646175.2012.695643

Lowe, J. (2016, June 3). Brexit campaigner Michael Gove says he's "glad" big economic bodies don't back Brexit. *Newsweek*. https://www.newsweek.com/michael-gove-sky-news-brexit-economics-imf-466365

Lundby, K. (2009). Media logic: Looking for social interaction. In K. Lundby (Ed.), *Mediatization: Concept, Changes, Consequences* (pp. 101–119). Peter Lang Inc.

Lupinacci, L. (2020). "Absentmindedly scrolling through nothing": Liveness and compulsory continuous connectedness in social media: *Media, Culture & Society*. https://doi.org/10.1177/0163443720939454

Lupton, D., & Southerton, C. (2021). The thing-power of the Facebook assemblage: Why do users stay on the platform? *Journal of Sociology*, *57*(4), 969–985. https://doi.org/10.1177/1440783321989456

Lusher, A. (2018, March 22). Suspended Cambridge Analytica CEO recalled to parliament over "inconsistencies" in evidence. *The Independent*. https://www.independent.co.uk/news/uk/home-news/cambridge-analytica-ceo-alexander-nix-recalled-parliament-select-committee-inconsistencies-evidence-mps-a8269296.html

Lyotard, J.-F. (1993). *The Postmodern Explained: Correspondence, 1982–1985*. University of Minnesota Press.

Macafee, T., & De Simone, J. J. (2012). Killing the bill online? Pathways to young people's protest engagement via social media. *Cyberpsychology, Behavior, and Social Networking*, *15*(11), 579–584. https://doi.org/10.1089/cyber.2012.0153

Maggs, J. (2020). The 'Channel Crossings' and the borders of Britain. *Race & Class*, *61*(3), 78–86. https://doi.org/10.1177/0306396819892467

Mann, R., & Fenton, S. (2009). The personal contexts of national sentiments. *Journal of Ethnic and Migration Studies*,35 (4), 517–534. https://doi.org/10.1080/13691830902764882

Marcus, G. E. (2003). The psychology of emotion and politics. In D. O. Sears, L. Huddy, & R. Jervis (Eds.), *Oxford Handbook of Political Psychology* (pp. 182–221). Oxford University Press.

Marshall, H., & Drieschova, A. (2018). Post-truth politics in the UK's Brexit referendum. *New Perspectives*, *26*(3), 89–105. https://doi.org/10.1177/2336825X1802600305

Martin, D. (2018a, March 27). What role did Cambridge Analytica play in the Brexit vote? *DW*. https://www.dw.com/en/what-role-did-cambridge-analytica-play-in-the-brexit-vote/a-43151460

Martin, G. (2018b, December 17). Shockwaves from French "yellow vest" protests felt across Europe. *The Conversation*. http://theconversation.com/shockwaves-from-french-yellow-vest-protests-felt-across-europe-108578

Martin, P. (2013). Racism, differentialism and antiracism in everyday ideology. A mixed-methods study in Britain. *International Journal of Conflict and Violence*, *7*(1), Article 1.

Marwick, A., Clancy, B., & Furl, K. (2022). Far-right online radicalization: A review of the literature. *Bulletin of Technology & Public Life*. https://doi.org/10.21428/bfcb0bff.e9492a11

Marwick, A. E., & boyd, danah. (2011). I tweet honestly, I tweet passionately: Twitter users, context collapse, and the imagined audience. *New Media & Society*, *13*(1), 114–133. https://doi.org/10.1177/1461444810365313

Marwick, A. E., & Partin, W. C. (2022). Constructing alternative facts: Populist expertise and the QAnon conspiracy. *New Media & Society*, 14614448221090200. https://doi.org/10.1177/14614448221090201

Maton, K. (2003). Reflexivity, relationism, & research: Pierre Bourdieu and the epistemic conditions of social scientific knowledge. *Space and Culture*, *6*(1), 52–65. https://doi.org/10.1177/1206331202238962

Matthews, J. (2015). Framing alleged Islamist plots: A case study of British press coverage since 9/11. *Critical Studies on Terrorism*, *8*(2), 266–283. https://doi.org/10.1080/17539153.2015.1042305

McDonald, K. (2018). *Radicalization*. Polity Press.

McGranahan, C. (2017). An anthropology of lying: Trump and the political sociality of moral outrage. *American Ethnologist*, *44*(2), 243–248. https://doi.org/10.1111/amet.12475

McKenzie, L. (2017). The class politics of prejudice: Brexit and the land of no-hope and glory. *British Journal of Sociology*, *68*(S1), S265–S280. https://doi.org/10.1111/1468-4446.12329

Mellon, J., & Prosser, C. (2017). Twitter and Facebook are not representative of the general population: Political attitudes and demographics of British social media users. *Research & Politics*, *4*.

Meredith, J., & Richardson, E. (2019). The use of the political categories of Brexiter and Remainer in online comments about the EU referendum. *Journal of Community & Applied Social Psychology*, *29*(1), 43–55. https://doi.org/10.1002/casp.2384

Messaris, P., & Abraham, L. (2001). The role of images in framing news stories. In S. D. Reese, O. H. Gandy, & A. E. Grant (Eds.), *Framing Public Life: Perspectives on Media and Our Understanding of the Social World* (pp. 215–226). Lawrence Erlbaum.

Metz, M., Kruikemeier, S., & Lecheler, S. (2020). Personalization of politics on Facebook: Examining the content and effects of professional, emotional and private self-personalization. *Information, Communication & Society*, *23*(10), 1481–1498. https://doi.org/10.1080/1369118X.2019.1581244

Miles, R., & Brown, M. (2003). *Racism* (2nd ed.). Routledge.

Millington, G. (2010). Racism, class ethos and place: The value of context in narratives about asylum-seekers. *The Sociological Review*, *58*(3), 361–380. https://doi.org/10.1111/j.1467-954X.2010.01926.x

Mintchev, N. (2021). The cultural politics of racism in the Brexit conjuncture. *International Journal of Cultural Studies*, *24*(1), 123–140. https://doi.org/10.1177/1367877920935135

Mintchev, N., & Moore, H. L. (2019). Brexit's identity politics and the question of subjectivity. *Psychoanalysis, Culture & Society*, *24*(4), 452–472. https://doi.org/10.1057/s41282-019-00139-3

Mirrlees, T. (2018). The alt-right's discourse on "Cultural Marxism": A political instrument of intersectional hate. *Atlantis: Critical Studies in Gender, Culture & Social Justice*, *39*(1), Article 1.

Miskimmon, A., O'Loughlin, B., & Roselle, L. (2013). *Strategic Narratives: Communication Power and the New World Order*. Routledge. https://doi.org/10.4324/9781315871264

Mizen, P. (2015). The madness that is the world: Young activists' emotional reasoning and their participation in a local Occupy movement. *The Sociological Review*, *63*(S2), 167–182. https://doi.org/10.1111/1467-954X.12267

Modood, T. (2015). "Difference," cultural racism and anti-racism. In P. Werbner & T. Modood (Eds.), *Debating Cultural Hybridity: Multicultural Identities and the Politics of Anti-Racism*. Bloomsbury Publishing.

Mondon, A., & Winter, A. (2020). *Reactionary Democracy: How Racism and the Populist Far Right Became Mainstream*. Verso Books.

Montgomery, M. (2017). Post-truth politics?: Authenticity, populism and the electoral discourses of Donald Trump. *Journal of Language and Politics*, 16(4), 619–639. https://doi.org/10.1075/jlp.17023.mon

Moore, M., & Ramsay, G. (2017). UK media coverage of the 2016 EU Referendum campaign (p. 188). Centre for the Study of Media, Communication and Power.

Morelock, J., & Narita, F. Z. (2022). The nexus of QAnon and COVID-19: Legitimation crisis and epistemic crisis. *Critical Sociology*, 48(6), 1005–1024. https://doi.org/10.1177/08969205211069614

Moskalenko, S., & McCauley, C. (2021). QAnon: Radical Opinion versus Radical Action. *Perspectives on Terrorism*, 15(2), 142–146.

Moss, J., Robinson, E., & Watts, J. (2020). Brexit and the everyday politics of emotion: Methodological lessons from history. *Political Studies*, 68(4), 837–856. https://doi.org/10.1177/0032321720911915

Mouffe, C. (2019). The populist moment. *Simbiótica. Revista Eletrônica*, 06–11.

Mudde, C. (2004). The populist zeitgeist. *Government and Opposition*, 39(4), 541–563. https://doi.org/10.1111/j.1477-7053.2004.00135.x

Mudde, C. (2007). *Populist Radical Right Parties in Europe*. Cambridge University Press. https://doi.org/10.1017/CBO9780511492037

Mudde, C. (2019). The far right today. *Polity*. http://web.b.ebscohost.com.manchester.idm.oclc.org/ehost/ebookviewer/ebook/bmxlYmtfXzIyODM1NDZfX0FO0?sid=4f7c7609-7928-43dd-91b0-1ca459bef0d8@pdc-v-sessmgr02&vid=0&format=EK&lpid=navPoint-6&rid=0

Musolff, A. (2017). Truths, lies and figurative scenarios: Metaphors at the heart of Brexit. *Journal of Language and Politics*, 16(5), 641–657. https://doi.org/10.1075/jlp.16033.mus

Narusawa, M. (2013). Abe Shinzo: Japan's new prime minister a Ffar-right denier of history. *The Asia-Pacific Journal: Japan Focus*, 11(1). https://apjjf.org/2013/11/1/Narusawa-Muneo/3879/article.html

Nast, C. (2016, June 14). We should ban old people from voting. *British GQ*. https://www.gq-magazine.co.uk/article/eu-referendum-old-people-should-not-vote

National Audit Office. (2017). Homelessness. https://www.nao.org.uk/wp-content/uploads/2017/09/Homelessness.pdf

Nefes, T. S. (2013). Political parties' perceptions and uses of anti-semitic conspiracy theories in Turkey. *The Sociological Review*, 61(2), 247–264.

Newman, N. (2021). Reuters Institute Digital News Report 2021. Reuters Institute for the Study of Journalism. https://reutersinstitute.politics.ox.ac.uk/sites/default/files/2021-06/Digital_News_Report_2021_FINAL.pdf

Nicholls, B. (2019). Postmodernism in the twenty-first century: Jordan Peterson, Jean Baudrillard and the problem of chaos. In R. Overell & B. Nicholls (Eds.),

Post-Truth and the Mediation of Reality: New Conjunctures (pp. 57–78). Palgrave Macmillan.

Norris, P., & Inglehart, R. (2019). *Cultural Backlash: Trump, Brexit, and Authoritarian Populism*. Cambridge University Press.

North, S., Piwek, L., & Joinson, A. (2021). Battle for Britain: Analyzing events as drivers of political tribalism in Twitter discussions of Brexit. *Policy & Internet*, *13*(2), 185–208. https://doi.org/10.1002/poi3.247

Nussbaum, M. (2013). *Political Emotions: Why Love Matters for Justice*. The Belknap Press of Harvard University Press.

Oborne, P. (2021). *The Assault on Truth: Boris Johnson, Donald Trump and the Emergence of a New Moral Barbarism*. Simon and Schuster.

O'Dea, S. (2018). Leading social networks ranked by usage in the United Kingdom (UK) in January 2018. Statista. https://www.statista.com/statistics/611105/leading-social-networks-ranked-by-daily-use-in-the-united-kingdom-uk/

Ofcom. (2022). News Consumption in the UK: 2022 Overview of research findings. https://www.ofcom.org.uk/__data/assets/pdf_file/0024/241827/News-Consumption-in-the-UK-Overview-of-findings-2022.pdf

Ofcom. (2017, June 20). Rise of the Social Seniors revealed. Ofcom. https://www.ofcom.org.uk/about-ofcom/latest/features-and-news/rise-social-seniors

O'Neill, B. (2020, February 3). The Remainer elites are the true bigots of Brexit Britain. *Spiked*. https://www.spiked-online.com/2020/02/03/the-remainer-elites-are-the-true-bigots-of-brexit-britain/

Outhwaite, W. (Ed.). (2017). *Brexit: Sociological Responses*. Anthem Press. https://www.cambridge.org/core/books/brexit/8E600626B072D21686FDD2CE55A9BDBA

Overell, R., & Nicholls, B. (2019). Introduction. In R. Overell & B. Nicholls (Eds.), *Post-Truth and the Mediation of Reality: New Conjunctures*. Palgrave Macmillan.

Page, R. (2018). *Narratives Online: Shared Stories in Social Media*. Cambridge University Press.

Palfrey, J., & Gasser, U. (2008). *Born Digital: Understanding the First Generation of Digital Natives*. Basic Books.

Papacharissi, Z. (2015). *Affective Publics: Sentiment, Technology, and Politics*. Oxford University Press.

Papacharissi, Z., & Trevey, M. T. (2018). Affective publics and windows of opportunity: Social media and the potential for social change. In G. Meikle (Ed.), *The Routledge Companion to Media and Activism*. Routledge.

Parker, S., Bennett, S., Cobden, C. M., & Earnshaw, D. (2022). "It's time we invested in stronger borders": Media representations of refugees crossing the English Channel by boat. *Critical Discourse Studies*, *19*(4), 348–363. https://doi.org/10.1080/17405904.2021.1920998

Patel, T. G., & Connelly, L. (2019). "Post-race" racisms in the narratives of "Brexit" voters. *The Sociological Review*, *67*(5), 968–984. https://doi.org/10.1177/0038026119831590

Paternotte, D., & Verloo, M. (2021). De-democratization and the politics of knowledge: Unpacking the cultural Marxism narrative. *Social Politics: International*

Studies in Gender, State & Society, *28*(3), 556–578. https://doi.org/10.1093/sp/jxab025

Peat, J. (2017, February 8). Vote Leave director admits they won because they lied to the public. *The London Economic*. https://www.thelondoneconomic.com/news/vote-leave-director-admits-won-lied-public/08/02/

Pedersen, M. A., Albris, K., & Seaver, N. (2021). The political economy of attention. *Annual Review of Anthropology*, *50*(1), 309–325. https://doi.org/10.1146/annurev-anthro-101819-110356

Pelinka, A. (2013). Right-wing populism: Concept and typology. In R. Wodak, M. KhosraviNik, & B. Mral (Eds.), *Right-Wing Populism in Europe: Politics and Discourse*. Bloomsbury Academic.

Pencheva, D. (2016, July 26). Brexit: How did news media play a role? | *PolicyBristol Hub*. https://policybristol.blogs.bris.ac.uk/2016/07/26/brexit-how-did-news-media-play-a-role/

Penney, J. (2018). Young People as Political Influencers on Social Media: Skepticism and Network Thinking. *Proceedings of the 9th International Conference on Social Media and Society*, 355–359. https://doi.org/10.1145/3217804.3217944

Pentzold, C., & Bischof, A. (2019). Making affordances real: Socio-material prefiguration, performed agency, and coordinated activities in human–robot communication. *Social Media + Society*, *5*(3), 2056305119865472. https://doi.org/10.1177/2056305119865472

Pepin-Neff, C., & Cohen, A. (2021). President Trump's transgender moral panic. *Policy Studies*, *42*(5–6), 646–661. https://doi.org/10.1080/01442872.2021.1952971

Petley, J. (2018a). "A Wave of Hysteria and Bigotry": Sexual Politics and the "Loony Left." In J. Curran & I. Gaber (Eds.), *Culture Wars: The Media and the British Left* (2nd ed.). Routledge.

Petley, J. (2018b). "Not funny but sick": Urban myths. In J. Curran, I. Gaber, & J. Petley (Eds.), *Culture Wars: The Media and the British Left* (2nd ed.). Routledge.

Phillips, J., & Yi, J. (2018). Charlottesville paradox: The "Liberalizing" alt-right, "Authoritarian" left, and politics of dialogue. *Society*, *55*(3), 221–228. https://doi.org/10.1007/s12115-018-0243-0

Piazza, R., & Lashmar, P. (2017). Jeremy Corbyn according to the BBC: Ideological representation and identity construction of the Labour Party leader. *Critical Approaches to Discourse Analysis across Disciplines*, *9*(2), Article 2.

Pilkington, H. (2016). *Loud and Proud: Passion and Politics in the English Defence League*. Manchester University Press.

Pilkington, H. (2019). "Field observer: Simples." Finding a place from which to do close-up research on the "far right." In E. Toscano (Ed.), *Researching Far-Right Movements: Ethics, Methodologies, and Qualitative Inquiries*. Routledge.

Pilkington, H. (2020). Understanding "right-wing extremism": In theory and practice (Young People's Trajectories through Anti-Islam(Ist) and Extreme Right Milieus: Country Level Report). DARE: Dialogue about Radicalisation and Equality. http://www.dare-h2020.org/uploads/1/2/1/7/12176018/d7.1_united_kingdom_1.pdf

Pilkington, H., & Vestel, V. (2021). Young people's trajectories through anti-Islam(ist) and extreme-right milieus: Cross national synthesis report. DARE: Dialogue about Radicalisation and Equality. https://www.dare-h2020.org/uploads/1/2/1/7/12176018/d7._2_-_cross_country_synthesis_final.pdf

Puar, J. (2013). Rethinking homonationalism. *International Journal of Middle East Studies*, *45*(2), 336–339. https://doi.org/10.1017/S002074381300007X

Quattrociocchi, W., Scala, A., & Sunstein, C. R. (2016). *Echo Chambers on Facebook* (SSRN Scholarly Paper ID 2795110). Social Science Research Network. https://doi.org/10.2139/ssrn.2795110

Rader, E., & Gray, R. (2015). Understanding User Beliefs About Algorithmic Curation in the Facebook News Feed. *Proceedings of the 33rd Annual ACM Conference on Human Factors in Computing Systems*, 173–182. https://doi.org/10.1145/2702123.2702174

Reality Check. (2019, July 25). Brexit: Does the UK owe the EU £39bn? *BBC News*. https://www.bbc.com/news/uk-politics-48586677

Reddy, W. M. (2001). *The Navigation of Feeling: A Framework for the History of Emotions*. Cambridge University Press.

Rhodes, J. (2010). White backlash, "Unfairness" and justifications of British National Party (BNP) support. *Ethnicities*, *10*(1), 77–99. https://doi.org/10.1177/1468796809353392

Rhodes, J., & Hall, N.-A. (2020). Racism, nationalism and the politics of resentment in contemporary England. In J. Solomos (Ed.), *Routledge International Handbook of Contemporary Racisms*. https://public.ebookcentral.proquest.com/choice/publicfullrecord.aspx?p=6121551

Ribeiro, M. H., Calais, P. H., Almeida, V. A. F., & Meira Jr, W. (2017). "Everything I disagree with is #FakeNews": Correlating political polarization and spread of misinformation. *ArXiv:1706.05924 [Cs]*. http://arxiv.org/abs/1706.05924

Richardson, J. E. (2015). "Cultural Marxism" and the British National Party: A transnational discourse. In *Cultures of Post-War British Fascism*. Routledge.

Risso, L. (2018). Harvesting Your Soul? Cambridge Analytica and Brexit. *Brexit Means Brexit?* the Symposium, Akademie der Wissenschaften under Literatur, Mainz. http://www.adwmainz.de/fileadmin/user_upload/Brexit-Symposium_Online-Version.pdf#page=75

Robertson, D. G., & Amarasingam, A. (2022). How conspiracy theorists argue: Epistemic capital in the QAnon social media sphere. *Popular Communication*, *20*(3), 193–207. https://doi.org/10.1080/15405702.2022.2050238

Rogers, R. (2020). Deplatforming: Following extreme internet celebrities to telegram and alternative social media. *European Journal of Communication*, *35*(3), 213–229. https://doi.org/10.1177/0267323120922066

Rone, J. (2021). "Enemies of the people"? Diverging discourses on sovereignty in media coverage of Brexit. *British Politics*. https://doi.org/10.1057/s41293-021-00157-9

Rone, J. (2022). Far right alternative news media as "indignation mobilization mechanisms": How the far right opposed the Global Compact for Migration. *Information,*

Communication & Society, *25*(9), 1333–1350. https://doi.org/10.1080/1369118X.2020.1864001

Rooduijn, M. (2019). State of the field: How to study populism and adjacent topics? A plea for both more and less focus. *European Journal of Political Research*, *58*(1), 362–372. https://doi.org/10.1111/1475-6765.12314

Rosa, J. M., & Ruiz, C. J. (2020). Reason vs. emotion in the Brexit campaign: How key political actors and their followers used Twitter. *First Monday*, *25*(3). https://doi.org/10.5210/fm.v25i3.9601

Rose, J. (2017). Brexit, Trump, and post-truth politics. *Public Integrity*, *19*(6), 555–558. https://doi.org/10.1080/10999922.2017.1285540

Ross Arguedas, A., Robertson, C. T., Fletcher, R., & Nielsen, R. K. (2022). Echo chambers, filter bubbles, and polarisation: A literature review. Reuters Institute for the Study of Journalism. https://reutersinstitute.politics.ox.ac.uk/echo-chambers-filter-bubbles-and-polarisation-literature-review

Royall, F. (2020). The Gilets Jaunes protests: Mobilisation without third-party support. *Modern & Contemporary France*, *28*(1), 99–118. https://doi.org/10.1080/09639489.2019.1676217

Ryan, L. (2020, June 8). 'Led by the science': The changing role of experts from Brexit to Covid19. *The British Sociological Association*. https://es.britsoc.co.uk/led-by-the-science-the-changing-role-of-experts-from-brexit-to-covid19/

Rzepnikowska, A. (2019). Racism and xenophobia experienced by Polish migrants in the UK before and after Brexit vote. *Journal of Ethnic and Migration Studies*, *45*(1), 61–77. https://doi.org/10.1080/1369183X.2018.1451308

Saini, R. (2017, March 23). "Racial self-interest" is not racism: Populist correctness gone mad? *Media Diversified*. https://mediadiversified.org/2017/03/23/racial-self-interest-is-not-racism-populist-correctness-gone-mad/

Sanchez, G. J. (1997). Face the nation: Race, Immigration, and the rise of nativism in late twentieth century America. *The International Migration Review*, *31* (4), 1009–1030. https://doi.org/10.2307/2547422

Saurette, P., & Gunster, S. (2011). Ears wide shut: Epistemological populism, argutainment and Canadian conservative talk radio. *Canadian Journal of Political Science / Revue Canadienne de Science Politique*, *44*(1), 195–218. JSTOR.

Savolainen, L. (2022). The shadow banning controversy: Perceived governance and algorithmic folklore—Laura Savolainen, 2022. *Media, Culture & Society, Online First*. https://journals.sagepub.com/doi/full/10.1177/01634437221077174

Sayer, A. (2011). *Why Things Matter to People: Social Science, Values and Ethical Life*. Cambridge University Press.

Sayer, D. (2017). White riot—Brexit, Trump, and post-factual politics. *Journal of Historical Sociology*, *30*(1), 92–106. https://doi.org/10.1111/johs.12153

Scatamburlo-D'Annibale, V. (2019). The "Culture Wars" reloaded: Trump, anti-political correctness and the Right's "free speech" hypocrisy. *Journal for Critical Education Policy Studies*, *17*(1), 69–119.

Schrieberg, D. (2016, July 1). *Angry Old People Shouldn't Be Allowed To Vote*. Forbes. https://www.forbes.com/sites/davidschrieberg1/2016/07/01/angry-old-people-shouldnt-be-allowed-to-vote/

Schuster, J. (2013). Invisible feminists? Social media and young women's political participation. *Political Science*, *65*(1), 8–24. https://doi.org/10.1177/0032318713486474

Schwartz, C., Simon, M., Hudson, D., & Hudson, J. (2020). A Populist Paradox? How Brexit Softened Anti-Immigration Attitudes. *British Journal of Political Science*. https://www.cambridge.org/core/journals/british-journal-of-political-science

Sealy, T. (2014). Multiculturalism is dead or how civic stratification shows us it hasn't yet lived. *Essex Graduate Journal of Sociology*, 167–182.

Sengul, K. (2021). "It's OK to be white": The discursive construction of victimhood, "anti-white racism" and calculated ambivalence in Australia. *Critical Discourse Studies*, 1–17. https://doi.org/10.1080/17405904.2021.1921818

Skeggs, B. (1997). *Formations of Class & Gender: Becoming Respectable*. Sage.

Skeggs, B., & Loveday, V. (2012). Struggles for value: Value practices, injustice, judgment, affect and the idea of class. *British Journal of Sociology*, *63*(3), 472–490. https://doi.org/10.1111/j.1468-4446.2012.01420.x

Sloan, L. (2017). Who Tweets in the United Kingdom? Profiling the Twitter population using the British social attitudes survey 2015. *Social Media + Society*, *3*(1), 1–11.

Smith, A. M. (1994). *New Right Discourse on Race and Sexuality: Britain, 1968–1990*. Cambridge University Press.

Smith, N. (2016, July 30). Who are the Corbynistas? *BBC News*. https://www.bbc.com/news/uk-politics-36922609

Solomos, J. (2003). *Race and Racism in Britain* (3rd ed.). Palgrave Macmillan.

Somers, M. R. (1994). The narrative constitution of identity: A relational and network approach. *Theory and Society*, *23*(5), 605–649. https://doi.org/10.1007/BF00992905

Souliotis, N., & Alexandri, G. (2017). From embedded to uncompromising neoliberalism: Competitiveness policies and European Union interscalar relations in the case of Greece. *European Urban and Regional Studies*, *24*(3), 227–240. https://doi.org/10.1177/0969776416630582

Spiering, M. (2004). *British Euroscepticism* (pp. 127–149). Brill. https://doi.org/10.1163/9789401201087_007

Spindler, W. (2015, December 8). *2015: The year of Europe's refugee crisis*. UNHCR. https://www.unhcr.org/news/stories/2015/12/56ec1ebde/2015-year-europes-refugee-crisis.html

Spring, M., & Webster, L. (2019, May 30). European elections: How disinformation spread in Facebook groups. *BBC News*. https://www.bbc.com/news/blogs-trending-48356351

Steber, M. (2018). Fundamentals at stake: The Conservatives, industrial relations and the rhetorical framing of the miners' strike in 1984/1985. *Contemporary British History*, *32*(1), 60–77. https://doi.org/10.1080/13619462.2017.1408536

Stein, J. (2016). *How trolls are ruining the internet*. http://time.com/4457110/internet-trolls/

Steinfeldt, J. A., Foltz, B. D., Kaladow, J. K., Carlson, T. N., Pagano, Jr., L. A., Benton, E., & Steinfeldt, M. C. (2010). Racism in the electronic age: Role of online forums in expressing racial attitudes about American Indians. *Cultural Diversity and Ethnic Minority Psychology*, *16*(3), 362–371.

Stephens, P. (2005). Britain and Europe: An unforgettable past and an unavoidable future. *The Political Quarterly*, *76*(1), 12–21. https://doi.org/10.1111/j.1467-923X.2005.00652.x

Stewart, B. (2020). The rise of far-right civilizationism. *Critical Sociology*, *46*(7–8), 1207–1220. https://doi.org/10.1177/0896920519894051

Stockemer, D., Niemann, A., Unger, D., & Speyer, J. (2020). The "refugee crisis," immigration attitudes, and Euroscepticism. *International Migration Review*, *54*(3), 883–912. https://doi.org/10.1177/0197918319879926

Stockham, R. (2015, February 23). Is UKIP a racist party? These 15 comments would suggest so. *Left Foot Forward*. https://leftfootforward.org/2015/02/is-ukip-a-racist-party-these-15-comments-would-suggest-so/

Suler, J. (2005). The online disinhibition effect. *International Journal of Applied Psychoanalytic Studies*, *2*(2), 184–188. https://doi.org/10.1002/aps.42

Sunstein, C. R. (2018). *#Republic: Divided Democracy in the Age of Social Media*. Princeton University Press.

Supran, G., & Oreskes, N. (2021). Rhetoric and frame analysis of ExxonMobil's climate change communications. *One Earth*, *4*(5), 696–719. https://doi.org/10.1016/j.oneear.2021.04.014

Sveningsson, M. (2014). "I don't like it and I think it's useless, people discussing politics on Facebook": Young Swedes' understandings of social media use for political discussion. *Cyberpsychology: Journal of Psychosocial Research on Cyberspace*, *8*(3), Article 3. https://doi.org/10.5817/CP2014-3-8

Swami, V., David, B., Laura, W., & Adrian, F. (2018). To Brexit or not to Brexit: The roles of Islamophobia, conspiracist beliefs, and integrated threat in voting intentions for the United Kingdom European Union membership referendum. *British Journal of Psychology 109*(1), 156–179. https://doi.org/doi:10.1111/bjop.12252

The Independent. (2018, July 27). Final say: The misinformation that was told about Brexit during and after the referendum. *The Independent*. https://www.independent.co.uk/news/uk/politics/final-say-brexit-referendum-lies-boris-johnson-leave-campaign-remain-a8466751.html

Thomas, E., & Titheradge, N. (2018, August 16). Manchester mosque sermon "called for armed jihad," say scholars. *BBC News*. https://www.bbc.com/news/uk-44729727

Thorbjørnsrud, K., & Figenschou, T. U. (2022). The alarmed citizen: Fear, mistrust, and alternative media. *Journalism Practice*, *16*(5), 1018–1035. https://doi.org/10.1080/17512786.2020.1825113

Thorson, K., Cotter, K., Medeiros, M., & Pak, C. (2021). Algorithmic inference, political interest, and exposure to news and politics on Facebook. *Information, Communication & Society*, *24*(2), 183–200. https://doi.org/10.1080/1369118X.2019.1642934

Transgender Europe. (2022, November 8). TMM Update Trans Day of Remembrance 2022. *Transrespect versus Transphobia*. https://transrespect.org/en/tmm-update-tdor-2022/

Treib, O. (2014). The voter says no, but nobody listens: Causes and consequences of the Eurosceptic vote in the 2014 European elections. *Journal of European Public Policy*, *21*(10), 1541–1554. https://doi.org/10.1080/13501763.2014.941534

Trotta, D. (2017, February 23). Trump revokes Obama guidelines on transgender bathrooms. *Reuters*. https://www.reuters.com/article/us-usa-trump-lgbt-idUSKBN161243

Tucker, J. A., Guess, A., Barbera, P., Vaccari, C., Siegel, A., Sanovich, S., Stukal, D., & Nyhan, B. (2018). *Social Media, Political Polarization, and Political Disinformation: A Review of the Scientific Literature* (SSRN Scholarly Paper ID 3144139). Social Science Research Network. https://doi.org/10.2139/ssrn.3144139

Turcotte, J., York, C., Irving, J., Scholl, R. M., & Pingree, R. J. (2015). News recommendations from social media opinion leaders: Effects on media trust and information seeking. *Journal of Computer-Mediated Communication*, *20*(5), 520–535. https://doi.org/10.1111/jcc4.12127

Tyler, K., Degnen, C., & Blamire, J. (2022). Leavers and Remainers as "kinds of people": Accusations of racism amidst Brexit. *Ethnos*, 1–18. https://doi.org/10.1080/00141844.2022.2155208

Valluvan, S., & Kalra, V. S. (2019). Racial nationalisms: Brexit, borders and Little Englander contradictions. *Ethnic and Racial Studies*, *42*(14), 2393–2412. https://doi.org/10.1080/01419870.2019.1640890

van Dijck, J. (2012). Facebook as a tool for producing sociality and connectivity. *Television & New Media*, *13*(2), 160–176. https://doi.org/10.1177/1527476411415291

van Dijck, J. (2013). *The Culture of Connectivity: A Critical History Of Social Media*. Oxford University Press.

van Dijck, J., & Poell, T. (2013). Understanding social media logic. *Media and Communication*,*1*Issue (1), 13. https://doi.org/10.17645/mac.v1i1.70

van Dijk, T. A. (2000). New(s) racism: A discourse analytical approach. In S. Cottle (Ed.), *Ethnic Minorities and the Media: Changing cultural boundaries*. Open University Press. https://pdfs.semanticscholar.org/dc0e/d424307e8c84360bac6d031d6bc299d92c19.pdf

Van Raemdonck, N. (2019). *The Echo Chamber of Anti-Vaccination Conspiracies: Mechanisms of Radicalization on Facebook and Reddit* (SSRN Scholarly Paper ID 3510196). Social Science Research Network. https://papers.ssrn.com/abstract=3510196

Vasilopoulou, S., & Wagner, M. (2017). Fear, anger and enthusiasm about the European Union: Effects of emotional reactions on public preferences towards European integration. *European Union Politics*, *18*(3), 382–405. https://doi.org/10.1177/1465116517698048

Venditti, S., Piredda, F., & Mattana, W. (2017). Micronarratives as the form of contemporary communication. *The Design Journal*, *20*(sup1), S273–S282. https://doi.org/10.1080/14606925.2017.1352804

Vera Espinoza, M., Hadj-Abdou, L., & Brumat, L. (2018, December 7). Global Compact for Migration: What is it and why are countries opposing it? *The*

Conversation. http://theconversation.com/global-compact-for-migration-what-is-it-and-why-are-countries-opposing-it-106654

Verbalyte, M., & Scheve, C. von. (2018). Feeling Europe: Political emotion, knowledge, and support for the European Union. *Innovation: The European Journal of Social Science Research*, *31*(2), 162–188. https://doi.org/10.1080/13511610.2017.1398074

Verduyn, P., Lee, D. S., Park, J., Shablack, H., Orvell, A., Bayer, J., Ybarra, O., Jonides, J., & Kross, E. (2015). Passive Facebook usage undermines affective well-being: Experimental and longitudinal evidence. *Journal of Experimental Psychology: General*, *144*(2), 480–488. https://doi.org/10.1037/xge0000057

Vertovec, S., & Wessendorf, S. (2010). *The Multiculturalism Backlash: European Discourses, Policies and Practices*. Taylor & Francis Group. http://ebookcentral.proquest.com/lib/manchester/detail.action?docID=472487

Virdee, S., & McGeever, B. (2018). Racism, Crisis, Brexit. *Ethnic and Racial Studies*, *41*(10), 1802–1819. https://doi.org/10.1080/01419870.2017.1361544

Vošner, H. B., Bobek, S., Kokol, P., & Krečič, M. J. (2016). Attitudes of active older internet users towards online social networking. *Computers in Human Behavior*, *55*, 230–241. https://doi.org/10.1016/j.chb.2015.09.014

Vraga, E. K., Thorson, K., Kligler-Vilenchik, N., & Gee, E. (2015). How individual sensitivities to disagreement shape youth political expression on Facebook. *Computers in Human Behavior*, *45*, 281–289. https://doi.org/10.1016/j.chb.2014.12.025

Vromen, A., Loader, B. D., Xenos, M. A., & Bailo, F. (2016). Everyday making through Facebook engagement: Young citizens' political interactions in Australia, the United Kingdom and the United States. *Political Studies*, *64*(3), 513–533. https://doi.org/10.1177/0032321715614012

Wahl-Jorgensen, K. (2019). *Emotions, Media and Politics*. Polity Press.

Waldner, L., K., & Dobratz, B. A. (2019). Rapport, respect, and dissonance: Studying the white power movement in the United States. In E. Toscano (Ed.), *Researching Far-Right Movements: Ethics, Methodologies, and Qualitative Inquiries*. Routledge.

Walker, M., & Matsa, K. E. (2021). *News Consumption Across Social Media in 2021*. Pew Research Center. file:///C:/Users/cxnh/Downloads/PJ_2021.09.20_News-and-Social-Media_FINAL.pdf

Walker, P., Topping, A., & Morris, S. (2020, June 12). Boris Johnson says removing statues is "to lie about our history." *The Guardian*. https://www.theguardian.com/politics/2020/jun/12/boris-johnson-says-removing-statues-is-to-lie-about-our-history-george-floyd

Walkerdine, V. (2020). "No-one listens to us": Post-truth, affect and Brexit. *Qualitative Research in Psychology*, *17*(1), 143–158. https://doi.org/10.1080/14780887.2019.1644407

Ward, M. (2014). They say bad things come in threes: How economic, political and cultural shifts facilitated contemporary anti-immigration activism in the United States. *Journal of Historical Sociology*, *27*(2).

Watts, J. (2018, January 4). Tony Blair attacks Labour's "mistaken" stance on Brexit. *The Independent*. https://www.independent.co.uk/news/uk/politics/brexit-blair-corbyn-attack-labour-approach-confusing-mistaken-a8140521.html

Wellings, B. (2012). *English Nationalism and Euroscepticism*. Peter Lang UK. https://doi.org/10.3726/978-3-0353-0285-1

Wells, K., & Watson, S. (2005). A politics of resentment: Shopkeepers in a London neighbourhood. *Ethnic and Racial Studies*, *28*(2), 261–277. https://doi.org/10.1080/01419870420000315843

Williams, M. L., Sutherland, A., Roy-Chowdhury, V., Loke, T., Cullen, A., Sloan, L., Burnap, P., & Giannasi, P. (2022). The effect of the Brexit vote on the variation in race and religious hate crimes in England, Wales, Scotland and Northern Ireland. *British Journal of Criminology*, azac071. https://doi.org/10.1093/bjc/azac071

Williams, R. (1977). *Marxism and Literature*. OUP Oxford.

Wilson, J. (2020, June 6). What is antifa and why is Donald Trump targeting it? *The Guardian*. https://www.theguardian.com/world/2020/jun/06/what-is-antifa-trump-terrorist-designation

Winter, A. (2017, August 17). Charlottesville, far-right rallies, racism and relating to power. *OpenDemocracy*. https://www.opendemocracy.net/en/charlottesville-far-right-rallies-racism-and-relating-to-power/

Wodak, R. (2015). *The Politics of Fear: What Right-Wing Populist Discourses Mean*. SAGE Publications Ltd. https://uk.sagepub.com/en-gb/eur/the-politics-of-fear/book237802

Wollebæk, D., Karlsen, R., Steen-Johnsen, K., & Enjolras, B. (2019). Anger, fear, and echo chambers: The emotional basis for online behavior. *Social Media + Society*, *5*(2), 2056305119829859. https://doi.org/10.1177/2056305119829859

Worth, O. (2017). Whither Lexit? *Capital & Class*, *41*(2), 351–357. https://doi.org/10.1177/0309816817711558c

Yamamoto, M., Kushin, M. J., & Dalisay, F. (2015). Social media and mobiles as political mobilization forces for young adults: Examining the moderating role of online political expression in political participation. *New Media & Society*, *17*(6), 880–898. https://doi.org/10.1177/1461444813518390

Ylä-Anttila, T. (2018). Populist knowledge: "Post-truth" repertoires of contesting epistemic authorities. *European Journal of Cultural and Political Sociology*, *5*(4), 356–388. https://doi.org/10.1080/23254823.2017.1414620

Zappettini, F. (2019). The Brexit referendum: How trade and immigration in the discourses of the official campaigns have legitimised a toxic (inter)national logic. *Critical Discourse Studies*, *16*(4), 403–419. https://doi.org/10.1080/17405904.2019.1593206

Zhang, X., & Davis, M. (2022). E-extremism: A conceptual framework for studying the online far right. *New Media & Society*, 14614448221098360. https://doi.org/10.1177/14614448221098360

Zhou, Y., & Pinkleton, B. E. (2012). Modeling the effects of political information source use and online expression on young adults' political efficacy. *Mass Communication and Society*, *15*(6), 813–830. https://doi.org/10.1080/15205436.2011.622064

Zhuravskaya, E., Petrova, M., & Enikolopov, R. (2020). Political effects of the internet and social media. *Annual Review of Economics*, *12*(1), 415–438. https://doi.org/10.1146/annurev-economics-081919-050239

Zuboff, S. (2019). *The Age of Surveillance Capitalism: The Fight for a Human Future at the New Frontier of Power*. Profile Books.

Index

9/11. *See* September 11 terror attacks

Abbott, Diane, 124–25, 166, 167
affect. *See* emotions in politics
affordances: connected, 40, 43, 63, 89, 96, 117, 176; definition of, 52–53; role of, 4, 10, 38–45, 51–76, 80, 176
age, impact of, 9
agency, 15, 24, 42–47, 52–54, 58, 66–69, 73–76, 90, 93, 94, 95, 100–1, 169–70, 173–74, 176–77
algorithms, role of, 4, 14, 38–42, 51–52, 51–58, 64, 73–76, 89, 177–78
The Alt-Right, 4, 5, 16, 87–89, 102, 117, 121, 140–41, 142, 150, 170, 177–78
alternative right-wing news outlets, 37, 39, 130, 150
anti-communism, 89–90, 137–42, 175–76
anti-leftism, 31, 33–36, 42, 83–85, 88–90, 95–97, 102, 113, 117, 119–42, 146, 148, 150–51, 154–55, 159–63, 167, 169–71, 174–78, 180
anti-Semitism, 86, 121
attention economy, 52, 54, 61–62, 66, 75, 177
austerity, 31–34, 110, 176. *See also* Global Financial Crisis of 2008

automation, logic of. *See* algorithms, role of

banning of social media accounts, 56, 69, 73–76, 136–37. *See also* censorship
Bannon, Steve, 5
The BBC, 35, 37, 130–31, 132–33, 152, 153, 154
big data analysis. *See* social media analysis
Blair, Tony, 149
bots, 10, 178
Breitbart News, 5, 88
Britain First, 7
British National Party (BNP), 121

Cambridge Analytica, 1–2, 4, 6–7, 178
Cameron, David, 6, 25, 122
censorship, 44, 58, 68, 69, 73–75, 84, 92, 133–37, 142, 154, 163. *See also* banning of social media accounts; political correctness
Channel 4, 131
Channel crossings, 101, 107, 109
civilizationism, 96, 104, 113–14, 117. *See also* racism: differentialist
clash of civilizations. *See* civilizationism
Clegg, Nick, 136

Clinton, Hillary, 130, 166
Cold War, legacy of, 9, 88, 120–21, 138, 175–76
conflict in online interactions, 22, 23, 42–43, 70–73, 75, 94, 123, 154–55
conservatism, 9, 16, 34, 85–86, 89–90, 120–22, 148, 151, 174–75
conspiracy theories: Cultural Marxism, 83, 88–89, 96, 104, 120–29, 133, 140–42, 150, 170, 176–78; Great Replacement, 86–89, 96, 102, 117, 141, 177–78; QAnon, 40–41, 71, 159, 170, 180; role of, 14, 28–29, 31, 40–41, 44, 71, 82, 85–89, 95–96, 141–42, 154, 158–59, 170, 177–78
Context collapse, 70
Corbyn, Jeremy, 33, 35, 124–25, 138–39, 141, 175
corruption, 32, 90, 131, 138–40, 165–66, 175
counter-knowledge. *See* knowledge, weaponization of
Covid-19 pandemic, 150, 179
Cox, Jo, 80

Davis, David, 152
declinism. *See* nostalgia
deindustrialization, 34, 45
democracy, threat to, 1, 2, 3, 16, 31, 46, 85, 89–91, 91–93, 95–96, 100, 130, 136, 174, 179
discursive opportunities, 13, 24–25, 25–31, 47–48
disempowerment. *See* agency
disinformation, 10, 99, 104, 116, 145–48, 178. *See also* misinformation

echo chambers, 4, 22–23, 40, 42–45, 48, 101
emotion in politics, 52, 75, 101, 146, 150, 167–71; affective public, 81; emotional regime, 147, 151, 159, 169–70. *See also* wellbeing
English Defence League (EDL), 7, 121. *See also* "Tommy Robinson"
environmental politics, 122, 170, 179
epistemic capital, 124, 145–72, 177, 180
EU referendum of 2016, 6, 30, 38, 45–46, 96, 100, 122–23, 130, 139, 140–42, 145–48, 155; campaign, 1, 2, 6, 7, 10, 16, 27, 30, 31, 38, 58, 85, 92, 95, 99, 100, 102, 109–10, 111, 116, 125, 145, 148, 174; result, 2–3, 8–10, 46, 75, 123–24, 133, 149, 169
European elections of 2014, 6, 45
exit deal negotiations between UK and EU, 12, 27, 46, 90–91, 131, 140–41, 151, 155, 163, 174
extremism. *See* far-right: terrorism; Islamist terrorism; radicalization

Facebook, corporate entity of. *See* Meta
The Facebook Papers, 57, 177
fact-signaling. *See* knowledge, weaponization of
far-right, 4–5, 15–17, 31, 61, 69, 101, 117, 134, 150; mainstreaming, 5, 101–2, 117, 178, 179, 180; terrorism, 5, 86, 121; transnational reach, 14–15, 17, 38, 40–41, 43–44, 85–89, 96, 99, 101–2, 104, 117, 119, 121–22, 124, 127, 130–31, 140–42, 170, 177–78
Farage, Nigel, 7, 27, 28, 44, 45, 84, 111, 159, 170. *See also* UKIP
fatigue, social media, 72–73, 74
filter bubbles, 4, 22–23, 40–42, 45, 48. *See also* algorithms, role of

Gab, 55, 56, 69, 179
GB News, 179
gender, 33, 34, 83, 85, 115, 120–21, 125–29, 135, 142, 179; feminism, 88, 89, 114, 122, 126; femonationalism, 113–14, 132; transphobia, 5, 10, 126–28, 179
General Election: of 2015, 6; of 2019, 3
gilet jaunes protests, 43, 44, 67, 93, 105
globalism, 71, 83, 93
Gove, Michael, 148

grand narrative. *See* metanarrative
"grooming gangs" scandal, 27, 33, 84, 101, 112, 115, 128, 132, 136–37

hegemony, cultural, 15, 36, 88–89, 121, 146, 170, 175, 178, 180
higher education, 88, 129–30
history, contested, 161–62
homophobia. *See* sexuality

identitarianism, 5
illiberalism, 16, 70, 174, 181
immigration, opposition to. *See* racism: cultural; racism: differentialist; racism: nativism
infinite scroll, 54
influencers, 31, 62
interpretivism, 10–11
Iraq War, 28–29
Islamist terrorism, 28–29, 107–8, 111, 168, 175
Islamic State (IS). *See* Islamist terrorism
Islamization, imagined threat of, 83, 86, 89, 112, 115–16, 117, 121, 134–35, 178. *See also* racism: Islamophobia; conspiracy theories: Great Replacement
isolationism, economic, 46, 80, 100, 148, 174

January 6 Capitol Hill insurrection, 5, 40, 179
Johnson, Boris, 3, 7, 101, 114, 131, 135, 148

Khan, Sadiq, 136
knowledge, weaponization of, 15, 145–72, 177–78, 180

Labour Party, 32–35, 83, 120, 122, 124–25, 141, 149, 175–76
the "left behind," 3, 11, 48

Macron, Emmanuel, 93
Manchester Arena attack of 2017, 168

May, Theresa, 2, 12, 27, 90, 122, 152, 174
media literacy, 9
media distrust, 36, 37–38, 41, 42, 53–54, 65, 81, 83, 84, 129–43, 150, 154–55, 159–60, 161, 175
memes, 61
Merkel, Angela, 136, 140, 163
Meta, 1, 57, 58, 136, 177
migrant crisis, European, 30–31, 41, 47, 101, 102, 111, 136, 175
Miller, Gina, 122
misinformation, 101, 116, 135, 145, 147–48, 158. *See also* disinformation
moderation of content on social media platforms. *See* censorship
multiculturalism, 10, 25–26, 28, 31, 33, 37, 83, 95, 102–3, 110, 114, 117, 119, 121–22, 129, 131, 135, 142, 149, 174, 179

narrative, 14, 79–153; counter-, 81, 176; meta-, 14, 89–97, 140, 153, 174; ontological, 84, 158–59
National Health Service (NHS), 32, 33, 109, 138, 155
nationalism, 4, 11, 44, 80, 100, 110, 135–36, 139, 145, 151
neoliberalism, 9, 25, 35–36, 88, 120, 122, 125, 140, 159
nostalgic nationalism, 4, 7, 90–91, 91–95, 100, 107–8

Obama, Barack, 127
online disinhibition effect, 43

People's Vote campaign. *See* second referendum, campaign for
polarization, 4, 10, 22, 35, 43; affective, between Leave and Remain identities, 43, 101, 116, 119, 122–23, 147, 175–76
political correctness, 28, 38, 83, 92, 120, 121, 129–37, 140, 142
political engagement, definition of, 8

populism, right-wing, 13, 14, 21, 24, 25, 35, 41, 42, 45, 47, 48, 52, 70, 73, 75, 80, 91, 95, 99, 119, 137, 148, 176, 179; actors and campaigns utilizing, 1–3, 5, 27, 43–45, 84, 121, 124, 127, 148–49, 179; affinity with social media, 22–23; anti-elitism tenet of, 31–34, 85; contested definition and use of, 15–18, 175; discourse, 11, 15, 82, 85, 100, 161, 178; epistemological, 149–50, 163–67, 180; people-centrism tenet of, 38, 46, 85, 90, 96, 108, 174; transnational, 4, 6, 44, 79, 82, 113, 117, 130, 140–41, 170, 173, 179
post-colonial melancholia. *See* nostalgic nationalism
post-truth, 2, 15, 99, 145–72, 180
Powell, Enoch, 103, 105

racism, 15–18, 25, 30–32, 46, 61, 68–69, 79, 92, 96, 99–117, 132, 167, 175, 178–79; cultural, 6, 14, 17, 25–26, 46–47, 84, 101, 105–8, 116, 175; denial of, 84, 105, 111, 135; differentialist, 14, 101, 102–5, 116, 175; Islamophobia, 4, 6, 14, 17, 25–30, 33, 35, 36, 46–47, 64, 69, 83–84, 86, 101, 103–6, 111–17, 132, 135–36, 159, 161, 167–68, 175; nativism, 4, 6, 14, 17, 25–26, 30, 32, 44, 47, 61, 85–86, 100–1, 108–10, 112, 116, 121, 175; post-race, 100; racialization, 17, 30–31, 85, 99–100, 105, 107, 110–11, 117, 166, 175
radicalization, 4, 10, 22–24
Reddit, 55
Rees-Mogg, Jacob, 7, 84, 131, 159, 166
regime of truth, 15, 146, 151, 153–54, 169–70, 177, 180
Remainers, representations of, 42, 66, 84, 87, 91, 100, 119, 122–25, 155–64, 169–70, 175–77
Right victimhood, 15, 34, 43, 58, 97, 117, 119–43, 145–46, 169, 176, 180

RT (formerly Russia Today), 28

Scottish independence, 2
second referendum, campaign for, 2, 38, 45, 46, 90, 122, 154
September 11 terror attacks, 4, 23, 26–28, 37, 47, 154, 175
sexuality, 88, 113, 120, 121, 127–28, 132, 142, 179; homonationalism, 113, 128, 132
sharing, logic of, 14, 52, 62–69, 74–76
social media analysis, 10–11, 12, 24, 47–48, 80, 181
social media logic, 14, 43, 52–53, 74–76
sociopolitical opportunities, 14, 24–25, 31–38, 47–48
Soros, George, 87
Spencer, Richard, 102
surveillance capitalism, 14, 52, 58, 64, 75, 177
Syrian conflict, 28–29, 103, 111

tabloid news, 2, 45, 120–23, 135
technological opportunities, 13, 24–25, 38–45, 47–48, 173, 178
Thatcher, Margaret, 9, 14, 35, 120–21, 130, 175
"Tommy Robinson," 7, 23, 44, 69, 84, 132, 136–37, 152–53, 159–60, 166–67. *See also* EDL
trade unionism, 34–36
transphobia. *See* gender: transphobia
Trump, Donald, 4, 5, 36, 40, 41, 43, 44, 84, 124, 127, 131, 132, 145, 148, 165–66, 167, 179
Twitter, 8, 55, 56

UKIP, 6, 23, 26, 27, 28, 32, 44, 45, 67, 79, 99, 100, 102, 106, 121, 141. *See also* Farage, Nigel
Ukraine, Russian invasion of, 179
Unite the Right rally of 2017 in Charlottesville, 5, 162
United Nations Global Compact for Migration, 104, 117, 153

vaccine hesitancy, 22, 40, 150, 179
vigilantism, online, 69
visuality, logic of, 14, 44, 52, 60–62, 64, 74–76, 106
Vote Leave. *See* EU referendum of 2016: campaign

war on terror. *See* September 11 terror attacks
wellbeing, 70, 72–73
Whiteness, 12–13, 17, 27, 65, 88, 95, 104; methodological, 11; White complicity, 13; White victimhood, 5, 15, 33–34, 43, 68, 83, 85, 96, 99–117, 129, 131, 134, 167, 169, 174–76; White working class, 2, 11, 32–34, 100, 123, 155–56; White supremacism, 86, 101, 117. *See also* conspiracy theories: Great Replacement

yellow vest protests. *See* gilet jaunes protests
YouTube, 40–41, 138, 170

About the Author

Natalie-Anne Hall is a postdoctoral research associate in the Department of Communication and Media, Loughborough University, UK. Her research focuses on everyday engagement with contentious knowledge and politics online, particularly racist and right-wing ideologies. She holds a PhD in sociology from the University of Manchester, UK.

Milton Keynes UK
Ingram Content Group UK Ltd.
UKHW030052161223
434468UK00002B/34